JAPANESE COOKING

For The

AMERICAN TABLE

Susan Fuller Slack

HPBOOKS

HPBooks
Published by The Berkley Publishing Group
200 Madison Avenue
New York, NY 10016

Book design by Richard Oriolo
Cover design by James R. Harris
Cover photograph by George de Gennaro Studios
Interior illustrations by Michelle Burchard
Some illustrations are from *Treasury of Japanese Designs & Motifs for
Artists & Craftsmen* by Carol Belanger Grafton, 1983,
Dover Publications, Inc.
Haiku poems on pages 13 and 225 reprinted by permission from
A Little Treasury of Haiku, translated by Peter Beilenson, 1908,
Avenel Books by Peper Pauper Press.

First edition: February 1996

Published simultaneously in Canada.

Library of Congress Cataloging-in-Publication Data

Slack, Susan Fuller.
Japanese cooking for the American table / Susan Fuller
Slack.—1st ed.
p.   cm.
Includes index.
ISBN 1-55788-237-1
1. Cookery, Japanese.   2. Cookery—Japan.   3. Japan—
Social life and customs.   I. Title.
TX724.5.J3S583   1996
641.5952—dc20   95-21289
                                                             CIP

Printed in the United States of America

10 9 8 7 6 5 4 3 2 1

CONTENTS

This book is dedicated to Todd, Shawn, Nicholas and Joshua who experienced the simplicity and beauty of Japanese life and came to love the incredibly diverse cuisine. A road once taken is never forgotten! These associations have encouraged the development of lifelong friendships. May these ties elevate their lives to a new level of awareness, enhanced by a rich well of memory and experience.

ACKNOWLEDGMENTS

Heartfelt thanks to: Editor, Jeanette Egan, who skillfully brought this collection of recipes, drawings and memories to life. Her hard work and dedication are reflected on every page.

Special thanks to my husband, Buddy, who assisted in countless ways during the book's creation and was chief cook and bottle washer, par excellence, during my long hours spent at the computer.

Special thanks to:

Kayoko and Kazumasa Tazoe, Osaka, Japan, for sharing technical information on Japanese cuisine and culture, for many delicious meals shared with me, and most of all, for their special friendship.

Dee Bradney for her recipe testing, research and remembrances of Japan.

Cathy Fillion.

Frank S. Kawana, President, Yamasa Enterprises, Los Angeles, for sharing his considerable knowledge on seri-neihan.

Martha Johnson of Eden Foods for providing me with research materials and a "taste" of the many fine natural foods they import from Japan.

Brenda Parnell and Chef Fujimura of the Nippon Center Yagoto in Greenville, South Carolina.

Mineko Tsuchitani, Tokyo, Japan, for translations.

Chieko Hardy for her gracious assistance.

Jeff Hamano and David J. Kuff of Zojirushi America Corporation.

Mrs. Setsuko Manabe, Tokyo, Japan.

Dr. Yoshitaka Sakakibara, Director of Japanese Language Program, University of South Carolina.

Michelle Burchard, Artist.

The Japanese words used in this cookbook are written in *Romaji*, a method of writing that transcribes the Japanese syllabic alphabet into roman letters. The romanized words are based on the widely used Hepburn system, also called the *hyojun shiki* or standard system. It evolved from a sixteenth-century romanization system based upon the Portuguese language. The Hepburn system was named after missionary/physician James Curtis Hepburn (1815–1911). He helped unify the system and popularized it by adopting its usage for the publication of educational books.

Following a common practice, I have used the acute accent mark (´) to indicate that when the vowel e is placed at the end of a word, it is pronounced as "ay" instead of being silent. This occurs in words such as saké or agé.

The length of a vowel can change the meaning of a word. Pronounce *okashi* with a long i and it will mean "strange." Say the word with a short i and it becomes "confection." A macron, or short straight mark, placed horizontally over a vowel indicates that the sound doubles in length when pronounced.

In compound words such as *su-zuké* (rice vinegar pickles), hyphenation indicates a phonetic change. Z replaces *tsu* from the word *tsukemono* (pickles). I have also placed hyphens between the syllables of some words to help simplify pronunciation.

PREFACE

Japan—A Trip to Wonderland

The first time I went to live in Japan, I felt I had fallen topsy-turvy into an exotic land of enchantment surely as mystical as the one Alice discovered as she peered through the looking glass. To paraphrase the words of nineteenth-century author Lafcadio Hearn, it was "a land of strangeness and charm." Every aspect of the Japanese culture was enigmatic but none more so than the exquisite cuisine. Never before had I encountered such an incredible array of foodstuffs like those I found in department-store food emporiums, bustling markets, teahouses, restaurants, sidewalk sales and festivals. It seemed to me that on every corner a street vendor was beckoning me to sample exotic, mouthwatering snacks such as fish-shaped pancakes, octopus fritters and savory fish stew. Horns and bells announced the arrival of small food carts as they made their way through peaceful residential streets selling roasted sweet potatoes, bean curd, chestnuts and boiled corn.

An early morning trip to an auction at the Tsukiji Fish Waterfront was a confusing yet invigorating ritual in which auctioneers and bidders used an incomprehensible set of signals to move thousands of pounds of fresh fish. A city within a city, Tsukiji was once the site of a segregated foreign settlement for the *gaijin,* or foreigner. Over 1,000 shops and stalls make up the adjacent market, where I purchased several of my favorite pieces of Japanese kitchenware.

Elsewhere in Japan, I purchased exquisite miniature vegetables, baskets of beautifully arranged, tiny edible flowers and apples, hand-wrapped with tissue and ribbons. In bakeries, I sampled breads shaped like sea creatures and sponge cakes that resembled small fruits and animals. Refrigerated counters were filled with dazzling varieties of impeccably fresh fish and shellfish. Handsome, handcrafted wooden tubs held mounds of fermented miso paste, colorful pickled vegetables, exotic sea vegetables and crisp rice crackers.

My small son and I were guests at Torikyo, an exclusive *ryokan* (inn) on the Izu peninsula. Our suite, once the apartment of a well-known military hero in the 1930s, was named *akebono,* or "beautiful sunrise." With our hosts, we dined at a low table on tatami floors. Each guest received a dozen beautiful lacquer and porcelain dishes, every one filled with exquisite, delicious foods. Our kimono-clad maid kept a watchful eye as we feasted on miniature seascapes of raw fish and seaweed, delicate braised fern tips

and soft-shell crab tempura clothed in a crisp, ethereal batter. Later, we were served fine *gyokuro* tea, sweet rice cakes and peeled tangerines in a treasured ebony basket made of aged, sooty bamboo from an old country farmhouse. We admired the formal gardens just outside our shoji door. The adjacent wall opened up to a panoramic view of the sea. Small wonder the name of this inn translates to "paradise."

On another occasion, high in the snow-misted mountains of Kyoto, I dined equally well in a rustic *minshuku,* or public lodge. The comfort level didn't match Torikyo's, but the togetherness and communal fun shared with other guests made the experience worthwhile. In the dining room, everyone huddled under the *kotatsu* (a low table that is heated from below), drank saké and sang songs after feasting on *mizutaki,* or chicken hot pot. Fortunately, my friend, Aya Yoshikawa, persuaded the chef to share his secrets for cooking this savory dish, so you can experience the taste, if not the memories, in your own home.

At the Kaiede family's farmhouse in Gifu Prefecture, my son and I took part in the winter ritual of *mochitsuki,* pounding glutinous rice to make soft, chewy rice cakes called *mochi.* Chances are you don't have a hollowed tree stump and mallet or even an electric rice pounder, but you can capture the essence of *mochi* with the easy recipe on page 201. For the Japanese, *mochi* is closely associated with New Year's celebrations and has felicitous associations.

—Susan Fuller Slack

INTRODUCTION

Tradition & Transformation

The wonder of Japan is not to be sought in the countless borrowings with which she has clothed herself. . . . No, the real wonder is the wearer. For the interest of the costume is much less in its beauty of form and tint than in its significance as idea— as representing something of the mind that devised or adopted it.

—LAFCADIO HEARN

◉

From early times Japan has been receptive to new ideas from other cultures. In the same manner, the Japanese have adopted foreign foods and culinary customs and incorporated them into Japanese society. But in the process, these foods and ideas have been altered to suit the Japanese taste and mind. They may resemble their Western counterparts but have taken on the trappings of Japanese tradition and been transformed into something entirely new. Western foods have become side dishes, selected because of their compatibility with rice. *Tonkatsu,* a fried pork cutlet (page 156), is a delicious example. The spicy sauce for *tonkatsu* is made from Worcestershire sauce and ketchup, the only Western sauces to hold wide appeal. Worcestershire sauce became a favorite topping for plain rice in western Japan around 1940. *Ebi furai* (fried shrimp) and Curry Rice (page 196) are other examples. The name for cooked white rice, *gohan,* becomes *meshi* when mixed with ingredients and *raisu* when served on a plate with a sauce.

Chinese cuisine is also very popular, in part due to employees returning from jobs overseas. Interestingly, foreign cuisines in Japan are mainly prepared by Japanese chefs rather than by nationals of the region where the foods originated. The fusion of East-West cuisine is strengthening in America as well as in Japan. We are beginning to realize the positive health benefits to be gained from adding Japanese foods to our diet. Understanding each other's cuisine and customs is an important avenue to successful international exchange.

A Culinary Tour of Japan

The emphasis on seasonal foods and food presentation is apparent throughout the four major islands of Japan. Partly due to mountainous terrain and other natural divisions, regional foods and cooking techniques are diversified.

Sparsely populated Hokkaido in the north is famous for dairy products, Sapporo, ramen and salmon. The finest *konbu* for soup stock comes from cold waters off the coast. Hearty stews and one-pot dishes are served here with the onset of freezing winter winds.

The main island of Honshu boasts two main culinary areas: the eastern Kanto plains region, where Tokyo lies, and the western Kansai plains region, which includes Osaka and Kyoto. Tokyo is the embodiment of modern Japan with first-class international restaurants. By contrast, Kyoto, once the ancient capital Heian-Kyo, offers a taste of the elegance and refinement of old Japan.

Shikoku is the smallest of the four major islands. It is famous for the wheat noodle, *udon,* most notably in the area of Kagawa Prefecture, where people eat the noodles three or four times a day. This small area has hundreds of *udon* factories and ships noodles worldwide.

South beyond Shikoku is Kyushu. Fine shiitake mushrooms and some of the best seafood come from this area. This was Japan's first contact point with the West when Portuguese settlers arrived in the sixteenth century. Foreigners introduced baking and new forms of deep-frying. Due to Chinese influence, pork is popular in Kyushu. *Shippoku-ryōri,* a merger of Japanese and Chinese cuisine, is popular here. This influence becomes stronger as we move southward into the Ryukyu Islands, which were under Chinese rule for four hundred years.

Planning Japanese Menus

A simple Japanese breakfast consists of rice, soup and a side dish. This is called *ichihan, ichiju,* and *issai.* The side dish might include grilled fish, an egg, boiled vegetables or a bit of fried tofu.

Lunchtime is a simple affair, perhaps a bowl of noodles, a plate of curry or Chinese fried rice. Away from home, there are unlimited restaurant choices or perhaps a modular box lunch, called the obentō or bentō.

The evening meal is comprised of three parts: soup, three side dishes and steamed rice with pickles and hot tea. Remember the saying *ichiju sansai:* "soup and three." The three side dishes are selected from the five cooking methods: fried (*agémono*), grilled (*yakimono*), steamed (*mushimono*), simmered (*nimono*) and raw (*sashimi*). Sashimi ("sliced fresh") doesn't require cooking, but it does require a demonstration of knife skills. A *nabémono*, or one-pot dish, can replace the three side dishes. Rice is such an important consideration, its inclusion is taken for granted. Well-seasoned side dishes, or *okazu*, are primarily served to stimulate one's appetite for eating the rice. In Japan, etiquette dictates that rice and *okazu* be eaten alternately, one bite at a time. Saké, a rice-based alcoholic beverage, and cooked rice are considered interchangeable and thus never served at the same time. If saké is drunk with the side dishes, the rice is eaten at the end of the meal.

An aesthetic of asymmetry underlies the Japanese view of table settings. Small dishes, designed to match the foods, provide a strong sense of the season. Food arrangement on the dishes follows a prescribed formula and often represents nature in an abstract form. Color schemes and seasonal motifs often convey a feeling of felicity and festivity. In ancient times, foods were eaten on small tray-tables, a Chinese influence. The lacquered tables of the nobility were brushed with gold dust. Tray-tables are not in everyday use now, but are reserved for *cha-kaiseki* (tea ceremony cuisine) or other special occasions. Rare Edo-period woodblock prints depict the first Nagasaki foreigners using "exotic" large tables and chairs.

Since early times, Japanese food philosophy has been guided by the ancient Chinese principle of yin/yang—opposing but balancing forces. As in China, five is a fortuitous number. Foods are prepared by the five culinary arts mentioned before. Century-old Japanese cookbooks instruct that foods should reflect the five flavors (sweet, sour, salty, hot, bitter) and the five colors (white, black, red, green and yellow). Today's Japanese cooks rely on the primary tastes of sweet, sour, salty and bitter.

Because of busy life-styles, most of us prefer a casual style for daily meals. In this case, choose as an entrée one dish from the five cooking methods mentioned above. Serving sizes can be increased. A Western rendition of a Japanese meal might include miso soup, fish and vegetable tempura, rice, salad, pickles, ice cream and green tea or beer. Or you could incorporate one or two Japanese dishes into your favorite Western meal.

When creating menus, refer to the principles of Western meal planning. Select dishes that meet nutritional needs and offer contrasts in cooking methods, ingredients, textures, colors and flavors. Fish is so important, it might be repeated in a meal two or three times. Except when noodles are served, offer generous servings of rice. Japanese foods are convenient to serve; many are do-ahead and can be eaten warm or room temperature.

Warm saké, called the "lubricant of society," is especially appreciated during the wintertime. Saké is now being brewed to be served chilled. Beer's thirst-quenching properties make it a popular summertime drink. In fact, it is now the preferred drink of most Japanese. A small glass of plum wine, perhaps over crushed ice, is valued for its medicinal properties, particularly for stomach disorders. A small glass would be pleasing as an aperitif or after-dinner drink.

Japanese Table Etiquette

One of the most important points of etiquette when eating with Japanese friends is to begin the meal with an offering of thanks by saying, *"Itadakimasu."* At the end of the meal, it is polite to say, *"Goshisosama deshita,"* indicating that you have appreciated such a wonderful feast.

Chopstick Etiquette

The Japanese custom of eating with chopsticks (*ohashi* or *hashi*) was adopted from China almost 2,000 years ago. It is believed the first chopsticks were connected and resembled tweezers rather than two separate sticks. Early records indicate spoons were once used with chopsticks, but eventually the spoons completely disappeared. This was partly because few except the nobility could afford them, since they were made of precious metals. Bamboo, a natural resource, was widely available for chopsticks.

The rules of chopstick and table etiquette were developed by court aristocracy and Buddhist clergy between the twelfth and fifteenth centuries. Later, during the Edo period (1600–1868), these customs became popular throughout the land. The use of a single pair of chopsticks during a Japanese meal is in sharp contrast to the numerous knives, forks and spoons necessary for a Western meal. Each family member often has his or her own personal set of chopsticks and a container for storing them. To facilitate the use of chopsticks, foods are usually precut into bite-size pieces, or in pieces small enough to be eaten politely in two or three bites. Hard-to-eat foods can be maneuvered by sliding the chopsticks under small portions and lifting the foods to the mouth. It is also proper to lift the soup bowl or rice bowl and carry food to the mouth. Japanese chopsticks can vary in shape but are shorter and lighter than Chinese chopsticks and much easier to use.

Chopsticks for everyday use are made of bamboo, pine, cypress and white birch. Many restaurants use soft wooden chopsticks (*warabashi*) that are attached at the top and enclosed in a paper wrapping. They are broken apart by the diner, then after the meal, slipped back into the paper wrapping for disposal. More formal chopsticks are often slightly longer and made of cedar, ivory or lacquered wood inlaid with abalone or mother-of-pearl. Smaller chopsticks are made especially for children, and longer chopsticks of metal or bamboo are available for cooking purposes.

Some of the earliest traditional rules governing chopstick etiquette are still in use today: At the beginning of the meal, chopsticks should be picked up with one hand, then placed in the other hand for eating. Moisten chopsticks before use by dipping them into soup or hot tea.

Reverse your chopsticks to the clean ends before helping yourself from the communal serving dish. A common pair of serving chopsticks can be provided. Do not lean your chopsticks against a food dish. Special chopstick rests (*hashi-oki*) are available. Place the eating end of chopsticks directly on the rest, pointing to the left. Do not scrape your chopsticks together to remove pieces of food. Do not point with your chopsticks during a meal. Lay your chopsticks down when you are being given a second serving.

Chopsticks have played an important role in religious ceremonies. At Buddhist funerals, special chopsticks are used to pass the cremated bones of the deceased between family members. Because of this custom, food must never be passed from person to person with chopsticks. Do not allow your chopsticks to stand upright in dishes of food—a taboo also related to funerary customs.

Additional Points of Etiquette

- Remove the rice bowl lid with left hand; place it to the left, facing upward.
- Remove soup bowl cover with right hand; place it to the right.
- Leave a little rice in your bowl if you wish a second helping.
- If you have finished, do not leave a single grain of rice in your bowl.
- Don't remove solid foods from soup without lifting bowl from the tray.
- Don't place food with liquid sauces in your rice bowl.
- Don't eat any more meat after pickles and tea have been consumed.

Eating Out in Japan

Specialty restaurants in Japan are named after the type of food they serve, combined with the suffix *ya,* meaning "shop." A few specialty restaurants include the *tempura-ya, soba-ya, sushi-ya* and *yakitori-ya.* The *ro-*batayaki-ya specializes in grilled foods and resembles a country farmhouse with a hearthside grill.

Styles of Cuisine in Japan

Chā-kaiseki is the grand cuisine of Japan, served before the formal tea ceremony. The word *kaiseki* comes from the ancient practice of meditating Zen priests who put warm stones into their robes to soothe their stomachs, taking the edge off their hunger. An exquisite but simple meal is served on precious porcelain, lacquer or pottery dishes, according to prescribed rules.

Kaiseki-ryōri was developed in the eighteenth century. This cuisine was influenced by *cha-kaiseki* but does not demand the same disciplines. Japanese-style banquet dishes are served while guests leisurely enjoy cups of warm saké. This type of *kaiseki* began as light snacks served at poetry-party gatherings. *Kaiseki ryōri* is available in tranquil garden restaurants called *ryōtei.*

Kappo-ryōri is the expensive cordon-bleu cuisine of Japan, prepared by highly skilled chefs and served in prestigious (*kappo*) restaurants. *Kappo* cuisine can be found in Japanese-style inns called *ryōkan.* The finest seasonal ingredients are chosen for set meals that are prepared daily. It is usually necessary to have contacts to arrange reservations.

Yushiki-ryōri is the ancient cooking of the Imperial Court, served only at very special occasions.

Honzen-ryōri is the ceremonial dinner served within court circles and for the warrior class.

Kyo-ryōri is the cuisine of Kyoto, which is a lighter, more delicate variation of *kaiseki.*

Kaitei-ryōri is the nutritious, delicious everyday family cooking of Japan. Recipes are handed down through families from generation to generation.

Kyodo-ryōri is the regional, country-style cooking of Japan and is served in quaint, rustic restaurants. In each restaurant, the most famous foods of the area can be sampled.

Nihon-ryōri offers a tremendous variety of simple Japanese-style foods served in family-style restaurants called *nihon ryōri-ya.* Colorful plastic food models called *sampuru* (samples) offer diners a glimpse of the tempting selections offered within.

Shojin-ryōri is the delicious and incredibly varied cuisine of the Zen Buddhist monks, who were forbidden to eat animal protein for centuries. Tofu is an important protein substitute and is prepared in limitless ways.

Shokudo-ryōri is a mixture of Western-, Japanese- and Chinese-style foods. It is served Western-style in inexpensive restaurants, department stores, airports, museums and other public places. There usually are displays with plastic models of the foods at the entrances.

Chuka-ryōri is Chinese-style food that is served in inexpensive neighborhood restaurants. Fried rice, or *chahan,* and a variety of ramen dishes are popular offerings.

Tea (Cha)

Ryokucha, or green tea, is the indispensable beverage of Japan. Green tea is produced by steaming newly harvested tea leaves before drying. This process inhibits the action of an enzyme that causes fermentation and darkening. Naturally fermented black tea is enjoyed in China, India and the Western world. Tea leaves are harvested from May through September. The quality varies, depending on the area of production, how early the leaves are picked, the size of the leaves and even the position of the leaves on the bushes. Tea leaves contain an amino acid that adds a distinct sweetness to the tea. Perhaps this explains the popularity of the dish called *ocha-zuké,* which in its simplest form is hot green tea poured over cooked rice.

Green tea is processed into leaf form and powdered form. Top-quality leaf tea, called *gyokuro* (jewel dew), comes from the first summer picking of protected young leaves from the tops of the bushes. These leaves will be dried into long, thin, tightly curled rolls. *Gyokuro* is expensive and is sipped for appreciation and not for quenching thirst. *Matcha,* or *hikicha,* is powdered green tea made from the same leaves as *gyokuro.* This expensive powdered tea is used mainly for the traditional tea ceremony.

Sencha is a good medium-quality tea

picked after the first trim. It is served in homes and often in sushi bars. *Bancha* is a popular lower-quality tea made from older leaves picked later in the season. It is served without charge in restaurants as a thirst-quenching beverage. *Kukicha,* the next grade after *bancha,* is made from the oldest leaves along with the stems and twigs of the bush. This is often rated as the healthiest grade of tea because of the low caffeine content. *Bancha* and *kukicha* are often roasted to give them a rich nutty flavor. Roasted *bancha* is refreshing in the summer when chilled and garnished with lemon or orange slices.

Genmaicha is sometimes called popcorn tea because it is a combination of *bancha* and partially popped brown rice. This tea is sometimes served in inexpensive restaurants.

Other teas include cold barley tea (*mugicha*) and a festive tea made by pouring hot water over salted preserved cherry blossoms. Medicinal teas, including those made from lotus root, mugwort, dried mushrooms and burdock root, are also popular.

Tea Ceremony

For the Japanese, the act of drinking tea can be more than a simple means of taking refreshment. Throughout the past four hundred years it has evolved into a highly stylized and refined art known as *cha-no-yu,* or the tea ceremony.

Brick-shaped loaves of tea were introduced into Japan from China in the eighth century. Powdered green tea (*matcha*) was brought to Japan by Zen monks returning from China in the twelfth century. Originally, tea was consumed for its medicinal properties and used as a mild stimulant to stay awake during all-night meditation. Tea drinking eventually spread to the nobility, who freely dispensed it during tea-tasting contests and extravagant social gatherings. Under the influence of the dominant samurai class, the formal etiquette for serving tea evolved. In the sixteenth century, the tea master, Sen-No-Rikyu, simplified the tea ceremony and developed it into the form still known today.

There are many types of tea gatherings, held in accordance with the changing seasons, the guests, the time of day and the occasion. Tea ceremonies are held to celebrate occasions, such as sunrise or sunset, New Year's festivities, the Doll Festival, a full moon or even the first plum blossoms of spring. The ceremony is often held in a special tea room or outdoors in a tranquil setting and is frequently preceded by a special light meal (*cha-kaiseki*). Moist tea sweets (*namagashi*), such as the jellied sweets in the Desserts & Confectionery chapter, are served after the meal. Then the host or hostess prepares frothy thick green tea (*koicha*) according to the prescribed ritual. The tea is passed in a single bowl and offered to each guest for sipping. Thin tea (*usucha*), in individual bowls, and dry sweets (*higashi*) are served next. Each guest receives a cup of thin tea. After the tea has been served, guests spend time examining and appreciating the tea articles, an essential part of the ceremony. *Cha-kaiseki* is an amalgamation of food and art—all in preparation for a simple cup of tea!

The tea ceremony is conducted according to a set of rules which might seem complex; each motion has special meaning. The formal manners, the spiritual hush of the occasion and the ritualized ceremony reflect the Zen philosophy that enlightenment can be reached only through meditation. The tea ceremony is regarded as a means of physical, mental and spiritual discipline.

The spirit of the tea ceremony is based upon the Zen principle of oneness with nature. Followers strive to recognize real beauty in the plain and simple. A moss-covered stone in the tea garden, a perfect flower on display in the tea room, the tranquillity of the ceremony and even the astringent taste of the green tea become objects of appreciation. *Cha-no-yu* is a living tradition in Japan and a symbol of the culture. *Chado* (the way of tea) has affected the everyday lives of the people as well as the arts, religion, architecture, ceramics, literature and calligraphy of Japan.

Brewing Tea

When brewing a pot of Japanese tea, several factors should be considered. The correct amount of tea leaves must be steeped for an exact amount of time in good-quality water heated to a certain temperature. To brew tea, fill your teapot with hot water to warm it before use. Pour out the warming water; refill the pot with water heated to the correct temperature, depending on the type of tea being used (directions follow). Add the leaves and steep them for the recommended amount of time. The tea leaves will begin to sink to the bottom of the teapot when the tea is properly steeped. Never boil the tea leaves in the water. The Japanese prefer their tea without sugar, lemon or milk.

Powdered ceremony tea (*Matcha*) is prepared by the cupful. Blend about 2 teaspoons powdered tea with 1/2 cup hot water. Correct water temperature will vary with the season.

Top-quality leaf tea (*gyokuro*) is steeped in water heated to between 120F (50C) and 130F (55C) 1 to 2 minutes. One to 2 tablespoons tea are enough for 1 cup water. Correct water temperature is not as high as that required for lower grades of tea. If the water is too hot, it will destroy the aroma and make the taste too strong. *Gyokuro* is sipped in small amounts.

Good medium-quality leaf tea (*sencha*) is steeped in water heated to between 175F and 180F (80C) 1 to 2 minutes. One tablespoon tea is enough for about 2 1/2 to 3 cups water. *Sencha* is sipped in small amounts.

Coarse tea (*bancha*) is steeped in water heated to between 210F and 212F (100C) 2 to 3 minutes. Two to 3 tablespoons tea are enough for 3 to 4 cups water. The tea leaves can be used a second time.

Barley tea (*mugicha*) is simmered in water 3 to 4 minutes, then strained and chilled before serving. One-half cup roasted barley is enough for 1 1/2 to 2 quarts simmering water.

Saké

Saké was first used as a sacramental beverage during Shinto religious ceremonies. It is served on all important occasions in Japan, including holidays, festivals, wedding ceremonies and at the signing of important documents. *Tokkyushu* is "special grade" saké, a distinction made by government inspectors. The ranking system is based on aroma, taste and color. First-grade saké is *ikkyushu*. Second-grade is *nikkyushu*.

Saké doesn't improve with age. The annual quality stays basically the same; there are no vintage years. Except in summertime, when it is traditionally served cold, saké is always warmed. To warm saké, pour it into a small pottery or porcelain bottle called a *tokuri*. Place the bottle in a pan of hot water over low heat; warm saké to 100–110F (40–45C). In the wintertime, saké can be heated to a slightly warmer temperature. Warming mellows saké, releases its delicate bouquet and enhances the effect. Never allow saké to boil, or the aroma and taste will be destroyed. Pour warm saké into tiny cups called *sakazuki*.

Individual servings of cold saké are served in a small cedar measuring box (*masu*) with a small amount of salt placed near one corner. The saké and salt should be downed quickly. Salt brings out the sweetness of saké. Traditionally the *masu* was filled to slightly overflowing to ensure a full measure for patrons who could only afford a single serving of saké.

Japanese etiquette precludes you from filling your own saké cup. Instead, each person holds the cup in his or her hands while the saké is poured by a companion or serving person. The act of receiving or pouring saké is called "receiving or performing *oshaku*." If you are offered more saké while your cup is full, the polite thing to do is to take a sip from your cup and present it for filling. If you do not wish any more, hold

your fingers, palm down, over your cup. If it is empty, turn the cup upside down.

Saké can be ordered in food shops as well as at the *izakaya,* sit-down saké shops, or inexpensive pubs found throughout Japan. Saké is always served as an accompaniment to foods and is never served alone. It is especially enjoyed with sashimi and other appetizing snacks known as *saké-no-sakana.* Some people feel that without several rounds of saké, many delicious meals in Japan might never be completed! The next time you drink saké, either in a restaurant or at home, put everyone in the right mood and toast them in the traditional manner by saying, *"Kampai!"*

Japanese Festivals & Celebrations

The festival, or *matsuri,* is an essential part of Japanese life. Each year countless neighborhood festivals are sponsored by shrines throughout Japan. Originally, all festivals centered around agricultural observances. Now these festive occasions provide an opportunity to celebrate the community as well as deities associated with the shrines.

New Year's celebration, or *O-Shogatsu,* is the most important *nenchūgyōji* or annual celebration. It is a time of welcome to the ancestral spirits and Toshigami, god of the incoming year. Preparations begin mid-December. Households are cleaned, personal obligations fulfilled, debts paid and holiday cooking begun. New Year's cuisine, or *osechi ryōri,* includes a variety of do-ahead dishes so the women can relax and enjoy the festivities. Often symbolic, New Year's foods are displayed in handsome stacked lacquered boxes called *jubako*. Each layer features a specific type of colorful food, creatively arranged in artistic patterns.

The Doll Festival, or Hina Matsuri, on March 3 is also known as the Peach Blossom Festival. To the Japanese, peach blossoms represent the virtues of gentleness, beauty and grace. During this celebration of womanhood, households with daughters display highly treasured ceremonial dolls on tiers of special shelves. At the top, a regal pair of Emperor and Empress dolls hold court. Young girls in exquisite, colorful kimonos with butterfly sleeves attend special tea parties to admire the dolls. I attended a party in honor of the Doll Festival at the home of Yukari Oya in Odawara. Guests sipped the thick, sweet rice beverage *amazaké* (page 246) and nibbled on pink rice puffs and chewy pink, green and white rice cakes, or *mochi*.

Japan celebrates Boys' Day, or the Tango Festival, on May 5, with hopes of good health for their sons and prayers to help them grow up to be strong, courageous men. Warrior dolls are displayed and colorful carp-shaped kites flown from tall poles and rooftops. *Mochi* stuffed with bean paste is a traditional children's favorite. Sweet Peanut Mochi (page 204) combines peanut butter and *mochi* to please the tastes of American children as well.

The Japanese believe the harvest moon in mid-August is of such great beauty it deserves its own celebration. Once a year, people gather for *tsukimi,* or moon-viewing parties, on balconies and hilltops, in parks or in other suitable moon-viewing sites. In traditional wooden homes, paper-covered shoji are opened wide so observers can gaze upon the magnificence of the full moon. During a special supper, there are toasts with saké. Haiku honoring the occasion is created. Japanese children are not watching for the man in the moon; they're searching for a Japanese rabbit who spends all his time pounding *mochi!*

In early April, the appearance of *sakura,* or cherry blossoms, initiates a time of celebration honoring friendships, the beauty of nature and the coming of spring. In the tradition of the Heian court aristocrats (794–1185), picnics and poetry are planned around special days when the blossoms are in full bloom. Bentō, or box lunches, are filled with snacks like sushi or Rice Balls (page 222). Seasonal rice balls are topped with the salted blossoms. My favorite treat is *sakura-mochi,* rice cakes stuffed with bean paste and wrapped in fragrant cherry leaves. Much to the sorrow of the picnickers making merry, cherry blossoms are short-lived. The playful force of a gentle spring breeze is often enough to send a confetti-like shower of blossoms through the air, ending their brief but beautiful existence.

GARNISHES

(Mukimono)

Bright red pepper pod . . .

It needs but shiny wings and look . . .

Darting dragon-fly!

—BASHO

An exquisite green leaf molded from fiery *wasabi*, a golden shower of chrysanthemum petals, a fisherman's net carved from a radish and draped over the glistening "catch" of sashimi and seaweed—all are part of the art of Japanese cuisine.

A major concern of the Japanese chef is that foods satisfy the soul as well as the body. Technical expertise enables him to produce tantalizing aromas and delicious flavors to satisfy the appetite. But equally important is his ability to create visual appeal to remind us of our close relationship with nature. The term *katachi-no-aji* means the "flavor of the shape." The chef understands that the eyes can taste as well as the tongue.

During the Edo period (1600–1868), Japanese cuisine flourished and developed into a highly stylized art. Knife-wielding cooks developed the art of *mukimono*, sculpting vegetables into fanciful shapes. Their inspiration was drawn from the tea ceremony, Japanese flower arranging and religious principles dating back to ancient Shinto. People were taught that humans were in partnership with nature; foods as well as garnishes should imitate the natural world. Even today, the ancient concept of *shun* dictates that each food has its own season and each season provides its own bounty.

Create your own unique style of food garnishing by following a few of those basic principles. Choose seasonal garnishes that add a complementary splash of color, contrasting textures and natural flavors. The beauty of a garnish has little to do with size or grandeur. A simple garnish such as an edible leaf or a tiny flower is appreciated as highly as a baby eggplant carved into a tea whisk or a giant radish cut into a gossamer net.

Take a cue from nature. The botanical trinity of pine, bamboo and plum is a felicitous decoration at the New Year. A single pine-needle shape might be cut from the skin of a citrus fruit. Real pine needles might be strategically placed on a food, as if they had just fallen from the branch of a tree. The bamboo represents virtue and fidelity. Use the leaves and young shoots to add color, seasonal drama and flavor. The plum sends forth its blossoms to signal the end of winter. Cherry blossoms herald the beginning of spring. Natural garnishes help create a sense of the season within us.

Score mushroom caps with a star-shaped cut; strip leaf-shaped patterns of outer rind from pieces of winter squash to reveal golden leaves hidden underneath. Delicate Egg Chrysanthemums evoke feelings of autumn; Vegetable Ikebana, of new flowers popping up in the spring.

Beyond the vast realm of vegetable sculpting, garnishings can be simple yet effective. Enhance foods with sesame seeds, fresh herbs, shreds of shiny black nori or tiny rings of green onion. Seasonal flowers, leaves or fresh herbs always pay tribute to nature.

Moritsuké, the ancient art of food arrangement, dictates that foods be piled up in individual portions, then colorfully decorated. This style is evident today in the presentation of ceremonial foods. Look to *kagami-mochi*, the symbolic stack of rice cakes on display during the Japanese New Year.

Garnishes from nature do not have to be the definitive embellishment. Consider other artistic sensibilities such as color, form and arrangement. Portion sizes, background settings and serving dishes all play an important role in building a total visual effect. Be certain each of these aspects conforms to the spirit of your meal.

Useful Garnishing Equipment

Cookie cutters

Canapé cutters

Japanese metal flower-shaped cutters

Japanese rice molds

Radish-rosette cutter

Combination citrus zester and citrus scorer

Straight paring knife

Curved paring knife

8- to 10-inch chef's knife

Japanese vegetable-cutting knife

Crinkle-edged vegetable-cutting knife

Vegetable peeler

Melon baller

Benriner cutter (see page 256)

Kitchen scissors

Assorted molds and cups for shaping rice

Wooden picks

Oriental bamboo skewers

Spray bottle for misting carved vegetables

Paper towels

Food color pastes

Self-sealing plastic bags

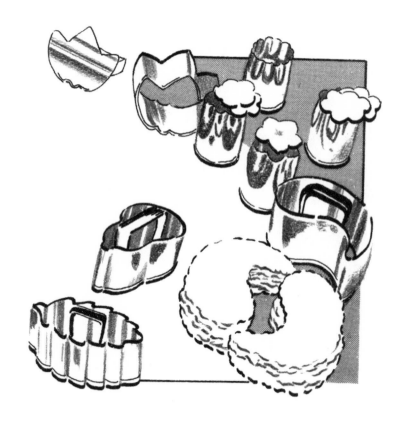

LEMON BASKETS

(Lemon Kago)

Lemon Baskets can be filled with condiments, sauces, salads, Sashimi (page 63), jelled *kanten* or ice cream.

1 large lemon, lime or orange per serving

◉ Cut off a thin slice from stem end of lemon to make a flat surface for basket to sit on. Plunge a small sharp knife horizontally into middle of lemon or a little above. Cut around lemon, leaving a 1/3-inch strip going across the top of the lemon to form the handle. Carefully cut out pulp from under handle and remaining portion of basket.

VARIATIONS

LEMON CUP

◉ Slice off the upper third of a lemon. Use a small spoon to scoop out pulp from lemon bottom and lid. Prop lids against filled cups. Refrigerate until serving time.

SCALLOPED LEMON SLICES

◉ Using a paring knife or lemon zester, remove several evenly spaced thin vertical strips of peel down the length of a lemon. Cut lemon into thin slices.

GREEN-ONION THREADS

◉ Place green stem end of a green onion on a cutting board. Cut stem open lengthwise. With the point of a small paring knife, shred stem lengthwise into threads. Place threads in a bowl of iced water to curl. Thickness of threads can be varied.

HANDMADE SEAWEED BASKETS

(Konbu No Hana Kago)

Fill these tasty edible baskets with rice crackers, nuts or small pieces of fried foods such as Tempura (page 152).

1 (6-inch) square *dashi konbu* (kelp) per basket
1 (10-inch) dried-gourd strip (*kampyo*) per basket, soaked in salted water

6 to 8 cups vegetable oil or peanut oil

◉ Dip *konbu* in a large bowl of warm water; gently flex occasionally 2 to 3 minutes to soften. Pat dry. To shape small basket, lay *konbu* on a cutting surface. Place a 6-inch saucer on top. Using a small sharp knife, trim around saucer. Press circular piece of *konbu* inside a 4 1/2-inch foil tart pan. Crease *konbu* around bottom of tart pan to help set shape. Flute edges.

◉ Make a few short slits on bottom of *konbu* to prevent blistering and splattering when fried. Make a small horizontal slit 1/2 inch from top edge of each side of basket. Insert 1 end of soaked gourd strip into 1 slit; tie it into a knot. Insert other end of gourd strip into opposite slit; tie as before. Handle will be limp until fried. Fill basket with loosely crushed foil to support handle and shape it.

◉ Thoroughly dry basket in pan several hours or overnight. In a wok or shallow pan, heat oil to 360F (180C). Remove basket from pan; discard foil. Using long tongs, carefully hold basket upside down in hot oil a few seconds to set shape of handle. Turn and fry side knots. Set basket upright in hot oil. With a large spoon, pour oil inside basket. Tilt on all sides for even browning. Basket will have a rich, brown lacquered look after frying. Don't overcook or it will taste bitter. Drain on paper towels.

◉ *Makes 1 basket.*

SCORED SHIITAKE MUSHROOMS

These sculpted mushrooms can be braised (Seasoned Shiitake Mushrooms, page 122) and added to box lunches or cooked in one-pot dishes.

◉ Use fresh shiitake or, if dried, rehydrate in warm water 30 minutes. Cut off stems. Using a small paring knife, make a shallow cut slightly at an angle across middle of mushroom cap on the top side. Make a second cut, at an opposite angle, parallel to the first one. Pull out the thin V-shaped piece of mushroom between cuts. Make a similar pair of cuts crossing the first cut in the center, at right angles. Remove the thin piece of mushroom between the second pair of cuts. Mushroom cap will appear fluted with a cross pattern.

◉ Any mushroom with a large flat cap can be decorated this way. Mushroom caps are also attractive with star shapes cut into the tops.

PINE-NEEDLE GARNISH

◉ Cut a 1 1/4 x 1/2-inch piece of lemon peel. On a cutting surface, place lemon peel with a short side toward you. Using a small sharp knife, make a cut 1/8 inch from right side. Cut should start from bottom and go 2/3 way to top edge of lemon piece. Turn peel and repeat cut on opposite side. Pull up 2 side strips and cross over center section.

VARIATION

◉ This garnish can also be made with strips of *kamaboko*, carrot or other vegetables.

PINWHEEL SHRIMP
(Uzu Sugata Ebi)

This pair of shrimp will spin merrily in a bowl of soup. Add them to your most delicious *suimono*—a clear elegant soup.

2 medium-size raw shrimp per pinwheel	1 tablespoon cornstarch Water

◉ Peel shrimp, leaving tails intact. Make a shallow cut lengthwise down the back of each shrimp. Rinse out dark vein. On a cutting board, lay 1 shrimp on its side with tail curling left. Place second shrimp on its side with tail curling right. Fit shrimp together with backs meeting. In a small bowl, make a thick paste with cornstarch and a few drops of water. Put a dab of paste between shrimp. Pin shrimp together with 2 wooden picks. In a medium-size saucepan, bring water to boil. Add shrimp. Reduce heat to low; poach shrimp pinwheels 2 to 3 minutes. Drain; cool slightly. Remove wooden picks.

◉ *Makes 1 pinwheel.*

CHERRY TOMATO FLOWERS

◉ With a sharp knife, cut cherry tomatoes into quarter sections without cutting all the way through to stem end. Gently remove seeds. Use scissors to trim sections to form attractive petal shapes. Chill tomato flowers in iced water. Fill with *wasabi,* mustard or other condiments as desired.

TURNIP ROSE DECORATION

This rose is strictly for looks; it will add a beautiful touch to your table decorations or floral centerpieces.

1 (1/2-lb.) well-shaped round turnip	Rose leaves

◉ Using a Benriner cutter, a French mandoline or large sharp chef's knife, cut turnip into paper-thin slices, about 1/16 inch thick. Soak in a briny, salt-water solution 1 hour. Slices will soften. Drain slices.

◉ Make a cut on 1 slice from center to edge. Overlap cut edges tightly, forming a cone shape. Mold 5 or 6 slices securely around turnip cone. Set the flower upright on a small serving dish. Mold remaining turnip slices around it to resemble a rose in full bloom. Secure petals with 5/8-inch carpenters' brads, finishing nails or U-shaped pins. Gently bend back tops of slices to resemble rose petals. Drop rose into iced water; leave several hours to "bloom." Add fresh rose leaves for garnish.

◉ *Makes 1 flower.*

EGG CHRYSANTHEMUM
(Tamago Kiku)

Beautiful flowers evoke a sense of the season. Add a touch of fall to your food platters with these attractive egg chrysanthemums.

1 extra-large egg per flower
Pinch of salt
1 or 2 drops yellow food coloring

Vegetable oil
Thin slices of pink pickled ginger,
    cut in fine shreds

◉ In a small bowl, beat egg, salt and food coloring. Heat a 10- or 11-inch skillet over medium-high heat. Wipe skillet with a paper towel that has been dipped in oil. Pour beaten egg into oiled skillet. Swirl skillet so egg covers bottom of skillet. Reduce heat to low. Cook 1 minute or until egg is set. Remove skillet from heat. Carefully turn egg sheet over; cook 30 seconds. Turn cooked egg out of skillet. Cool 5 minutes.

◉ Fold 2 opposite sides of egg sheet so they meet in center. Fold egg sheet in half again, starting from a folded side. Using a small knife, make short slits, 1/2 inch apart, down the side with the double fold. Make slits no deeper than one-fourth to one-half the width of the folded piece. Beginning at 1 end, carefully roll up the egg sheet. Set flower on the base. Secure with wooden picks. Gently spread open flower petals. Place a small amount of ginger in center of flower.

◉ *Makes 1 flower.*

EGG CREPES
(Usu Yaki Tamago)

The skill of the Japanese chef is determined by the thinness of his egg crepe.
Shredded egg crepes are used as an ingredient in Japanese dishes and
as an attractive garnish.

2 large eggs	1/4 teaspoon cornstarch
1 tablespoon mirin	1/4 teaspoon salt

◉ Place all the ingredients in a small bowl; beat with a whisk. Strain mixture into a small bowl. Heat an 8-inch nonstick skillet over medium heat. Wipe skillet with a paper towel that has been dipped in oil. Pour 2 tablespoons egg mixture into oiled skillet. Swirl skillet so egg mixture covers bottom of skillet in a very thin sheet. If pan is too hot, egg will not swirl properly. Cook 30 seconds or until set. Carefully turn crepe; cook about 15 seconds. Turn crepe out of skillet to cool completely before cutting.

◉ When cool, roll up crepe. With a sharp knife, cut in strips from 1/8 to 1/4 inch wide.

◉ *Makes 6 crepes.*

VARIATION

EGG PANCAKE

◉ A thicker pancake can be made using the entire amount of egg mixture and cooking it in a 9- or 10-inch skillet.

VEGETABLE IKEBANA

Use vegetables to create floral garnishes for your special dishes or for a centerpiece for your next party.

◉ To make simple flowers, cut 1/4-inch-thick slices from turnips, large carrots, daikon radish or jicama. No need to peel the vegetables. Cut flower shapes using assorted sizes of cookie cutters, Japanese metal flower cutters or canapé cutters. Drop the flowers into iced water to crisp. They can be refrigerated overnight. Cut flowers will enhance platters or can be eaten as dippers.

◉ For arrangements, flower shapes can be tinted if necessary. I prefer to add color by cutting centers from colorful vegetables, then attaching them to the vegetable flowers with toothpicks. Cover bamboo skewers with green onion stems. Make a few short stems and a few longer stems. Push the pointed end of each covered skewer into a vegetable flower. Push the other ends into a hollowed acorn squash, melon or other suitable food container. It may help to push skewers into a potato half inside the vegetable container to hold flowers in place. Tuck blanched leek stems into the arrangement base; pull up and tuck in the ends to create loops of various sizes to correspond with the arrangement.

ONION FLOWER

◉ Remove outer skin from an onion. Using a paring knife or a V-shaped wedge cutting tool, insert knife into center of onion. Make V-shaped cuts around middle of onion, cutting about halfway through. Hold onion under hot running water and separate layers. Flowers can be tinted in bowls of water with food coloring added. Various centers can be inserted. For a layered flower, stack layers attractively, beginning with largest and ending with smallest.

◉ *Makes 1 flower.*

CARROT SPIDER MUM

● Cut 10 or 12 (4-inch-long) paper-thin strips from a large carrot, using a Benriner cutter or a French mandoline. Using a small knife, make 5 lengthwise cuts, about 2 inches long, in center of each strip. Cut outside strips apart on each slice, trimming ends into a point. Fold ends of a carrot strip together. Push a regular thick carrot slice onto 1 end of a short bamboo skewer. This will keep carrot petal from sliding down toothpick. Push a folded carrot strip onto bamboo skewer. Fold remaining strips; push onto same skewer. When all strips are on skewer, push another thick carrot slice on top of the skewer to hold petals in place. Gently pull alternate carrot strips to left and right on skewer to build a flower shape. Drop flower into a small bowl of iced water to chill. Before using, trim skewer so it does not show on garnish.

● *Makes 1 flower.*

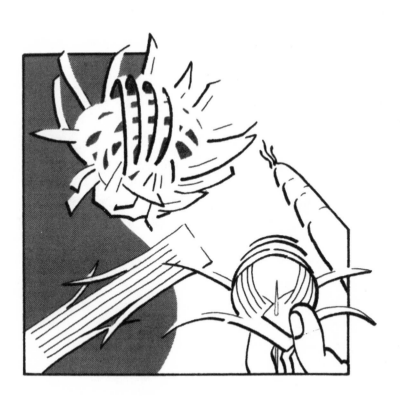

JAPANESE NOODLE FAN

Noodle fans add an elegant touch to serving plates of tempura or other foods.

◉ Hold a small bundle of somen noodles together by one end. (If you prefer, use chopsticks to hold noodles.) Dip the other end of the noodles into prepared tempura batter. Lower noodles into hot oil while holding the unbattered end a safe distance above the oil; cook a few seconds or until the batter sets. Drop noodle bundle into the oil to spread open into a fan. Cook 30 to 45 seconds; remove from oil with chopsticks. Arrange on serving plate.

◉ *Makes 1 fan.*

CARROT FANS

◉ From a large carrot, cut rectangular pieces 1 1/2 inches long, 1 inch wide and 1/2 inch thick. Cook pieces in boiling water 1 minute, drain and rinse with cold water. Using a small paring knife, starting 1/2 inch from edge of 1 long side, make 4 or 5 cuts at right angles to and through opposite long side of each carrot piece. Strips should remain attached. Let stand in iced water at least 20 minutes to spread open.

◉ *Makes 3 or 4 fans.*

Lotus Blossom

◉ Peel a large onion; cut a flat area on base. Secure onion for cutting by inserting 2 long metal skewers through bulb close to flat base. Run skewers, parallel to base, in opposite directions. With a sharp knife, slice onion in half, down to skewers, then in quarters, then in eighths. If onion is large, it may be possible to cut it further into sixteenths. Cook onion 1 to 2 minutes in boiling water. Remove skewers; submerge onion in iced water. When cooled, gently open up the petals. Store Lotus Blossom in iced water until needed; drain well. Garnish with lily-pad leaves or trimmed vegetable leaves.

◉ *Makes 1 blossom.*

APPETIZERS

(Zensai)

◉

Zensai are tantalizing small portions of artistically arranged foods which serve to stimulate the appetite and increase the pleasure of drinking saké. In a formal Japanese meal, *zensai* are served after the first cup of saké but before the clear soup and sashimi courses. In a less formal context, a variety of *zensai* (under different names) might comprise the evening meal for a group of tired workers stopping off for a few drinks after a hard day at the office.

According to the encyclopedic study *An Inquiry into Japanese Cooking*, the roots of *zensai* can be traced back to nineteenth-century *honzen-ryōri*, the formal court cuisine used for entertaining. Exquisite small portions of food were arranged in the inverted lids of inkstone boxes. Known as *suzuri-buta*, this dish evolved into *hiro-buta*, a complex variation of the original. Today, small appetizer assortments are still creatively served on unique serving trays.

The small exquisite foods of the tea cere-mony, or *chakaiseki,* have also influenced the development of *zensai.* From the sashimi course, *mukozuki,* to one of the final courses known as *hassun,* the foods are accompanied by ritual saké. For the *hassun* course, foods are served on a square lacquered tray, or *hassun,* in remembrance of the time when ceremonial foods were served on the lid of a writing box.

In the early 1900s, the word *zensai* was coined by the famous potter Kitaoji Rosanjin to mean "appetizer." He felt these diminutive portions of food could be beautifully crafted from food scraps such as shrimp heads, fish skin and vegetable stems—items normally dealt with in a much less interesting way!

Elegant *zensai* is served in tiny portions; just enough to "awaken the appetite." Many of the dishes throughout this book can be served as appetizers. Tiny salad-like portions of *aemono* or *sunomono* can become *zensai* when served before an elegant meal. Then they might be called *saki-zuki* or *tsuki-dashi.* *Tsuki-dashi* is sushi jargon for appetizers at the sushi bar.

Small is beautiful in Japan. It is the qual-ity of the appetizer, not the quantity, that counts! Only the freshest and finest ingredi-ents are used for *zensai.* Their colors, textures and flavors should be selected according to the season. Preparation for *zensai* can be as easy as slicing a piece of pickled radish, raw tuna or lotus root, which displays a natural design. Other *zensai* might require more preparation time, as a formal occasion may demand.

Japanese appetizers range from the tiny elegant foods known as *zensai* to the hearty mouthfuls known as *saké-no-tsumami.* The latter are served in places where men go drinking. The portions may not be large, but there are plenty of choices for sampling. *Tsumami* might be two or three pieces of sliced raw fish or tiny packages of seaweed tied with bows of shredded gourd. Rice is never served with *tsumami* because it does-n't go well with alcoholic beverages. How-ever, rice might be served at the end of the evening in the form of *ocha-zuké,* green tea poured over rice. Pickles are served on the side.

Another appetizer is called *otoshi,* com-plimentary snacks served in drinking estab-lishments. Spicy Glazed Sardines or Szechuan-Style Nuts & Bolts are so good, you won't want to eat just one! For a unique presentation, serve these *otoshi* in elegant Gyoza Baskets or in larger Handmade Sea-weed Baskets (page 17).

Kamaboko, steamed fish cake loaf, is cel-ebration food, well suited to be served as an appetizer. Created centuries ago, it was men-tioned in the *Kojiki,* the oldest chronicle of Japan compiled in A.D. 712. In the year 1115, records of an imperial celebration menu show how *kamaboko* was being served. *Kamaboko* is made from a homogenous pro-tein gel or fish paste called *surimi.* There are a number of *surimi* products resembling *kamaboko;* collectively they are called *neri-seihan.* They come boiled, steamed and fried; plain or flavored with vegetables and season-ings. Japanese markets carry an astonishing array. *Kamaboko* can be sliced and served or fashioned into whimsical shapes like the but-terflies on page 39. Another unique *neri-seihan* food is *chikuwa,* used to make Bamboo-Shaped Fish Rolls.

Because of their versatility, many appetizers can be served as other courses during a meal. Simmered Gobo & Bacon Rolls would be a delicious accompaniment for rice. In Kyoto, I ate tiny grilled oyster mushrooms from a golden leaf. Spicy Glazed Mushrooms would be just as impressive scattered on top of a Texas-size barbecued steak.

An assortment of *zensai* might satisfy today's urge for "grazing"—an American trend for entertaining whereby a variety of small dishes are offered in place of a single entrée. It may be that the concept of grazing is already deeply rooted in Japan, where saké is never served without *saké-no-sakana*—small appetizer portions that exist solely to complement the taste of saké.

SPICY GLAZED MUSHROOMS

(Shimeji Itame)

Fresh wild mushrooms are becoming available in supermarkets throughout the United States. For appetizers, I like to serve these mushrooms in a favorite handcrafted pottery leaf dish with saké or beer. Other times, I toss them with warm soba or serve them on a bed of baby mixed lettuce with a gingery dressing.

6 ounces tree oyster mushrooms (*shimejitaké*), ends trimmed, separated
6 ounces fresh shiitake mushrooms, stemmed and sliced
1 tablespoon vegetable oil
1 slice gingerroot, crushed
1 garlic clove, crushed

1 tiny red chile, halved and seeded
1 tablespoon light soy sauce (*usukuchi shoyu*)
1 tablespoon mirin
2 teaspoons butter
Pinch salt
2 teaspoons Japanese chives (*nira*) or regular chives

◉ Briefly rinse mushrooms under cool water. Gently press out water; pat dry on paper towels. In a wok or large skillet, heat oil over medium-high heat. Add gingerroot, garlic and chile. Stir-fry 1 minute until aromatic; discard. Add mushrooms. Stir-fry 1 minute. Add soy sauce and mirin. Cook 1 minute or until liquid evaporates. Stir in butter, salt and chives. Serve on a warmed serving plate.

◉ *Makes 4 servings.*

FRIED CHEESE ROLLS WITH NORI

(Cheese Iso Maki Agé)

These crispy cheese-stuffed pastries are wrapped in a "black belt" of nori. They promise to be a knockout at your next cocktail party! I discovered a similar snack at a grocery store demonstration in Tokyo.

Green Onion & Miso Dipping
   Sauce (page 33)
1 (8-oz.) box pasteurized process
   cheese spread, well chilled
1 tablespoon cornstarch mixed
   with 1 tablespoon water

1 sheet nori, cut in 1/2-inch
   strips
1 (10-oz.) package round *gyoza*
   skins (about 54 skins)
6 cups peanut oil or vegetable
   oil

◉ Prepare Green Onion & Miso Dipping Sauce; set aside. Cut cheese crosswise into 3 equal-size blocks. Cut each block into 6 slices. Cut each slice into 3 strips. You will have 54 strips. Place a cheese strip on lower half of a *gyoza* skin. Fold sides over to enclose cheese. Fold up bottom portion of skin; roll up into a tight cylinder. Seal edges with a tiny amount of cornstarch mixture.

◉ Wrap a narrow strip of nori around middle of each cylinder. Dampen ends of nori strips to seal. Cover with plastic wrap to prevent drying. In a wok or deep pot, heat oil to 360F (180C). Fry logs, a few at a time, in hot oil about 1 minute or until crisp and golden. Drain briefly on paper towels; place on a wire rack while frying remaining logs. Serve with dipping sauce.

◉ *Makes 8 to 10 servings.*

GREEN ONION & MISO DIPPING SAUCE

A rich-tasting, fat-free dip. Good as a dip for appetizers or as a sauce for grilled tofu or lightly cooked vegetables.

2/3 cup sweet white or yellow
    miso
3 tablespoons mirin
2 tablespoons sugar
2 tablespoons toasted sesame
    seeds

2 teaspoons fresh lemon juice
2 green onions, green parts only,
    finely minced

◉ In a small bowl, combine all ingredients.

◉ *Makes about 1 cup.*

PICKLED QUAIL EGGS

Red shiso turns this marinade a natural deep pink color. Quail eggs, a popular addition to the bentō, may not be available; use the smallest chicken eggs you can find. The pretty eggs will taste delicious. For a party I like to serve them in the middle of a tangled "nest" of puffed, fried rice stick noodles (*saifun*).

12 hard-cooked quail eggs, peeled
1/2 cup rice vinegar
2 tablespoons sugar

1/2 teaspoon salt
3 or 4 pickled red shiso leaves if
    available, well rinsed

◉ Place quail eggs in a small jar. In a small bowl, combine vinegar, sugar and salt. Stir well to dissolve sugar. Pour over quail eggs. Rinse shiso leaves well under cool water to remove excess salt. Tuck leaves into the jar. Cover and refrigerate 2 to 3 days. For each serving, thread 2 or 3 pickled eggs on a short skewer.

◉ *Makes 4 to 6 servings*

GYOZA BASKETS

Fill these attractive little pastry baskets with tiny portions of salads, pickles or appetizers. For a taste of something utterly seductive, paint the insides with melted chocolate, then fill with a tiny scoop of green tea or ginger ice cream.

About 6 cups peanut oil or vegetable oil	6 round *gyoza* skins, or more if desired

◉ In a wok or deep pot, heat oil to 325F (165C). Press each skin into a small metal tart pan or fluted brioche pan. Set one of the pans in a long-handled wire strainer. Lower pan slowly into hot oil, holding skin in place with a wooden spoon. If oil is too hot, skin will immediately lose its shape and float out of pan. Lift tart pan slightly out of oil and continually spoon hot oil over sides and into bottom of pastry basket. Fry until crisp and golden brown. With wooden spoon, hold the basket securely in the wire strainer. Tilt over oil, pouring out any oil inside. Cool pan and pastry basket 1 to 2 minutes. Lift cooled pastry basket out of pan. Drain briefly on paper towels; cool on a wire rack.

◉ Deep-fry remaining skins as above. Cool completely before use.

◉ *Makes 6 baskets.*

SPICY GLAZED SARDINES
(Tazukuri)

Once you taste these tiny sweet fish, I promise you won't want to stop. Add a sprinkle of Seven-Spice Powder (page 228) for a spicy taste. Serve as a delicious nibble in Gyoza Baskets (page 34) or over rice.

About 4 cups peanut oil or
    vegetable oil
1 (3-oz.) pkg. dried tiny sardines
1/4 cup soy sauce
2 tablespoons water

2 tablespoons mirin
3 tablespoons sugar
1 tablespoon toasted sesame
    seeds

◉ In a wok or deep saucepan, heat oil to 360F (180C). Place sardines in a large wire skimmer. Lower into hot oil. Fry 30 seconds. Drain on paper towels. In a small saucepan, bring soy sauce, water, mirin and sugar to a boil. Reduce heat to medium. Cook 5 minutes or until thick and syrupy; cool 3 to 4 minutes. Add sardines; mix well. Stir in sesame seeds.

◉ *Makes 4 to 6 servings.*

VARIATION

◉ Sardines can be dry-roasted in a hot skillet 3 to 4 minutes instead of being deep-fried.

MARINATED RADISH FANS

(Aka Kabu Sunomono)

Ordinary radishes are transformed into tiny fans which make a tasty hors d'oeuvre, a colorful salad or an attractive garnish.

Tangy Marinade (see below)
1 bunch large, well-shaped,
    oval radishes

TANGY MARINADE
1/2 cup rice vinegar

1/3 cup sugar
1/2 teaspoon salt
1/2 teaspoon sesame oil
1 (1-inch) square piece *konbu*
    (optional)

◉ Prepare marinade. Cut off radish tops; trim off root ends. Wash radishes in cool water; pat dry. On a cutting board, place a radish on its side between 2 chopsticks. Top and bottom of radish should be at right angles to chopsticks. Make a series of slices across radish down to chopsticks. Chopsticks will prevent knife from cutting all the way through radish. Repeat with remaining radishes.

◉ Add radishes to marinade. Refrigerate 30 minutes. If radishes are marinated longer than 1 hour, they will bleed and become bright pink. Remove radishes from marinade; shake off excess liquid. With your fingers, gently spread each radish open into a fan shape. Serve in small dishes.

◉ *Makes 3 or 4 servings.*

TANGY MARINADE

◉ Combine all ingredients in a medium-size bowl.

Marinated Radish Mums
(Kiku Aka Kabu Sunomono)

Use chopsticks to help with the cutting, as in the recipe for Marinated Radish Fans (page 36). Radish mums taste good and make an attractive garnish, too. For larger flowers, try the same technique with turnips. Spoon a small amount of salmon-roe caviar (*ikura*) in the center of each flower.

Tangy Marinade (page 36)
1 bunch large, well-shaped,
   oval radishes

◉ Prepare marinade; set aside. Cut off radish tops; trim off root ends. Rinse in cool water; pat dry. On a cutting board, place a radish on an end between 2 chopsticks. Make a series of slices across radish down to chopsticks. Chopsticks will prevent knife from cutting all the way through radish. Turn radish 90 degrees; make a series of similar parallel cuts at right angles to the first ones. Repeat with remaining radishes. Add radishes to marinade. Refrigerate 2 or 3 hours. Radishes will "bloom" into a flower shape. The red skins will bleed, tinting radishes pink. To serve, tap off excess liquid. Serve in small dishes.

◉ *Makes 3 or 4 servings*

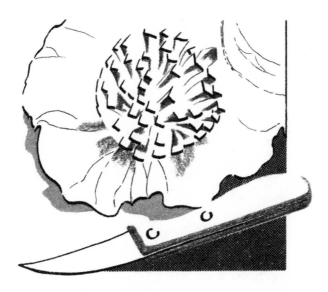

BAMBOO-SHAPED FISH ROLLS
(Takenoko Chikuwa)

Chikuwa ("bamboo wheel") fish cake cylinders were originally made from fish paste patted into elongated shapes around bamboo stalks. The paste was grilled over an open fire, then sold with bamboo stalks intact. Today, they are purchased hollow. They can be stuffed and eaten plain or dipped in Tempura Batter (page 152) and deep-fried. Serve as an appetizer, as part of the bentō lunch or add to stews during the last few minutes of cooking. Cut all the vegetables into uniform strips.

4 small hollow fish rolls (*chikuwa*)
1 teaspoon Wasabi (page 237)
4 or 5 fresh green beans, blanched
    and cut into matchstick strips
1/2 small carrot, cut into
    matchstick strips

1 (1-inch-wide) strip red bell
    pepper, cut into matchstick
    strips
Soy sauce

◉ Cut fish rolls in half crosswise. Using a small knife, spread insides with Wasabi. Gather a strip of each vegetable in a bunch; push into hollow center of one section of fish roll; trim ends. Continue stuffing remaining fish rolls. Slice each piece of fish roll on the diagonal into 2 pieces. Stand stuffed pieces on their flat ends to resemble bamboo shoots. Serve at once with soy sauce, or cover and refrigerate several hours.

◉ *Makes 16 appetizers.*

KAMABOKO BUTTERFLIES
(Chō Chō Kamaboko)

These attractive little appetizers will fly right into your mouth! *Narutomaki* is a pretty fish cake with attractive ridges on the outside and a pink and white pinwheel design inside. Pink and white symbolize felicity.

1 (6-oz.) pkg. steamed *narutomaki*
   or *kamaboko* (pinwheel design
   or plain)

Green onion stems
Soy sauce
Wasabi (page 237) to taste

◉ Slice fish loaf into 1/2-inch-thick pieces. Slice each piece through the middle to within 1/8 inch of base without cutting all the way through. You will have 2 attached flaps of fish loaf. Place each piece on a cutting surface with uncut side to your right. Make a short diagonal cut on uncut side in lower half. Slant-cut downward at a 45-degree angle. Spread flaps to make wings and tuck cut-off section inside flaps. Decorate each butterfly with green onion pieces to resemble antennae. Serve with soy sauce and Wasabi.

◉ *Makes 10 to 12 butterflies.*

SIMMERED GOBO & BACON ROLLS

(Gobo No Bacon Maki)

Yukari Ito, a close family friend from Setagaya-ku, Tokyo, shared this recipe and recommends it as a snack to accompany saké.

4 (5-inch) pieces *gobo* (burdock)

1 tablespoon vinegar

1 cup Sea Vegetable & Bonito Stock (page 46)

2 tablespoons mirin

2 tablespoons soy sauce

1 tablespoon saké

2 tablespoons sugar

4 bacon slices

◉ Scrape *gobo*. Soak in a small amount of water with vinegar 15 minutes. In a small saucepan, combine all remaining ingredients except bacon. Bring to a boil over high heat; immediately reduce heat to low. Add *gobo*. Cover and simmer 25 minutes or until tender. *Gobo* will retain texture but can be pierced easily with a knife. Cool in sauce.

◉ Remove *gobo*; shake dry. Reserve sauce. Wrap a bacon slice around each piece of *gobo* in a spiral fashion. Secure ends with wooden pick halves. In a small skillet, fry wrapped *gobo* over medium-low heat, turning several times so bacon cooks evenly. Wooden picks can be removed when bacon is half cooked. Watch carefully; if fat burns, remove *gobo*. Drain and wipe skillet; return *gobo* to skillet and continue frying until bacon is crisp. Pour off remaining fat. Pour reserved sauce over *gobo*, coating well. Cut each piece into 5 (1-inch) pieces. Put 4 or 5 pieces on each small serving plate. Spoon remaining sauce over each serving.

◉ *Makes 4 or 5 servings.*

STUFFED VEGETABLE CONFETTI

Lillian and Bunky Johnson served this spectacular appetizer as they entertained aboard the Captain's Gig while sailing down the Delaware. In Philadelphia, Bunky served as commanding officer of the USS *Forrestal*. This recipe was discovered on a junket to Japan. Because they are so pretty, Lillian says they remind her of "big pieces of edible confetti."

1 pound ground beef or pork
2 large eggs
1 medium-size yellow onion, finely chopped
2 tablespoons oyster sauce
1 large garlic clove, finely minced
Salt and black pepper to taste
2 teaspoons soy sauce

1 green and 1 red bell pepper, each cut into 4 strips
20 round mushrooms or small fresh shiitake mushrooms, wiped
1 Japanese eggplant, halved lengthwise

◉ Preheat oven to 350F (175C). In a medium-size bowl, combine all ingredients except bell peppers, mushrooms and eggplant. Stir ingredients well to combine. Cut pepper strips in half crosswise, making 16 pieces. Remove mushroom stems. Cut eggplant halves crosswise into 4 pieces. Spoon a small mound of filling onto each piece of vegetable. Moisten fingers; smooth tops and sides of meat mixture. Place in 1 or 2 lightly oiled baking dishes. Bake 15 to 20 minutes. Serve warm or at room temperature.

◉ *Makes 6 to 8 servings.*

SZECHUAN-STYLE
NUTS & BOLTS

You won't be able to eat just one bite, or two or three, of this irresistible snack. This recipe is a slight variation of one I developed for San-J International. It has become a favorite in their kitchens as well as mine. You'll enjoy it, too, especially with a cup of saké or beer.

2 cups Rice Chex cereal
1 cup dry-roasted peanuts
4 tablespoons melted butter
2 tablespoons San-J Szechuan
   Hot & Spicy Sauce
1 tablespoon sesame seeds

1/4 teaspoon celery salt
1 cup roasted green peas
   (Japanese *senbei*)
1 cup kaki no tané (Japanese
   rice crackers)
1 cup pretzel sticks

◉ Preheat oven to 275C (135F). Place cereal and peanuts in a large shallow pan. Melt butter in a small saucepan; blend in Szechuan sauce, sesame seeds and celery salt. Pour sauce evenly over cereal mixture, stirring gently to coat. Mix in green peas, rice crackers and pretzels. Spread mixture in a large baking sheet with sides. Bake 45 minutes, stirring every 15 minutes. Cool completely before serving.

◉ *Makes 8 cups.*

SPICY SEA HERB FISH
(Sakana Senbei)

Senbei, or baked rice cake, is an inexpensive, popular snack made from rice or wheat flour. It comes in a variety of interesting shapes and flavors. Several types are named after their shape. To capture the essence of *senbei,* I have dusted popular fish-shaped snack crackers with Japanese seasonings. *Ao-nori* is a powdered seaweed seasoning available in glass jars. If unavailable, grind a half sheet of preseasoned, toasted nori in a small electric coffee or spice grinder.

1 tablespoon plus 2 teaspoons
    vegetable oil
1 teaspoon sesame oil or
    shiso-flavored oil
1 generous tablespoon *ao-nori*
    (seasoned, crushed laver)

1 generous teaspoon poppy seeds
1 teaspoon ground red
    (cayenne) pepper
1/2 teaspoon garlic salt
1 (6-oz.) pkg. fish-shaped
    snack crackers

◉ Preheat oven to 325F (165C). In a medium-size bowl, stir together all the ingredients except crackers. Add crackers; gently mix with the seasoned oil until crackers are evenly coated. Spread crackers and seasoning on a baking sheet. Bake 10 minutes, stirring once or twice. Cool crackers; store in an airtight container.

◉ *Makes 2 cups.*

SOUPS

(Shirumono)

◉

Soups are among the most simple, satisfying foods of Japan. Two main varieties of soup are *suimono (osumashi)*, or clear broth, and *miso-shiru,* or broth thickened with miso (fermented bean paste). *Suimono* is served after the appetizer course of an elegant Japanese meal. It is an excellent accompaniment to sushi, and doubles as a replacement for a thirst-quenching beverage in the meal. *Suimono* and *miso-shiru* are served year-round. Through the use of a great variety of fresh ingredients, they are a reflection of the changing seasons.

Suimono consists of four parts. The first is *dashi,* a Sea Vegetable & Bonito Stock. Made with dried kelp and bonito, *dashi*'s subtle, complex flavor guarantees the success of the soup. The second part is usually a bite-size piece of protein food, such as tofu, fish or chicken. The third part might be a complementary piece of seasonal vegetable. The fourth part is the seasoning or garnish. This is the final touch and might include a few drops of soy sauce, a certain spice or a tender herb selected in honor of the season. Clear soups and miso soups are sipped directly from the bowl. The solid ingredients are eaten with a pair of chopsticks.

The same principles of preparing clear soup apply when making miso soup. The only variation is the addition of the miso paste. You can add a single type of miso, such as the sweet white miso favored in Kyoto, or you can blend it with a darker paste to create a depth of flavor not found in the use of a single type. Several types of miso paste are commonly blended in *cha-kaiseki* (tea ceremony cuisine).

The soup is complete with the addition of the solid ingredients and seasoning. For a more substantial main-course meal, the protein in the soup can be increased.

For centuries, one of Japan's favorite breakfast foods has been a steaming-hot bowl of miso soup. Supplemented with protein-rich tofu and a nutritious leafy green vegetable, Savory Miso Soup is a powerhouse of good nutrition and an energizing way to start the day.

Miso soup is so beloved in Japan, it has been the favorite subject of poets and scholars throughout Japanese history. For centuries, it has been a staple food of the disciples of Zen. It is said that a young woman in Japan is ready to become a wife when she is able to make delicious miso soup. I have found that a cup of miso soup instantly satisfies nostalgic cravings of homesick houseguests from Japan. Thicker soups or stews, such as Country Vegetable Soup with Miso, feature the solid ingredients as the principal elements.

The foundation of a good soup in any country is the stock. *Dashi* is one of the great stocks of the world. But unlike meat or chicken stock, its preparation requires only a few minutes of effort. This advantage enables the Japanese to have fresh stock available daily for the preparation of meals. For centuries, the use of animal fat was unknown in Japan. Fats serve to add richness, flavor and substance to stock. The ingenious development of *dashi* was based upon the need to add these qualities to foods without the use of fats. Dried bonito (*katsuobushi*) and dried kelp (*konbu*) were selected because of their high amino acid content. These proteins are the natural source of the manufactured flavor enhancer monosodium glutamate. They provide a subtle flavor which enhances the taste of foods considerably. Dried shiitake mushrooms, high in similar flavor compounds, add even more flavor to the stockpot. Some people prefer stock made with small dried sardines, or *niboshi*. If used, remove heads and entrails to prevent bitter stock. Try a combination of half *niboshi* and half bonito shavings for an excellent variation.

The cuisine of Zen Buddhists, known as *shojin-ryōri*, bases its stocks mainly upon the use of vegetables, especially *konbu*. The long life span of the Okinawan people is attributed to the healthful properties of *konbu*, consumed in large quantities.

Some Japanese soups and stews are made with chicken stock, especially when the primary soup ingredient is chicken. It is possible to substitute chicken stock for Sea Vegetable & Bonito Stock in the recipes; however, the special flavor and unique character of the soups will be greatly diminished.

SEA VEGETABLE & BONITO STOCK
(Ichiban Dashi)

Dashi is the basis for Japan's delicate soups, simmered dishes and sauces. Do not boil this mild-tasting stock after adding the kelp or bonito, or the stock may taste too strong. The strained bonito can be dried in a hot skillet with sesame seeds and salt for a tasty rice topping. Stronger stocks and Second-Quality Stock (see below) can be successfully used for noodle broths, noodle dipping sauces, stews or simmering vegetables. *Dashi* can be refrigerated or frozen. Keep frozen *dashi* cubes in the freezer for the times you will need small amounts for cooking.

1 (5- to 6-inch) length of top-quality *dashi konbu* (kelp), lightly wiped
4 1/2 cups bottled spring water or tap water

1/2 cup dried-bonito shavings (*hana-katsuo*)

◉ Make 2 or 3 slits in *konbu* with a small knife. In a medium-size saucepan, place *konbu* and water over medium-low heat. (Some cooks allow a 30-minute soak before heating.) Heat slowly about 10 minutes, bringing water to the boiling point. Remove *konbu* from pan; do not boil or stock may be too strong. Add bonito shavings. After 1 minute, shavings will partially sink. Immediately strain stock through 3 layers of dampened cheesecloth, a coffee filter or a fine strainer. Do not press shavings to remove liquid. Use at once, or refrigerate up to 3 days. Recipe can be doubled.

◉ *Makes about 4 cups*

VARIATION

SECOND-QUALITY STOCK

◉ In a medium-size saucepan, combine 3 1/2 cups water and strained bonito shavings and *konbu* from Sea Vegetable & Bonito Stock. Bring to a boil. Remove from heat;

steep 30 minutes. Bring back to a boil; add 1/4 cup fresh bonito shavings. Remove from heat. When shavings settle to the bottom of the pan, strain stock. Use at once, or refrigerate up to 3 days.

◉ *Makes about 3 cups.*

HEARTY VEGETABLE BROTH

Create a hearty broth by simmering vegetables in *dashi-jiru,* Japanese soup stock.
Refrigerate leftover bits of raw vegetables in airtight plastic bags just
for this purpose.

◉ Prepare 1 recipe Sea Vegetable & Bonito Stock (opposite). For a vegetarian version, omit the bonito shavings. For a stronger *konbu* flavor, soak the sea vegetable in the measured amount of water at least 2 hours.

◉ For a mushroom-flavored broth, toss 4 or 5 medium-size dried shiitake mushrooms into 4 cups *dashi.* If you have time, let them stand several hours, or cover the pan and simmer 10 minutes over low heat. Trim and discard mushroom stems. Slice caps; if desired, add back to the soup pot.

◉ For a more complex vegetable flavor, add to stock 2 or more ingredients such as sliced carrot, daikon radish, cabbage, green onion, leek or gingerroot. Strain stock to remove vegetables. Serve the delicious broth hot, or use it as a soup base.

◉ Embellish a cup of vegetable broth with bite-size pieces of tofu, cooked vegetables, noodles, minced green onion or a few drops of soy sauce.

CUSTOM MISO SOUP

Prepare the Sea Vegetable & Bonito Stock as directed on page 46. Customize your soup with 1 Protein Selection and 1 or 2 of the Complementary Ingredients. Always choose ingredients that reflect the season. Tender vegetables and uncooked meat and seafood can be simmered directly in the stock a few minutes before the miso is added. Generally, use 1 level tablespoon of your favorite miso paste for each cup of stock. You may need to increase the amount of sweet white miso. Adjust amounts depending on the saltiness of each miso and personal taste. Experiment with blending light and dark miso. The Seasoning/Garnish can be stirred into the pot of hot soup or added to individual bowls of soup.

PROTEIN SELECTION
1 piece diced Fish Cake Tempura
  (page 158)
1 small fresh fish fillet, cubed
1/2 recipe Tofu Treasure Balls
  (page 148)
1/2 skinned, boned, cooked
  chicken breast half, diced
4 or 5 medium-size raw shrimp,
  peeled and cleaned
Crabmeat
15 cherrystone clams, scrubbed,
  soaked in salt water and simmered
  4 minutes in 1 quart water
3 ounces shredded pork
1/4 lb. cubed bean curd
Slices of *kamaboko* or *chikuwa*

COMPLEMENTARY INGREDIENTS
1/2 cup soaked *wakamé,* cut
  into smaller pieces

2 mountain potatoes (*sato imo*),
  peeled, diced and cooked
1 small regular potato, peeled,
  diced and cooked
2-inch piece daikon radish,
  peeled, simmered and cubed
Pieces of deep-fried *mochi*
1 piece blanched *abura-agé*
  (fried tofu pouch), cut into
  thin strips
1 or 2 cabbage leaves, shredded
Unsprayed chrysanthemum
  petals of 1 flower, separated
1 package *enokidaké*
  mushrooms, ends trimmed,
  rinsed
4 small fresh round mushrooms,
  sliced
1/2 carrot, cut into flower shapes
  or matchstick strips

1/4 small *kabocha* pumpkin or
acorn squash, cooked, peeled
and cubed

12 snow peas, strings removed

6 to 8 small blanched sliced okra

1/4 cup sliced bamboo shoots

6 or 8 fresh baby green beans,
French-cut

SEASONING/GARNISH

1 or 2 minced green onions

Powdered *sansho* pepper

Seven-Spice Powder (page 228)

Few drops soy sauce

3 shredded *shiso* leaves

Fine strips of lemon peel

2 to 3 teaspoons ginger juice
(see *Graters*, page 257)

Mitsuba leaves or flat-leaf parsley

Snipped chives

SAVORY MISO SOUP

(Miso-shiru)

Miso-shiru is one of the true flavors of Japan. It is a favorite breakfast food served with rice, an egg, grilled fish and pickles. In Japanese mythology, miso was considered a gift of the gods.

4 cups Sea Vegetable & Bonito
Stock (page 46)

1/2 cup chopped fresh kale,
mustard greens or spinach

2 generous tablespoons red miso

1 tablespoon white miso

1/4 lb. silken tofu, cut into
1/2-inch cubes

1 green onion, minced

◉ In a medium-size saucepan, heat stock over medium-low heat. Add kale or mustard greens. Simmer 8 minutes. If spinach is used, simmer 2 minutes. Combine red and white miso in a small bowl. Dilute with a few tablespoons hot stock; stir into simmering soup. Add tofu. Turn off heat; do not allow to boil after miso is added. Ladle soup into 4 or 5 Japanese soup bowls or other soup bowls. Garnish with green onion. Top with lids. Serve at once.

◉ *Makes 4 or 5 servings.*

TEAPOT SOUP
(Bobin Mushi)

During a trip to Kyoto, I visited the famous Kiyomizu Temple. My plans were to make a quick trip up the steep, narrow lane to the temple. Three hours later, my plans were dashed when I found myself less than halfway there. I had become entranced with the enchanting folk crafts and *Kyo-yaki* (Kyoto ceramics) spilling out of the shops lining "Teapot Lane." I discovered a cache of unique little ceramic teapots meant for serving soup instead of tea. The lid for each pot became the serving dish when turned upside down. Here is my recipe for teapot soup. You probably don't have a collection of these unique little pots, so serve the soup in a 1 1/2-quart, wide-mouth ceramic teapot. Offer small serving bowls on the side. Your friends and family will still be charmed!

3 1/2 cups Chicken Stock with
    Ginger (page 51)
3 small fresh shiitake mushrooms,
    stemmed and sliced
1 tablespoon light soy sauce
    (*usukuchi shoyu*)
1 tablespoon mirin
Salt to taste
3 small okra pods, blanched
    30 seconds and sliced
2 oz. bamboo shoots, sliced
1/2 chicken breast, skinned,
    boned and diced

4 small raw shrimp, peeled
4 gingko nuts (*ginnan*) (optional)
4 pieces ball- or flower-shaped
    wheat gluten (*fu*), soaked, or
    4 thin slices from a large
    carrot, cut into flower shapes
1 green onion, thinly sliced
4 trefoil sprigs (*mitsuba*), shiso,
    watercress or flat-leaf parsley
4 lemon wedges

◉ Place stock in a medium-size saucepan; add mushrooms, soy sauce, mirin and salt. Bring to a simmer over medium-low heat. Add okra, bamboo shoots and chicken; cook 5 minutes. Add shrimp, gingko nuts, if using, and wheat gluten or carrots. Simmer 2 minutes longer. Add green onion and trefoil. Warm teapot with hot water; drain. Fill with soup. Cover and serve. With a small ladle, fill soup bowls. Pass lemon wedges.

◉ *Makes 4 or 5 servings.*

CHICKEN STOCK WITH GINGER
(Tori No Sumashi-jiru)

This excellent stock is a good base for many Japanese soups and other dishes.

1 (3 1/2- to 4-lb.) chicken
2 to 3 lbs. chicken parts
    (backs, necks, wings)
5 green onions or 2 leeks,
    halved and well rinsed

4 (1/4-inch-thick) slices peeled
    gingerroot, crushed
About 5 quarts bottled spring
    water or tap water

◉ Rinse chicken and chicken parts under cool running water. Remove any fat pads. Place all ingredients in a stockpot over medium-high heat. When stock bubbles, immediately reduce heat to low. Simmer, uncovered, 30 minutes, skimming off foam that forms on top. Do not boil or stir stock. After 30 minutes, remove breast and thigh meat from whole chicken if desired; reserve for another use. Continue simmering stock 1 1/2 to 2 hours longer. If water level becomes low, add a little more water.

◉ Strain into a large pan; discard solids. For greater clarity, stock can be strained again through a strainer lined with several layers of dampened cheesecloth. Cool stock, uncovered, 1 hour. Refrigerate up to 3 days. Skim off surface fat before using stock. Stock should be brought to a boil before use. Defatted stock can also be kept frozen in smaller amounts for 1 to 2 months. To concentrate stock flavor, boil it to reduce by 1/3 to 1/2. Add salt as needed or as suggested in recipes. Recipe can be halved.

◉ *Makes about 5 quarts.*

CREAMY CORN POTAGE WITH CRABMEAT
(Tomorokoshi No Kani-jiru)

On the island of Okinawa, this delicate creamy soup is a great favorite in restaurants.

3 1/2 cups Chicken Stock with
  Ginger (page 51)
1 cup fresh whole-kernel corn
  from 2 large ears or 1 (9-oz.)
  pkg. frozen whole-kernel or
  cream-style corn
1 tablespoon saké
1/2 teaspoon sugar
1 teaspoon salt

Dash ground black pepper
1 tablespoon minced baked ham
2 1/2 tablespoons cornstarch
1/4 cup chicken broth or water
2 to 3 oz. flaked crabmeat,
  carefully picked over
1 large egg white, slightly beaten
2 small green onions,
  thinly sliced

◉ In a medium-size saucepan, heat stock and corn over medium heat 5 minutes. Strain hot mixture into a medium-size bowl. Puree corn in a blender or food processor fitted with a steel blade. Add a small amount of stock. Press pureed corn back into hot stock through a fine strainer. Discard any corn pulp left in strainer. Heat stock mixture over medium heat. Stir in saké, sugar, salt, pepper and ham.

◉ In a small bowl, blend cornstarch and 1/4 cup chicken broth or water. Increase heat. When soup boils, add cornstarch mixture, stirring constantly until thickened. Reduce heat to low. Stir in crabmeat. Remove from heat. Drizzle in beaten egg white, stirring with chopsticks in a circular motion. Add green onions. Ladle hot soup into bowls.

◉ *Makes 6 to 8 servings.*

JAPANESE DUMPLING SOUP

(Gyoza-jiru)

This hearty meal in a bowl can be found in noodle shops or a *chuka-ryori-ya*, a Japanese restaurant that serves Chinese food. The dishes are usually influenced by both cuisines. To make *wonton mein*, add 3/4 pound cooked noodles and 1/2 cup sliced bamboo shoots.

6 cups Chicken Stock with
   Ginger (page 51)
2 medium-size dried shiitake
   mushrooms
1 teaspoon salt, or to taste
1 tablespoon saké or dry white
   wine
2 teaspoons light soy sauce
   (*usukuchi shoyu*)
1 teaspoon plus 1 tablespoon
   sesame oil

Dash of ground black pepper
1/2 carrot, cut into thin
   matchstick strips
1 cup fresh spinach, rinsed
   and torn
2 teaspoons salt
1/2 recipe Pan-Fried Pork &
   Cabbage Dumplings
   (page 98) (about 24), uncooked
2 thin green onions, finely
   minced

◉ Prepare stock. Soak mushrooms in a bowl of warm water 30 minutes. Squeeze dry; cut off stems. Slice mushrooms. Place stock in a large pot with mushrooms, 1 teaspoon salt, saké, soy sauce, 1 teaspoon sesame oil and pepper. Bring to a boil. Add carrot and spinach. Cook 1 minute. Keep warm on low heat.

◉ In a large pot, bring 2 1/2 quarts water and 2 teaspoons salt to a boil. Drop dumplings into water; reduce heat to medium-low. Simmer 3 to 4 minutes or until dumplings rise to the top. With a slotted spoon, place 3 or 4 dumplings in each serving bowl. Ladle hot soup over dumplings. Add a few drops sesame oil and some green onion to each portion. Serve at once.

◉ *Makes 6 servings.*

SAVORY RICE PORRIDGE
(ZOSUI)

This hearty rice porridge is a great way to use leftover rice.

2 medium-size dried shiitake
    mushrooms
4 cups Chicken Stock with
    Ginger (page 51)
1 tablespoon soy sauce
3 cups Basic Cooked Rice
    (page 194), cooled
1 chicken breast half, skinned,
    boned and cut into 1/4-inch
    cubes
2 tablespoons shredded carrot
1/3 cup tiny cooked shrimp
    or crabmeat

1/4 cup chopped pickled
    mustard greens
3 green onions, minced
About 1 teaspoon salt
2 teaspoons saké
1 tablespoon mirin
1 large egg, slightly beaten
6 tablespoons Cabbage &
    Shiso Pickle with Lemon
    (page 231) or shredded
    beni shōga

◉ Soak mushrooms in a bowl of warm water 30 minutes. Squeeze dry; cut off stems. Mince mushrooms; set aside. In a large saucepan, bring stock and soy sauce to a boil. Rinse rice in a fine strainer to remove excess starch; add rice to stock. Reduce heat; simmer 5 minutes. Add chicken to rice mixture; simmer 3 minutes. Stir in carrot, shrimp, mustard greens, green onions and reserved mushrooms; simmer 1 minute. Add salt, saké and mirin; stir until blended.

◉ Remove pan from heat. Drizzle in egg, stirring with a pair of chopsticks in a circular motion. Ladle hot stew into individual bowls. Garnish each serving with 1 tablespoon Cabbage & Shiso Pickle with Lemon.

◉ *Makes 6 servings.*

COUNTRY VEGETABLE SOUP WITH MISO
(Yasai No Miso-Jiru)

Japanese country foods reflect the season's best, whether it be a newly dug country potato or a crisp, juicy daikon radish just pulled from the earth. Ladled into handmade pottery bowls, this hearty soup would make a fine lunch. Offer a side dish of rice balls or sushi on edible plates made from leaf-shaped pieces of fried *konbu*. In the manner of vegetable soups, you can substitute any hard-to-find ingredient with another. Blue is the farmer's color in Japan; the countryside is awash in indigo blue. To frame the setting with another country touch, arrange the dishes on a rustic blue tablecloth or place mats.

6 cups Sea Vegetable & Bonito
  Stock (page 46)
2 dried shiitake mushrooms
1 tablespoon safflower oil
3 small peeled, cubed *sato-imo*
  (country potatoes) or 1 small
  sweet potato, cut into chunks,
  soaked in salt water 15
  minutes
2 inches peeled daikon radish,
  sliced in half-moon shapes
  (*hangetsu-giri*)

1 small carrot, cut into 1/4-inch
  diagonal slices
2 to 3 ounces shredded lean pork
1/2 cake *konnyaku*, cut into
  1/4-inch rectangles and
  blanched 2 minutes
4 tablespoons red or white miso
  paste or a blend thereof
1 tablespoon light soy sauce
  (*usukuchi shoyu*)
Ground black pepper to taste
2 green onions, finely chopped

◉ Prepare stock. Soak mushrooms in a bowl of warm water 30 minutes. Squeeze dry; cut off stems. In a large saucepan, heat oil over medium heat. Sauté mushrooms, *sato-imo,* onion, radish and carrot 3 minutes. Stir in pork; cook 30 seconds. Add stock and konnyaku. Simmer 10 minutes or until vegetables are tender. Remove surface foam. Blend miso with a little hot stock; stir into soup pot. Add soy sauce, pepper and green onions. Serve hot.

◉ *Makes 4 or 5 servings.*

DASHI-NO-MOTO
(Instant Dashi)

Homemade *dashi* is quickly made and undeniably tastes best, but instant *dashi* is fine to use in a pinch for soup or on occasions when you need a cooking stock. In Okinawa, I watched cooks shake the powder directly into stir-fry dishes as a seasoning.

3 to 4 cups water	1 envelope *dashi-no-moto* powder

◉ In a 2-quart saucepan, simmer water over medium heat. Stir in *dashi* powder; simmer 2 minutes. Use at once.

◉ *Makes 6 cups.*

VARIATIONS

◉ To use *dashi* granules (*hon dashi*), use about 1/4 teaspoon per cup boiling water.

◉ To use the liquid concentrate (*katsuo dashi*), use 1/2 teaspoon per cup hot water.

CONSOMMÉ WITH SNOW PUFF MUSHROOMS IN CUCUMBER RINGS

(Enoki To Kyuri No Suimono)

The preparation of soup in Japan can be an art in itself and often the measure of a good cook. Peering into a bowl of *suimono*, or clear soup, is like viewing nature's artistry in miniature. At the same time, the soup should embody the aesthetic concept of *shibusa:* refined, understated beauty. Serve this elegant consommé at your most special occasion.

Like miso soup, *suimono* seems to taste best served in Japanese lacquerware. As your guests lift the lids of their bowls, they will be surrounded by a delectable aroma offering a subtle hint of the sea. Sometimes, hot soup in a covered lacquer bowl creates a vacuum, making it difficult to remove the lid. If this happens, gently press the sides of the bowl while removing the lid.

1 small Japanese cucumber, peeled	1/2 teaspoon salt, or to taste
1 bunch *enokidaké* (snow puff mushrooms), ends trimmed, rinsed	1 teaspoon light soy sauce (*usukuchi shoyu*)
4 cups Sea Vegetable & Bonito Stock (page 46)	4 or 5 slivers of lemon peel

◉ Cut ends off cucumbers; discard. Using a long thin knife or iced-tea spoon, hollow out cucumber. Cut into 8 to 10 rings, about 1/4 inch thick. Insert a cluster of mushrooms into pairs of cucumber rings. Prepare stock. Add salt and soy sauce. Ladle steaming-hot soup into lacquer soup bowls. Place 1 pair of stuffed cucumber rings and 1 sliver of lemon peel into each bowl of soup. Cover with lids; serve at once.

◉ *Makes 4 or 5 servings.*

NEW YEAR'S SOUP

(Ozoni)

The preparation for this special holiday soup can be done in advance; assemble the ingredients and add hot soup at the last minute. Filled with a variety of flavors and textures, this recipe for ozoni is similar to the type served in Southern Japan. For a hearty country-style version, dissolve 3 or 4 tablespoons of your favorite miso paste in the hot stock.

4 cups Sea Vegetable & Bonito Stock (page 46) or Chicken Stock with Ginger (page 51)
2 tablespoons light soy sauce (*usukuchi shoyu*)
1 tablespoon saké
Salt to taste
1 tablespoon mirin
1/2 chicken breast, skinned, boned and diced
5 small Scored Shiitake Mushrooms (page 18)

1 cup sliced napa cabbage
5 slices *narutomaki* or *kamaboko* (fish loaf)
5 Grilled Mochi (page 201)
5 Carrot Fans (page 26) or carrot slices cut into flower shapes
10 snow peas
2 small green onions, thinly sliced

◉ Pour stock into a medium-size saucepan; add 1 tablespoon of the soy sauce, the saké and salt. Bring stock to a simmer over medium-low heat. In a small bowl, combine remaining soy sauce and mirin; add chicken and marinate 5 minutes.

◉ Add mushrooms, chicken, cabbage and *narutomaki* to stock; simmer 5 minutes. Grill rice cakes (page 201). Place 1 rice cake in each of 5 soup bowls. Ladle hot soup into bowls, dividing solid ingredients equally. Place 1 carrot fan and 2 pea pods in each bowl. Garnish with green onions.

◉ *Makes 5 servings.*

SASHIMI & SUSHI

Beyond Fuji, the new moon
Casts her silvery net seaward,
My fishing boat, my catch
Captured by moonbeams.

—SUSAN FULLER SLACK

Freshness makes its most subtle statement in the form of sashimi—fresh, chilled raw fish. My first inquisitive taste was in Tokyo several years ago. With a flash of steel, a sushi chef, or *shokunin,* deftly performed his magic act, cutting exceptionally fresh fish into a variety of thin slices. Several pieces were arranged carefully upon a bed of garnishes, or *tsuma.* Often selected to represent the season, garnishes play an important role by adding color, texture and flavor. On the side, a tiny dish of soy sauce and a small green cone of *wasabi,* a type of horseradish. My first bite of raw fish was a pleasant surprise. The taste was clean and

mild, the texture tender and the smell like a fresh ocean breeze. There was no hint of the fishiness sometimes detected in "fresh fish" prepared at home. But I would caution that your first taste of *wasabi* be approached as if entering a steaming Japanese hot tub: Don't leap in; inch your way in a little bit at a time!

Sashimi, most representative of Japan's seafood dishes, is made from the highest quality seasonal fish which are dressed to be served raw. Freshness is so desirable that the concept is often carried to an extreme. Dancing shrimp, or *odori,* requires that live prawns be quickly cleaned and served for immediate consumption. Although the presentation of sashimi is usually less dramatic, it is regarded as more than just a plate of raw fish. Sashimi might be artistically arranged on the serving plates with fresh herbs and sea vegetables to remind one of a miniature landscape.

Japanese housewives can purchase excellent sashimi at their local markets; they have developed a skill for recognizing the freshest fish at its flavorful best. You can duplicate sashimi in your own kitchen if you observe the golden rule: Purchase only the freshest seasonal fish and live shellfish with tightly closed shells. Sea bream, bonito, tuna, salmon and carp hold the most cultural and seasonal significance in Japan. Salmon is rarely served raw except by the Ainu people of northern Hokkaido, who freeze it outdoors in the fall. Good sashimi can be made using the seasonal best of whatever fish is available in your area. It is best to use only saltwater fish for sashimi; freshwater fish could harbor parasites.

Seek the advice of a trusted fishmonger who will guide you in making your fish selections. If you request it, he will scale, gut and fillet your fish in preparation for slicing. Frozen fish is best avoided, although fresh-caught tuna can be successfully frozen. Give careful thought to slicing your fish for serving. The shape and firmness of each fish will help determine the proper cut. The firmer the flesh, the thinner it can be sliced. The thickness of each cut can affect the fish's final flavor.

Not all sashimi is served completely raw. Tosa Prefecture on Shikoku Island is famous for its bonito fishing. One specialty is flame-seared bonito; grilled just enough to color the skin. The fish is chilled in iced water, then marinated in an acidic liquid for a brief time. Fish for sashimi can also be quickly passed through boiling water. The technique of *kami-jio*, or "paper salting," requires that fish fillets be layered with handmade *washi* paper while being salted. The paper is salted, never the fish.

The merits of good sashimi depend upon freshness, flavor and texture alone, but good sushi results from a careful blending of vinegar and rice. Sushi originated in Southeast Asia as a method of fish preservation. In the beginning, fresh fish were layered with large amounts of salt. Later they were pressed between layers of steamed rice. The formation of organic acids caused the rice to ferment and add flavor to the fish. Harmful bacteria were destroyed during the fermentation process. At first, the rice was discarded, but eventually it was eaten, too. Layered carp and rice (*funa-zushi*) is a descendant of the earlier type of pressed sushi. It is still made today at Lake Biwa, near Kyoto. Pressed-box sushi (*oshi-zushi*) became increasingly popular in the Kyoto area, where it is a specialty today. Sushi Canapés and the Sushi Birthday Cake are my modernized versions of the traditional pressed layered sushi.

Impatient to devise a quicker method for sushi, the Japanese seasoned rice with vinegar to create a sour taste. Pickled foods (*namasu*), such as vinegared fish and beef, were pressed on top. *Wasabi* was added for its antibacterial properties as well as for its good flavor.

Fresh sliced tuna is one of the most popular toppings for sushi rice. *Otoro* tuna is the grade containing the most fat. The pale marbled flesh is located near the belly section of the fish. *Otoro* is highly prized and expensive. *Chutoro* tuna is a less-fatty grade located in the midsection. Bright red *akami*, the leanest part near the backbone, is an excellent choice for dieters.

Many people like to eat sushi but without the raw fish. Beef lovers will appreciate the Spicy Grilled Beef Sushi. Stuffed Tofu Puffs and Kansai-Style Scattered Sushi, the "chef salad" of sushi, are popular in Japanese home cooking.

A skillful sushi chef can prepare sushi with amazing speed. He instinctively gathers the correct amount of vinegared rice for hand-pressed sushi and molds it with one hand into a perfectly shaped bite-size oval. Apprentice chefs spend years perfecting these skills, often practicing with huge tubs of soybean pulp (*okara*) instead of wasting precious rice. Each movement has been calculated and the timing must be exact. Every grain of rice must be coaxed into the same direction.

The expertise of the sushi chef is the result of years of apprenticeship and hard work. Perhaps the skill cannot be duplicated, but the taste of delicious sushi can be recreated in your own kitchen. The secret bears repeating—prepare the finest ingredients with care and reverence. The essence of such careful food preparation is in itself a religion, a belief in the total supremacy of nature.

SASHIMI DIPPING SAUCE

(Tosa-joyu)

The alcohol can be burned off the saké and mirin if you wish. It mellows the flavor of the sauce. This sauce keeps for months and improves with age. If you prepare sashimi often, double the amount. If the sauce seems strong for your taste, dilute portions with a little *dashi*.

3/4 cup soy sauce
2 teaspoons rice vinegar
3 tablespoons mirin
3 tablespoons tamari

2 tablespoons saké
1 tablespoon dried bonito
  shavings

◉ Combine all the ingredients in a medium-size bowl. Cover tightly. Allow mixture to steep 48 hours. Strain through a fine-mesh strainer. Store in an airtight container.

◉ *Makes about 2 1/4 cups.*

SASHIMI ROSES

(Bara Sashimi)

The size of the sashimi roses can be varied according to the width and thickness of the fish strips. Pick the petals and dip them in *wasabi* and soy sauce or tangy Lemon Soy Dipping Sauce (page 65).

1 fresh, firm, chilled 1-inch-thick
  white-fish fillet, skinned
3 to 4 oz. thinly sliced smoked
  salmon or lox, cut into 2
  1-inch strips
Shredded daikon radish

Fresh shiso leaves
Wasabi Leaves or cones
  (page 237)
Soy sauce or Lemon Soy
  Dipping Sauce (page 65)

◉ Cut fish fillet into rectangular pieces about 2 inches wide. Slice each piece diagonally across the grain into 1/8-inch-thick slices. Lay 6 slices in a long row with short ends overlapping, leaving about 1/4 of top of each piece showing. Starting at the bottom, carefully roll up pieces into a single roll. Set roll upright. Bend back tops of slices to resemble rose petals. Shape smoked salmon strips into roses using this method. Or roll a single slice loosely into a cone shape and stand it upright. Wrap remaining slices around cone shape, overlapping them to resemble a rose. Carefully bend back tops of slices to resemble rose petals. On each serving plate, place 1 white and 1 pink sashimi rose. Garnish each with shredded daikon, shiso leaves and a cone or leaf of *wasabi*. Serve with soy or dipping sauce.

◉ *Makes 3 or 4 servings.*

SASHIMI

Slightly dampen your knife and cutting board before beginning. Use clean cuts, not a sawing motion, so your fish does not tear. Present an array of your favorite sashimi cuts on individual chilled plates or on a chilled platter. Allow 5 or 6 pieces per person. Serve with the appropriate garnishes and Sashimi Dipping Sauce (page 61) or the lighter Lemon Soy Dipping Sauce (page 65).

PAPER-THIN CUT (USU-ZUKURI) (1)

◉ Firm-fleshed white fish fillets, such as halibut and sea bass, can be cut into 1/16-inch diagonal slices across the grain. These slices are often placed on a platter, overlapping in a circular flower-shaped design. A decorative edible garnish is usually placed in the center. The thin slices can be rolled up to form a flower rosette.

THIN CUT (SOGI-ZUKURI) (2)

◉ Similar to paper-thin cut but slices are slightly thicker, about 1/8 inch.

DOMINO CUT (HIRA-ZUKURI) (3)

◉ This common rectangular cut is excellent for many fish such as tuna, flounder, red snapper and yellowtail. Make clean 3/8-inch straight cuts across the grain through rectangular bars of fish. Firmer-fleshed fish can be cut into thinner slices. Pieces can be cut slightly at an angle if desired. Use the blade of the knife to push slices to the side as they are cut, creating a stacked domino effect.

◉ A similar cut, called *hiki-zukuri,* is used for fragile fish, which require careful handling. Each cut piece of fish is lifted to the plate instead of being pushed to the side of the board with the knife.

THREAD CUT (ITO-ZUKURI) (4)

◉ An excellent method for cutting squid or other thin pieces of fish fillets. Slice fish into 1/16-inch strips; arrange small flower-like piles on each serving plate. For a delicious and attractive presentation, toss squid strips with *masago,* tiny bright orange smelt eggs. Hollowed-cucumber cups or tiny leaf-lined baskets are handy serving containers for string-cut fish.

CUBE CUT (KAKU-ZUKURI) (5)

◉ Tuna and other thick fillets of fresh fish can be cut into a cube cut. Cut lengthwise strips of fillets about 3/4 inch wide; cut into 3/4-inch cubes. The strips can be neatly wrapped in sheets of nori, sealed with wasabi, then cut into cubes. Garnish with toasted sesame seeds.

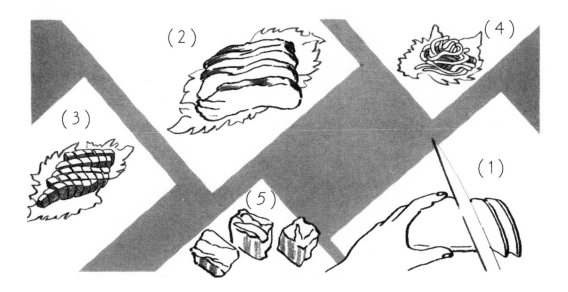

LEMON SOY DIPPING SAUCE
(Ponzu)

In Japan, this tangy sauce is made with a citrus fruit called *yuzu*. The juice is referred to as *ponzu*. This blend goes well with thinly sliced raw fish that have light flesh, such as flounder or sea bream. It is also a good dipping sauce for Chicken Hot Pot (page 130). If you are on a low-salt diet, dilute a little soy sauce with *dashi* and lemon juice to taste.

1/2 cup soy sauce
1/4 cup fresh lemon juice
2 tablespoons mirin
3 tablespoons water

2 to 4 tablespoons rice vinegar
1 tablespoon dried bonito
    shavings (optional)

◉ In a small bowl, combine all ingredients. Cover and steep 2 to 3 hours; strain if bonito shavings are used. Sauce can be steeped longer for a more pronounced bonito flavor.

◉ *Makes about 1 1/4 cups.*

TREASURE SHIP SASHIMI
(Takara Buné)

Celebrate Japanese New Year with this spectacular whole fish. The fish is prepared using the three-piece cut, or *sanmai-oroshi*. Decorate it with carved-vegetable flowers (page 24). The Japanese like to display this spectacular fish in a beautiful black lacquer dish shaped like a boat. Sometimes a talented chef will cut an edible net from daikon radish and cast it partially over the fish, as if it has just been caught.

1 (1 1/2- to 2-lb.) fresh, whole,
   undressed red snapper or
   sea bream
Fine long shreds of carrot and
   daikon radish

Fresh lemon slices
Wasabi (page 237)
Soy sauce

◙ Rinse fish under cool water; place on damp cutting surface. Grasp fish by the tail and run a fish scaler or sharp knife toward head of fish. Scrape around fish until completely scaled. Rinse well. Clean cutting board. Replace fish on cutting board with head to the left and belly facing you. Slide knife under pectoral fin near head; cut off head. A larger fish may require another cut on the opposite side. Reserve head. Using a sharp knife, slit open belly of fish; remove viscera. Rinse out cavity under cool water. Be sure air bladder and blood clots are removed. Pat dry.

◙ Using a sharp boning knife, make a shallow slit just above the backbone, going from head to tail. Make firm steady cuts along slit, separating meat from backbone and ribs. Hold cut edge of fillet and raise it as separation progresses. When fillet is completely separated, turn fish over to the other side. Cutting from neck area, repeat process. Cut skeleton crosswise just above tail. Reserve tail with head.

◙ To skin fillets, place them on cutting surface, skin-side down. Using a serrated fish knife, make a small cut separating tip of tail flesh from skin. Grasp skin with your left hand. In your right hand, knife should be laying almost parallel to skin and cutting board. Begin cutting flesh away from skin, sawing knife gently from right to left. Pull skin tightly as flesh is being scraped away. Check fillets for any small bones and remove with tweezers or a sharp knife. Trim fillets into rectangular shapes. Wide fillets can be cut in half lengthwise. Make clean 3/8-inch cuts across grain of fillets. Some fillet portions can be cut into cubes.

◉ Place a large flat pile of shredded daikon and carrot on a serving platter. Arrange fish slices on platter to resemble body of uncut fish. Put fish head and tail into place; head should be facing left. Prop the tail up as if in motion. Garnish with lemon slices, Wasabi, shiso leaves or any other garnishes (page 69). Serve at once, or cover tightly and refrigerate up to 2 hours.

◉ *Makes 4 to 6 servings.*

"CLAM SHELL" SUSHI
(Hamaguri-zushi)

These attractive sea creatures are created from thin egg sheets, folded and stuffed with sushi rice. They are just as good with shrimp or crab salad. I like to serve them on a platter garnished with red and green *tosakanori*. This pretty seaweed resembles curly endive and is delicious marinated with rice vinegar and sugar. You could substitute curly-leaf lettuce if *tosakanori* isn't available.

5 large eggs	2 tablespoons mirin
1 teaspoon potato starch or	1/4 teaspoon salt
cornstarch	Vegetable oil
1 tablespoon *dashi* or water	Sushi Rice (page 72)

⬛ In a medium-size bowl, whisk eggs until just blended. Dissolve starch in *dashi*. Whisk into eggs along with mirin and salt. Strain mixture through a fine strainer into a medium-size bowl. Heat an 8-inch nonstick skillet over medium heat. Wipe surface with a paper towel moistened with vegetable oil. Pour about 3 tablespoons egg mixture into hot skillet; swirl to form a well-shaped circle. Reduce heat; cook about 1 minute or until egg is almost set. Do not brown bottom. Carefully turn egg circle over; cook 10 seconds longer. Turn egg circle out of skillet; cool.

◉ Continue making circles with remaining mixture. Fold egg circles into quarters. Heat a wooden-handled metal skewer in an open flame. Use skewer to brand 3 decorative lines on top of each folded egg circle, or mark with dark soy sauce. Stuff each shell with a generous tablespoon of Sushi Rice. If necessary, press shells to improve shapes. Arrange on a garnished serving platter. For individual servings, arrange 2 clam shells per plate.

◉ *Makes 4 or 5 servings.*

GARNISHES
(Tsuma)

Sashimi-no-tsuma are the garnishes that are important to the taste and appearance of sashimi and sushi. They serve to cleanse the palate between each bite. *Shiki-zuma* is the garnish arranged in a mound behind sashimi or as a bed under it. Thin shreds of daikon or carrot are excellent for this purpose. Available in Asian markets are special cutting boxes that allow you to create the long fine vegetable shreds the sushi chef cuts by hand. *Kazari-zuma* are the decorative garnishes used alongside. Pickled ginger, *wasabi* and soy sauce are the basic condiments served with sashimi or sushi. Red Maple Radish (page 233), grated fresh gingerroot and lemon slices are optional choices.

Small cones or leaves of Wasabi (page 237)
Pink Pickled Ginger Slices (page 229)
Long thin shreds of daikon radish or carrot
Green shiso leaves
Thin diagonal slices Japanese or European-style cucumber
Cucumber cups for holding condiments
Thinly sliced or shredded small green onions
Edible chrysanthemum flowers and leaves
Celery shreds
Daikon sprouts (*kaiwari daikon*)
Watercress or parsley
Daikon, carrots or turnips cut into flower shapes (page 24)
Thin slices of lemon

STUFFED TOFU PUFFS
(inari-zushi)

These delicious snacks are made from puffed squares of fried tofu, or *abura-agé*. Some people affectionately refer to them as "football sushi" because each puff resembles a football when stuffed. For tailgating, stuff the bags whole, with one side cut open. After stuffing, overlap the cut edges; place cut-sides down. Here I cut each *abura-agé* in half to make smaller party-size portions.

1/2 recipe Sushi Rice (page 72)
1 tablespoon toasted sesame seeds
10 square pieces *abura-agé* (tofu puffs)
1 1/2 cups Sea Vegetable & Bonito Stock (page 46)
2 tablespoons sugar
2 tablespoons light soy sauce (*usukuchi shoyu*)

1 tablespoon mirin
1 tablespoon saké
Shredded red pickled ginger (*beni shōga*)
Radish sprouts (*kaiwari daikon*), shredded shiso or flat-leaf parsley

◉ Prepare Sushi Rice; mix in sesame seeds. Combine 1/2 cup water and 2 tablespoons vinegar for moistening your hands. Divide rice into 20 portions, patting each into an oval shape. Place on a platter; cover with plastic wrap.

◉ Bring 4 cups water to a boil in a medium-size saucepan. Blanch 2 or 3 tofu pouches at a time, 1 to 2 minutes, to remove excess oils. Press under water with a wooden spoon. Drain and cool slightly; press out excess liquid.

◉ In a medium-size saucepan, stir together stock, sugar, soy sauce, mirin and saké. Bring to a boil over medium-high heat. Reduce to medium-low. Add tofu and simmer 12 to 15 minutes, turning occasionally. Sauce should be greatly reduced. Cool tofu in sauce. Press excess liquid from tofu. Cut each tofu puff in half to make 2 rectangles. Fill each piece with a rice oval. Top each with pickled ginger and radish sprouts. Serve immediately, or cover loosely with plastic wrap and serve within 2 to 3 hours; do not refrigerate.

◉ *Makes 20 pieces.*

◉ Add additional ingredients to the rice if you wish: 3/4 cup tiny cooked shrimp or shredded *surimi* seafood; 3 minced Seasoned Shiitake Mushrooms (page 122), or 1/2 cup Seasoned Vegetables for Sushi Rice (page 85).

LEMON MAYONNAISE

(Lemon Mayo)

Mayonnaise dressing is popular in Japan. This lemon-fresh version is delicious in sushi rolls, on simmered vegetables or on grilled or poached seafood. The *wasabi* variation is excellent in potato salad. Spread the delicate pink Plum Mayonnaise on your next chicken or turkey sandwich.

1 cup top-quality mayonnaise	1 teaspoon freshly grated
1 to 2 teaspoons fresh lemon juice	lemon peel

◉ In a medium-size bowl, combine all ingredients. Scrape into an airtight container or handy squeeze-tube bottle for easy use. Use immediately or refrigerate.

◉ *Makes 1 cup.*

VARIATIONS

WASABI MAYONNAISE

◉ Dissolve 2 teaspoons *wasabi* powder in 1 tablespoon mirin or lemon juice. Stir into mayonnaise.

PLUM MAYONNAISE

◉ Omit lemon juice and peel. Soak 8 *umeboshi* in water 3 hours to remove salt. Drain; remove pits. With a fork, mash pulp into a paste. Stir into mayonnaise. You can substitute 3 tablespoons prepared plum paste.

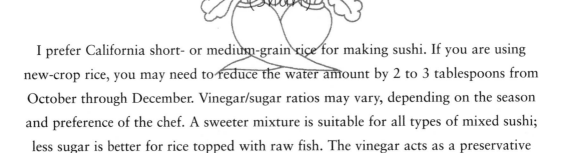

SUSHI RICE
(Sushi)

I prefer California short- or medium-grain rice for making sushi. If you are using new-crop rice, you may need to reduce the water amount by 2 to 3 tablespoons from October through December. Vinegar/sugar ratios may vary, depending on the season and preference of the chef. A sweeter mixture is suitable for all types of mixed sushi; less sugar is better for rice topped with raw fish. The vinegar acts as a preservative and kills parasites; the salt enhances the delicate sweet-sour balance of flavors.

2 cups California short- or medium-grain rice	SEASONED RICE VINEGAR (AWAZÉ-ZU)
1 (3-inch) piece dried *konbu* (kelp), lightly wiped	1/4 cup rice vinegar
2 1/3 cups bottled spring water or tap water	2 tablespoons sugar
	1 tablespoon mirin
	1 tablespoon saké
	1 1/2 teaspoons salt

◉ Place rice in a large bowl; fill with cool water. Swish your hand through the water; pour off and add fresh water. Repeat process until the water is fairly clear. Drain rice in a large strainer; tap gently to remove liquid. In a 3-quart saucepan, combine rice and *konbu* with the water; soak 15 minutes. Remove *konbu*.

◉ Bring rice to a rolling boil. Reduce heat to low. Cover saucepan with a tight-fitting lid. Simmer 15 minutes or until liquid is absorbed. Remove from heat. Let rice stand, covered and undisturbed, 15 minutes.

◉ Prepare Seasoned Rice Vinegar. With a damp wooden rice paddle or spoon, remove rice to a damp cedar rice mixing tub or a pottery or glass bowl. Hold paddle over rice; sprinkle with vinegar, letting it drip on rice. Add small portions, mixing each portion into rice with a gentle cutting and tossing motion. As the vinegar is added, fan rice to cool, remove moisture and add sheen. A partner to fan is helpful while you toss rice. A small electric fan works well, too. Mix in only as much dressing as the rice will absorb without becoming too moist. Use at once, or cover with a damp cloth. Do not refrigerate; rice becomes hard. Use within 6 to 8 hours.

◉ *Makes about 4 cups.*

SEASONED RICE VINEGAR (AWAZÉ-ZU)

◉ In a small saucepan, combine all ingredients. Heat gently, stirring until sugar dissolves. Cool.

SUSHI CANAPÉS

Sushi in "fancy dress" will be a welcomed guest at any party! Serve these on your nicest silver platter.

1 recipe Sushi Rice (page 72)
2 tablespoons rice vinegar
1 tablespoon Wasabi (page 237)
   or Lemon Mayonnaise
   (page 71)
1 tablespoon toasted sesame seeds
1 tablespoon capers

GARNISHES
Smoked salmon, sliced paper-thin
Small cubes of fresh tuna
Edible pea pods, blanched
   and chilled
Salmon-roe caviar
Black caviar
Fresh herbs (*kinomé*, flat-leaf
   parsley, shiso leaf)
Small cooked shrimp, halved
   lengthwise
Shaved pieces of baked ham,
   in small pieces

◉ Prepare Sushi Rice. Line an 11 x 17-inch baking pan with foil; lightly oil. In a small bowl, combine 1/2 cup water and 2 tablespoons vinegar for moistening hands. Press 3 cups rice evenly over lined pan. Dot rice with Wasabi; spread to cover. Sprinkle with sesame seeds and capers.

◉ Place remaining rice on top in small mounds. With damp hands, press rice mounds evenly over bottom layer of rice. Cover rice directly with plastic wrap. Place a slightly smaller pan on top; firmly press rice. Remove top pan and plastic wrap. Place a baking sheet on top of pan with rice. Firmly grasp pan and baking sheet; invert quickly. Cut rice into shapes using 2-inch metal cutters with sharp edges. Hearts, circles, diamonds, squares, half-moons, fans and flowers are attractive shapes. Carefully move rice shapes to a serving tray. Canapés may be shaped up to 4 hours ahead and tightly covered with plastic wrap.

◉ Add garnishes 1/2 hour before serving. Garnishing ideas: salmon slices or tuna rolled into free form flowers with 2 pea pod stems; salmon-roe caviar flower with a dab of black caviar in the center and herb leaves; whole shrimp or mound of ham with shiso leaf.

◉ *Makes 4 to 6 servings.*

Suggestions for Sushi Fillings

Use some of these suggested fillings to create your own combinations for sushi rolls or hand-rolled sushi cones.

Fresh tuna, yellowtail, red snapper or flounder fillets, cut into strips

Top-grade canned tuna or salmon (popular in Japan)

Cooked peeled shrimp, chopped

Crabmeat

Jalapeño chiles

Caviar

Kamaboko or *chikuwa,* cut into strips

Seafood *surimi* strips

Strips of smoked salmon

Strips of prosciutto

Avocado strips moistened with lemon juice

Japanese cucumber, cut into 1/4-inch-thick strips

Bell pepper strips

Sweet Omelet Roll (page 212)

Enoki-daké mushrooms, blanched

Japanese pickled vegetables, chopped or cut into strips

Cooked asparagus tips

Whole green beans, blanched

Cucumber strips

Strips of bamboo shoots

Seasoned Shiitake Mushrooms (page 122)

Seasoned Kampyo (page 123)

Seasoned Vegetables for Sushi (page 85)

Natto (fermented beans)

Cooked green-tea noodles

Pink Pickled Ginger Slices (page 229)

KOKESHI DOLL SUSHI

(Kokeshi-zushi)

An edible replica of the charming wooden doll so dear to little girls throughout Japan. Celebrate Japan's Doll Festival by preparing these sushi dolls with your children. The clever kids in my cooking classes always dress these "dolls" using the latest designer touches!

Sushi Rice (page 72)
4 (8 x 7 1/2-inch) sheets nori or
   pink bonito sheets
   (*té-maki-katsuo*)
Soaked *hijiki* or *aramé* sea
   vegetable (optional)

Shredded red pickled ginger
   (*beni shōga*)
Tiny flower-shaped candies
Small paper umbrellas

◉ Prepare Sushi Rice. Combine 1/2 cup water and 2 tablespoons vinegar for moistening your hands. Divide rice into 5 equal portions. Pinch off 1/4 of each portion to form heads. Roll large portions of rice into oblong shapes, about 4 x 2 inches. Shape a little wider at the bottom for dolls' bodies. Roll the small portions of rice into round balls. Flatten slightly at top and bottom; these will be dolls' heads.

◉ Pass shiny side of nori or bonito 2 or 3 times over the flame of a gas stove or over an electric burner on high heat. Do not overtoast or nori will crack when rolled. Cut sheets in half. Use 1/2 sheet to form a kimono for each rice doll. Trim length of sheets to wrap neatly around rice bodies, flaring slightly at the bottom. Using kitchen scissors, snip a small V shape at each neck. Cut 5 (4 x 3-inch) nori or bonito pieces for hair. Using small scissors, trim out a 1 1/2- to 2-inch square at the bottom of each piece for face. Fit the pieces over small rice balls; faces should be uncovered. Smooth over heads. Trim sides of hair so it slants toward mouth. Moisten base of rice-ball head with water and press it gently onto doll's neck; tilt head at an angle if desired.

◉ Trim tiny pieces of nori for eyes. If desired, use small threads of *aramé* sea vegetable for eyelashes. Use tiny pieces of red pickled ginger for mouth. Candy flowers can be used for kimono decoration or in doll's hair. Use your imagination to think of different ways to decorate the sushi dolls. The final touch might be a small paper umbrella tucked on the side.

◉ *Makes 5 kokeshi dolls.*

HAND-ROLLED
SUSHI CONES
(Té-maki-zushi)

Té-maki-zushi is great party food! Offer seasoned rice, sheets of nori and a wide variety of ingredients selected from the Suggestions for Sushi Fillings (page 75). Guests can stuff and fold their own. Given a little encouragement, the amateur sushi chefs will come up with dozens of unique specialty-of-the-house rolls!

1/2 recipe Sushi Rice (page 72)
1 (6- to 8-oz.) salmon fillet
    with skin
12 (8 x 7 1/2-inch) sheets nori,
    cut into 24 (5 1/2 x 3 1/4-inch)
    pieces
12 (7 x 4-inch) sheets pink bonito
    (*té-maki-katsuo*) or nori,
    cut into 12 pieces
3 tablespoons Wasabi (page 237)
Lemon Soy Dipping Sauce
    (page 65)
Salmon roe (*ikura*)

12 large poached shrimp,
    halved lengthwise
36 fresh shiso leaves or torn
    butter-lettuce leaves
1 small avocado, cut into strips
    and sprinkled with lemon juice
2 Japanese or 1 European
    cucumber, cut into thin strips
Pink Pickled Ginger Slices
    (page 229)
1 pkg. radish sprouts (*kaiwari
    daikon*) (optional), separated
3 tablespoons sesame seeds

◉ Prepare Sushi Rice. Combine 1/2 cup water and 2 tablespoons vinegar for moistening your hands. Shape rice into 36 neat portions, using 1 level tablespoon rice per portion. Place on a tray; cover loosely with plastic wrap until serving time. Grill salmon, skin-side up, in a broiler pan 4 to 5 minutes. Skin should be very crisp. When fish is opaque in thickest portion and begins to flake, remove from broiler. Cool, flake with fingers. Tear crisp skin into pieces. Place on serving plate.

◉ Prepare remaining ingredients; arrange on serving tray in separate piles. Pass shiny side of nori 2 or 3 times over the flame of a gas stove or over an electric burner on high heat. Do not overtoast or nori will crack when rolled. Place in a basket.

◉ Put Lemon Soy Dipping Sauce in a small pot for pouring. To fill each cone, place a shiso leaf or piece of lettuce at an angle on 1 side of a sheet of bonito or nori. Bottom of leaf should point toward bottom center of sheet. Top with a portion of rice. Spread rice with Wasabi. Add a small amount of salmon or shrimp and any remaining ingredients. Pull bottom left-hand corner of nori up over ingredients. Wrap long side around bundle and pull tightly into a cone shape. Sprinkle a few drops of sauce inside cone. Eat at once. Invite guests to make their own cones after you have demonstrated how to assemble the first. Amounts can be doubled.

◉ *Makes 36 pieces.*

Note

In Japan, sushi is never refrigerated because the rice becomes too firm. But leftovers containing fish must be quickly refrigerated to prevent spoilage. Bring to room temperature before serving.

Spicy Grilled Beef Sushi
(Bulgogi-zushi)

Popular in Japan, this superb Korean sushi uses unseasoned cooked rice. Use this basic rolling technique with seasoned Sushi Rice (page 72) for making any type of Japanese sushi roll.

Basic Cooked Rice (page 194)
5 (7 1/2 x 8-inch) sheets nori
About 1 tablespoon sesame oil
4 medium-size fresh shiitake
    mushrooms, stemmed and
    cut into strips
2 teaspoons plus 3 tablespoons
    soy sauce
1 (8-inch-long) piece pickled
    daikon (takuan)
1/3 cup rice vinegar
1/2 lb. fresh spinach, stemmed,
    blanched and chilled

3/4 lb. beef tenderloin, cut into
    1/2-inch-thick slices
1/2 teaspoon sugar
1 green onion, minced
1 large garlic clove, minced
Dash ground black pepper
2 tablespoons vegetable oil
4 to 5 tablespoons sesame seeds
Shredded red pickled ginger
    (beni shōga) (optional)

◉ Prepare Basic Cooked Rice. Cool and cover with a damp cloth; set aside. Rub sheets of nori sparingly with sesame oil. Pass shiny side of nori 2 or 3 times over the flame of a gas stove or over an electric burner on high heat. Do not overtoast or nori will crack when rolled.

◉ In a small bowl, sprinkle mushrooms with 2 teaspoons soy sauce. Cut daikon into strips 8 inches long and 1/2 inch square at each end. Place in a shallow glass bowl with vinegar. Marinate 30 minutes; drain well. Press water from spinach. Lay on paper towels in a long bunch; pat dry. On a plate, drizzle spinach with 1 teaspoon sesame oil.

◉ Stack the meat slices; cut into 1/2-inch-wide strips. In a bowl, mix beef, sugar, green onion, garlic, pepper and remaining 3 tablespoons soy sauce. Marinate 10 minutes; drain well. Heat oil in a skillet over high heat. Add meat strips; stir-fry 1 minute or until medium-rare. Remove from skillet; cool completely. Arrange meat, daikon, mushrooms and spinach on a tray.

● On the rolling edge of a bamboo sushi mat, place a sheet of nori, shiny-side down, with longest side running horizontally. Combine 1/2 cup water and 1/2 teaspoon salt for moistening your hands. In a damp measuring cup, measure 1 generous cup rice. Unmold in the middle of nori sheet. Pat rice over 3/4 of nori sheet, leaving top 1/4 uncovered. Lay 2 pieces beef, 2 pieces daikon, 4 or 5 mushroom strips and about 1/5 of spinach leaves in a long horizontal strip along the center of the rice. Sprinkle with sesame seeds.

● To form roll, lift edge of mat with your thumbs. Holding filling ingredients in place, roll mat and nori away from you to enclose filling. Roll to far edge of rice only, leaving uncovered portion of nori extended. Be careful not to catch end of mat in sushi roll. Tuck in any escaping grains of rice. Press mat firmly a few seconds to set shape. Moisten extending edge of nori with water and complete roll. Wrap mat completely around rice roll and press gently a few seconds. Remove mat. Tap ends on counter if necessary, to even up. Continue making rolls with remaining ingredients.

● Cut and serve, or store uncut in a loosely covered rectangular pan up to 1 1/2 hours; do not refrigerate. To cut rolls, wet a large sharp knife. Place rolls on a cutting board, seam-side down. Cut each roll in half with a swift clean cut. Clean and moisten knife between cuts. Cut each half into 3 or 4 pieces. Place pieces on a serving tray, cut-sides up. Serve with pickled ginger.

● *Makes 30 to 40 pieces.*

SUSHI BIRTHDAY CAKE
(Tan-joo-bi Kei Ki)

For the sushi-lover, this could be the best birthday cake ever!

Vinegared Cucumber Slices
  (see below)
Sushi Rice (page 72)
1 to 2 tablespoons Wasabi
  (page 237)
4 ounces smoked salmon, sliced
  paper-thin
3 or 4 Egg Chrysanthemums
  (page 22)
Stems and leaves made from
  trimmed, blanched green
  vegetables

Leaf lettuce leaves
Edible red fresh flowers (optional)

VINEGARED CUCUMBER SLICES
2 tablespoons fresh lemon juice
2 tablespoons rice vinegar
1/4 cup sugar
1/4 teaspoon salt
1 European or 1 large regular
  cucumber, sliced paper-thin

◉ Prepare Vinegared Cucumber Slices. Line a 9-inch round baking pan with foil. Lightly oil; set aside. Prepare Sushi Rice and Wasabi. Combine 1/2 cup water and 2 tablespoons vinegar for moistening your hands. In a damp measuring cup, measure half the rice. Pat evenly over bottom of lined pan. Spread with Wasabi; cover with smoked salmon. Drain cucumber slices; arrange over salmon layer. Dot cucumbers with remaining rice. With damp hands, spread evenly over top. Firmly but gently press on sushi cake. Cover with plastic wrap. Place a slightly smaller pan on top of rice; add a 1- or 2-pound weight. Press 2 to 3 minutes. Remove pan and plastic wrap.

◉ Prepare Egg Chrysanthemums in various sizes and vegetable leaves. To unmold cake, place a serving plate on top of cake in pan. Grasp pan and plate securely; invert quickly. Cake will fall onto plate. Peel off foil. Arrange a spray of Egg Chrysanthemums on top of cake; garnish with green stems and leaves. Arrange leaf lettuce and flowers around base. Slice small wedges using a large, wet, sharp knife. Don't refrigerate; serve within 2 hours.

◉ *Makes 8 to 10 pieces.*

VINEGARED CUCUMBER SLICES

◘ In a medium-size bowl, combine lemon juice, vinegar, sugar and salt. Stir well to dissolve sugar. Add cucumber slices. Cover and marinate in the refrigerator 3 to 4 hours. Drain well before use.

◘ *Makes about 1 cup.*

Stuffed Avocado Sushi

(Avocado-zushi)

A great way to serve "scattered" sushi!

1 recipe Kansai-Style Scattered Sushi without avocado and pickles (page 84)
5 or 6 large ripe avocados
Lemon juice
Fresh lettuce leaves
Pickled Ginger Slices (page 229)

◘ Prepare sushi ingredients; lightly toss together. Peel, pit and halve avocados. Enlarge avocado shells by scraping out a small amount of avocado flesh. Chop flesh; toss into sushi rice. Drizzle avocados with lemon juice. Scoop rice mixture into each avocado shell. Place each half on a lettuce-lined serving plate. Garnish with pickled ginger.

◘ *Makes 10 to 12 servings.*

KANSAI-STYLE SCATTERED SUSHI
(Chirashi-zushi)

Chirashi-zushi, or "scattered" sushi, is one of the easiest types of sushi to prepare.
Popular around the Osaka and Kyoto areas, the ingredients for the sushi rice are
scattered on top. A variation is *gomoku-zushi,* in which the ingredients are tossed
together with the rice. Many people like to make another nontraditional version in
which rice is mixed with some of the ingredients; others are scattered on top.

1/2 recipe Sushi Rice (page 72)
1/2 recipe Seasoned Vegetables for
    Sushi Rice (opposite)
1/2 recipe Seasoned Shiitake
    Mushrooms (page 122)
1 to 2 tablespoons toasted
    sesame seeds
2 green onions, thinly sliced
1/4 cup frozen petit green peas,
    thawed

1/2 lb. cooked seafood (shrimp,
    poached salmon, crabmeat
    or clams)
1 ripe avocado, peeled, cubed,
    and drizzled with lemon juice
Egg Crepes (page 23), cut
    into fine threads
1 sheet nori, finely shredded
Japanese pickled vegetables
    of choice

◉ Prepare Sushi Rice, Seasoned Vegetables for Sushi Rice and Seasoned Shiitaké
Mushrooms. Slice mushrooms into strips. Assemble all the ingredients. In a medium-
size bowl, lightly toss rice with sesame seeds and green onions. Scoop rice onto a large
attractive platter. On top of the sushi rice, scatter the vegetables, mushroom strips,
green peas and seafood. Top with avocado, crepe threads, nori and pickles. Spoon onto
small plates for eating with chopsticks.

◉ *Makes 4 to 6 servings.*

SEASONED VEGETABLES FOR SUSHI RICE

Several types of sushi call for a variety of julienne-cut vegetables to be simmered in a flavorful stock. Add the seasoned vegetables to Kansai-Style Scattered Sushi (opposite) or Stuffed Tofu Puffs (page 70), or use them to enhance the flavor of plain rice.

1 cup matchstick strips each of 1 or 2 vegetables: fresh green beans, bamboo shoots, carrots, celery or *gobo* (burdock)
1 cup Sea Vegetable & Bonito Stock or Second-Quality Stock (page 46)

1 tablespoon mirin
1 tablespoon saké
2 tablespoons sugar
2 teaspoons light soy sauce (*usukuchi shoyu*)

◉ Prepare vegetables of choice. In a medium-size saucepan, combine remaining ingredients; bring to a boil over high heat. Reduce heat to medium; add 1 vegetable. Simmer 2 or 3 minutes or until tender. Remove with a slotted spoon; cool completely. The second vegetable can be cooked in the remaining sauce.

◉ *Makes 1 or 2 cups.*

TERIYAKI WALNUT ROLL
(Kurumi Maki-Zushi)

The California roll was the first of a whole new genre of innovative sushi rolls. This led to other spinoffs such as jalapeño roll, the devil roll with hot-pepper sauce, Philadelphia roll with smoked salmon and cream cheese and the American dream roll with shrimp tempura. This plump vegetarian roll is a smorgasbord of interesting flavors and textures wrapped up in nori. The glazed walnuts add a rich "meaty" flavor to this roll, but if you prefer, they can be simply toasted.

Teriyaki Walnuts (see below)
1 recipe Sushi Rice (page 72)
Seasoned Shiitake Mushrooms
    (page 122)
Seasoned Kampyo (gourd strips)
    (page 123), cut into 7-inch
    lengths
1 recipe Sweet Omelet Roll
    (page 212), cut into strips
5 (7 1/2 x 8-inch) sheets nori
5 to 6 teaspoons Wasabi
    (page 237)

1/3 cup Japanese pickled
    vegetables of choice
2 tablespoons sesame seeds
Shredded pickled ginger

TERIYAKI WALNUTS
1 1/2 cups walnut halves
1/4 cup light corn syrup
1 tablespoon light soy sauce
    (*usukuchi shoyu*)
1 tablespoon light brown sugar

◉ Prepare Teriyaki Walnuts, Sushi Rice, Seasoned Shiitake Mushrooms, Seasoned Kampyo and Sweet Omelet Roll. Pass shiny side of nori 2 or 3 times over the flame of a gas stove or over an electric burner on high heat. Do not overtoast or nori will crack when rolled.

◉ Place a sheet of nori, shiny-side down and long side running horizontally, on edge of a bamboo sushi mat.

◉ Combine 1/2 cup water and 2 tablespoons vinegar for moistening your hands. Measure 1 cup rice; unmold in the middle of nori sheet. With damp hands, press rice over nori, leaving 1 3/4 inches uncovered at the top. Make a slight horizontal indentation along the center of the rice from end to end. Spread indentation with 1 teaspoon

Wasabi. Along the length of Wasabi, place 1/5 of walnuts, mushroom strips, kampyo and omelet. Sprinkle with pickled vegetables and sesame seeds.

◉ To form roll, lift edge of mat with thumbs. Hold ingredients in place with fingers and roll mat and nori to enclose filling. Roll to the far edge of the rice, leaving uncovered portion of nori extended. Tuck in escaping grains. Press mat firmly to set shape. Moisten extending edge of nori with water; complete roll. Wrap mat completely around rice roll; press gently for a few seconds. Unroll; tap ends on a counter to even. Repeat with remaining ingredients.

◉ Place rolls on cutting surface, seam-side down. Wet a large, sharp knife with water-vinegar mixture. With a clean cut, slice rolls in half; wipe and dampen knife between cuts. Slice each half into 3 (1 1/4-inch) pieces. Place on serving tray with ginger, or store uncut in a loosely covered rectangular pan up to 2 hours at room temperature. Do not refrigerate.

◉ *Makes 30 pieces or 4 to 5 servings.*

TERIYAKI WALNUTS

◉ Bring a small pot of water to boil. Blanch walnuts 30 seconds. Drain and pat dry on paper towels. Put walnuts in a large skillet over medium heat. Dry-roast, stirring often to prevent burning, 10 minutes or until aromatic.

◉ In a medium-size saucepan over medium heat, bring corn syrup, soy sauce and brown sugar to a boil. Add walnuts; cook 3 or 4 minutes or until soy sauce mixture develops large bubbles and is greatly reduced. Pour nuts onto a lightly greased pan. Cool completely. Nuts will become less tacky as they sit. Break apart and use as needed.

◉ *Makes 1 1/2 cups walnuts.*

CAROLINA ROLL
(Ura-maki)

Maki-zushi, or nori-wrapped rolls of rice, seafood and vegetables, is one of the most adaptable forms of sushi. Inventive sushi chefs can shape the ink-black nori to create kaleidoscope-like patterns of swirls and flower designs within each roll. To please Western sushi devotees, California sushi chefs created a variety of hybrid *maki-zushi.* *Ura-maki,* or reverse roll, features the nori rolled inside the rice. Rolls from other areas feature chiles, soft-shell crab, asparagus and even beef tartar.

2 cups Sushi Rice (page 72)
1 (3-oz.) pkg. cream cheese, softened
1 tablespoon Wasabi (page 237), or to taste
2 teaspoons minced fresh shiso leaves or basil
2 (7 1/2 x 8-inch) sheets nori, cut into 4 (7 1/2 x 4-inch) pieces

4 pieces smoked salmon or thinly sliced ham, in 7 1/2 x 3-inch strips
12 pickled okra pods, ends trimmed, patted dry
1/4 cup toasted black sesame seeds

◉ Prepare Sushi Rice. In a small dish, blend cream cheese, Wasabi and shiso; set aside. Pass shiny side of nori 2 or 3 times over the flame of a gas burner or electric burner on high heat. Do not overheat or nori will crack when rolled. Place a strip of nori, shiny-side down and long side running horizontally, on a flat surface.

◉ Combine 1/2 cup water and vinegar for moistening your hands. Measure 1/4 of the rice; unmold in the middle of nori sheet. With damp hands, press rice over nori. Cover a bamboo sushi mat with plastic wrap. Transfer nori, rice-side down, to the edge of the sushi mat. Spread 1/4 of the cream cheese mixture across the middle of the nori, from side to side. Lay a salmon strip on cream cheese. Top with a row of 3 okra pods.

◉ To form roll, lift edge of mat with thumbs. Hold ingredients in place with fingers and roll mat and nori to enclose filling. Roll to the far edge of the rice. Wrap mat completely around rice roll; press gently for a few seconds. Unroll; remove plastic wrap. Sprinkle 1 tablespoon sesame seeds over a small area on a cutting board. Roll sushi in sesame seeds. Cover loosely with plastic wrap; set aside. Repeat with remaining ingredients to make 3 more rolls.

◉ Place rolls seam-side down on cutting surface. Wet a large, sharp knife with water-vinegar mixture. With a clean cut, slice rolls in half; wipe and dampen knife between cuts. Slice each half into 3 (1 1/4-inch) pieces. Place on serving tray. Serve at once, or store uncut in a loosely covered rectangular pan up to 1 hour at room temperature.

◉ *Makes 24 pieces or 4 servings.*

Sushi Lingo

Most sushi chefs are pleased to hear their customers use the special lingo of the *sushi-ya*.

Baran	green plastic garnish
Hachi-maki	knotted headband of the sushi chef
Itamaé or *ita-san*	sushi chef
Maki-su	bamboo rolling mat
Oaiso	"the bill"
Ochoko	small saké cup
Ochoshi	small bottles used to pour saké
Otemoto	chopsticks
Oshibori	hand towel
Agari ("finished")	hot green tea
Gari	pickled ginger
Murasaki ("purple")	soy sauce (usually a rich house blend)
Ponzu	soy sauce dip with citrus (for sashimi)
Sabi or *namida*	*wasabi* (horseradish)
Sencha	upper-grade sushi bar tea
Tsuma	sashimi garnishes
Chakin-zushi	sushi with eel in a special egg wrapper
Charashi-zushi	sushi rice with ingredients on top
Fukusa-zushi	sushi wrapped in paper-thin egg sheet

Futo-maki	fancy thick roll
Gunkan-maki	"battleship" style of *nigiri-zushi*
Hoso-maki	one ingredient inside roll
Inari-zushi	stuffed bean curd pouches
Kappa-maki	cucumber roll
Maki-zushi	rolled sushi
Nigiri-zushi	hand-shaped sushi with topping
Nori	paper-thin sheets of seaweed
Nori-maki	rolled with nori
Oshi-zushi	pressed box sushi
Saké-no-kawa-maki	salmon skin roll
Shari	sushi rice
Tekka-maki	tuna roll
Te-maki	hand roll
Uméjiso-maki	uméboshi and shiso leaf roll
Anago	conger eel
Awabi	abalone
Ebi	shrimp
Hamachi	young yellowtail
Ika	squid
Ikura	salmon roe
Maguro	tuna
Tai	sea bream
Tako	octopus
Uni	sea urchin roe

Sushi Etiquette

- The pickled ginger on your plate is eaten to refresh the palate between each bite of sushi.
- A pair of sushi is one order.
- Use chopsticks to pick up a piece of sushi; turn it over so the fish is on the bottom. Dip fish side into the soy sauce. If you dip the rice side, it will fall apart.
- Eat sushi in one or two bites.
- Seasoned fish, such as anago or eel, should not be dipped in soy sauce.

CHARCOAL-GRILLED & PAN-GRILLED FOODS

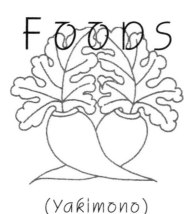

(Yakimono)

◉

Inside the drafty old wooden farmhouse, the rice farmer and his family gathered about the *robata yaki,* or sunken open-hearth firepit, to cook their evening meal. Attached to the soot-covered ceiling was a contrivance for holding a pot of vegetables over the hot fire. It wasn't the usual meal; tonight there was fresh salted fish grilling on the rack below. Later in the evening, the family huddled on tatami mats around the cozy fire, passing the long hours in spirited communion.

This vignette of old Japan is rarely experienced today. Nostalgic for open-hearth cooking and the old ways, many Japanese enjoy spending time at the *robata yaki-ya,* or hearthside grill restaurant. There, one can sit around an old-style cooking hearth or at a long counter that displays a bounteous array of seasonal foods on ice. In the style of the Ainus, a northern Caucasoid people, foods are passed to the diners on wooden paddles. One of the pleasures of the *robata* is *yakimono.*

Yakimono, or grilled foods, represents one of the oldest methods of Japanese cookery. There is an entire category of techniques for *yakimono,* "foods seared with intense heat." It includes charcoal-grilling, pan-grilling, oven-broiling and baking. But everyday Japanese home cooking is done on the stovetop or on tabletop grills.

As with the old rice farmer, it is a special day when I can dine on Salt-Grilled Trout (*Shio Yaki*). Cooked over an open fire, it became one of my favorite foods while in Japan. Fish is salted by a number of methods before grilling. It can be hand-salted, placed in a saline bath or lightly packed in salt for a short time. Salting extracts odors and keeps the flesh moist. Salt-grilled fish is a popular breakfast food.

Before grilling, foods might be inserted with two or more bamboo or metal skewers of appropriate length. Skewers help balance foods as they are turned on the grill. Skewers can be twisted inside cooked foods to determine their degree of doneness. Food is properly cooked if the skewer can be easily twisted with little resistance. To test fish, insert a bamboo skewer into the thickest portion of the flesh. Cooked fish yields easily; uncooked fish offers greater resistance. Don't overcook; the flesh continues cooking after being removed from the grill. Experience is your best guide for cooking fish to perfection. Soak skewers in cool water 30 minutes before use. The ends can be wrapped in foil to prevent burning. Reusable flat metal skewers hold foods more securely than round ones.

Foods for grilling are lightly seasoned and marinated 20 to 30 minutes, if at all. They might be basted with a soy sauce mixture, vegetable oil, or on occasion, butter. The end result of grilling should always be the same: Foods should be tender and juicy inside with a crusty appealing exterior.

Teppan yaki, or "cooking on an iron plate," is an age-old technique. Butter-Grilled Meat, Shellfish & Vegetables is an example of *batā yaki,* a recent variation in which foods are grilled in butter. Elevated to new heights, the art of *teppan* has taken on a theatrical quality as chefs slice, dice and entertain. At home, use a flat Japanese iron pan (*teppan*) or a heavy cast-iron skillet over a portable tabletop gas burner. You could also use an electric skillet. The rectangular *tamago yaki nabé* is an essential pan for making Sweet Omelet Roll. Like any good omelet pan, it must be carefully seasoned to give perfect results.

Charcoal-grilling can be accomplished on a regular barbecue grill, hibachi or tabletop grill. Start the charcoal fire 30 minutes in advance so the coals will be hot at cooking time. The Japanese prefer a smokeless, odorless charcoal, eschewing the aromatic woody aromas Americans adore. Preheat your tabletop grill 2 to 3 minutes. A Japanese stovetop fish-grilling pan (*sakana yaki*) is designed to hold fish securely between two wire grids for an occasional quick turn over the base pan. Several models are fitted with a ceramic heating element. As an alternative to charcoal-grilling, foods can be broiled in the oven by placing them on a rack fitted into a broiling pan. For best results, preheat the broiler and pan before the food is added. Place foods 4 to 5 inches from the heat source.

CHICKEN TERI YAKI

(Tori No Teri Yaki)

Teri means "shiny"; *yaki* is "grill." Poultry, meat or seafood is cooked on a hot grill or in a skillet, then glazed with a soy sauce mixture. This delicious chicken recipe could not be quicker or easier. If you prefer, marinate chicken in the entire amount of sauce, then grill over a hot charcoal fire.

6 chicken breast halves, boned
   and skinned
2 teaspoons grated gingerroot
Ground black pepper to taste
2 tablespoons light soy sauce
   (*usukuchi shoyu*)
2 tablespoons mirin

1 tablespoon saké
1/2 teaspoon sugar
1 tablespoon vegetable oil
1 garlic clove, crushed
Seven-Spice Powder (page 228)
   (optional)

◉ Flatten chicken slightly between sheets of waxed paper. Place in a rectangular baking dish. Add gingerroot and pepper. In a small bowl, combine soy sauce, mirin and saké. Add 2 1/2 tablespoons to the chicken. Stir sugar into remaining amount; set aside. Marinate chicken 10 to 15 minutes.

◉ Heat skillet with oil over medium-high heat. Add chicken; cook 4 to 5 minutes. Turn chicken; cook 4 to 5 minutes more or until chicken is almost done. If marinade drippings burn, remove chicken briefly to wipe pan. Pour reserved marinade and garlic over chicken. Turn chicken in sauce 1 minute or until well glazed. Remove chicken to serving plates. Sprinkle with spice powder if desired. Serve at once.

◉ *Makes 6 servings.*

SKEWERED EGGPLANT WITH PEANUT MISO SAUCE

(Nasu Dengaku)

One of the oldest methods of miso cookery is *dengaku*. The word is formed by Chinese characters meaning "rice paddy" and "music." About six hundred years ago, a popular entertainer danced on a single stilt in a folk play, probably in the vicinity of a rice paddy. After that, the name *dengaku* was used for skewered, grilled tofu spread with miso paste. Vegetable *dengaku* is also delicious, especially when made with eggplant, daikon radish, mushrooms and sweet potato.

Peanut Miso Sauce (see opposite)
1 (1 1/2-lb.) eggplant, peeled
2 tablespoons vegetable oil
2 green onions, minced

PEANUT MISO SAUCE
2 tablespoons cocktail peanuts
1/2 cup white or yellow miso
2 tablespoons brown sugar
2 green onions, minced
2 tablespoons saké
2 teaspoons light soy sauce
(*usukuchi shoyu*)

◉ Prepare sauce. Soak 12 to 14 (2-prong) Japanese pine-needle skewers or 24 to 28 thin (6- to 8-inch) bamboo skewers in water 30 minutes. Cut eggplant crosswise into 1-inch-thick rounds. Cut each slice into 2 semicircles. Push 1 pine-needle skewer or 2 bamboo skewers into the end of each piece. Brush both sides of eggplant pieces with oil.

◉ In a wok bring 4 cups water to a boil over high heat. Place eggplant on a steamer tray. Cover; place over boiling water. Steam 10 minutes or until barely tender. Remove steamer tray. Cool 5 minutes.

◉ Preheat broiler and broiling pan. Spread sauce over 1 side of each eggplant slice. Lightly oil hot broiling pan. Place coated eggplant sauce-side up on pan. Broil 4 to 5 inches from heat source, watching carefully, 1 to 2 minutes or until sauce begins to speckle. Garnish with green onions. Serve at once. To eat, push eggplant off skewers.

◉ *Makes 5 or 6 servings.*

PEANUT MISO SAUCE

◉ In a Japanese grinding bowl or food processor fitted with a steel blade, grind peanuts to a paste. Blend in remaining ingredients.

GRILLED MISO CHICKEN
(Tori No Miso-zuke Yaki)

Miso marinade adds a rich flavor to this country-style grilled chicken. Thigh meat
stays moist and tender, but boned chicken breasts are delicious, too.
The chicken can be sautéed in a skillet.

2 tablespoons light soy sauce (*usukuchi shoyu*)	1 teaspoon minced gingerroot
2 tablespoons saké	1 garlic clove, minced
2 tablespoons mirin	8 boned chicken thighs, skin intact
2 tablespoons light miso	1 tablespoon toasted sesame seeds
2 green onions, crushed and slivered	Seven-Spice Powder (page 228) (optional)

◉ Blend soy sauce, saké, mirin, miso, green onions, gingerroot and garlic in a rectangular baking dish. Coat chicken with mixture. Marinate 1 hour or refrigerate overnight, turning several times.

◉ Preheat a hibachi, portable tabletop grill or charcoal grill. Shake marinade off chicken; pat dry. Place skin-side down on hot grill. Grill 4 to 5 minutes. Turn chicken; grill second side 4 to 5 minutes or until golden brown and done inside. When chicken is done, sprinkle with sesame seeds and spice mixture.

◉ *Makes 4 servings.*

SAUTÉED HIJIKI, PORK & VEGETABLES
(Hijiki, Buta To Yasai Itami-ni)

Tangled black *hijiki* threads taste sweet and delicious. *Hijiki* is extremely rich in protein, calcium, and other minerals. Cut the meat and vegetables to match the shape of the soaked *hijiki*. For a vegetarian version, omit the pork.

3 medium-size dried shiitake
   mushrooms
1/4 cup dried *hijiki* (sea vegetable),
   rinsed in a strainer
3 tablespoons vegetable oil
1 large garlic clove, minced
3 green onions, finely shredded
1 large carrot, cut into
   matchstick strips
3 ounces thinly sliced pork loin,
   cut into matchstick strips

10 snow peas, cut into
   matchstick strips
1 cup fresh bean sprouts
1 teaspoon sugar
1 tablespoon soy sauce
1/2 teaspoon *dashi-no-moto*
   powder (instant *dashi*)
1 tablespoon mirin
1/4 cup chicken broth or water

◉ Soak mushrooms in a bowl of warm water 30 minutes. Squeeze dry; cut off stems. Cut caps into thin shreds. Put rinsed *hijiki* in a medium-size bowl; add warm water to cover. Soak 20 minutes. Rinse in a strainer under cool water. Press out water. Slice several times to make shorter lengths.

◉ Heat a wok or medium-size skillet over medium-high heat. Add 2 tablespoons of the oil. Add mushrooms, *hijiki*, garlic, onions and carrot. Stir-fry 2 minutes. Add pork strips and stir-fry 2 minutes, adding extra oil if needed. Add snow peas and bean sprouts. Stir-fry 1 minute or until vegetables are shiny with oil and hot. Mix in sugar, soy sauce, *dashi* powder and mirin. Add broth, cover pan and cook 1 minute. Remove lid. Stir mixture; cook until liquid is reduced. This dish is good served warm or at room temperature.

◉ *Makes 3 or 4 servings.*

BUTTER-GRILLED MEAT, SHELLFISH & VEGETABLES
(Batā Yaki)

When we prepare this *teppan yaki* dish, we become nostalgic for similar meals we've enjoyed at Sam's Anchor Inn in Okinawa. The chefs use generous amounts of butter and garlic for cooking the tabletop-grilled beef, seafood and vegetables. When you prepare this, don't forget to serve rice. There are potatoes in this dish, but in Japan they are viewed as another vegetable choice, never a substitute for rice.

Daikon Dipping Sauce
  (page 103)
3 garlic cloves, finely minced
1 large Bermuda onion, halved
  and cut crosswise into 1/4-inch
  slices
1 1/2 to 2 lbs. beef tenderloin or
  sirloin, cut into 1-inch cubes
3 large potatoes, peeled, cut into
  1-inch cubes, parboiled and
  cooled

2 small bell peppers, cut into
  strips
1/2 lb. button mushrooms, sliced
1 pound large uncooked shrimp,
  peeled and deveined
About 1/4 cup vegetable oil
About 1/4 cup butter, at room
  temperature
Salt and ground black pepper
  to taste
Cooked rice

◉ Prepare Daikon Dipping Sauce; pour into 5 or 6 small bowls. Arrange garlic, onion, beef, potatoes, bell peppers, mushrooms and shrimp on large serving platters.

◉ At the table, heat a portable tabletop griddle or electric skillet to high heat. Add 1 tablespoon oil and 1 tablespoon butter. Add 1/3 of garlic and onion and cook a few minutes. Add 1/3 of meat; cook to desired doneness. Add portions of remaining foods in the order listed. If possible, keep foods separate as they cook. Season with salt and pepper. Serve with rice and dipping sauce. Pass small plates on the side. Invite diners to help themselves from the griddle. Replenish griddle as foods are eaten.

◉ *Makes 5 or 6 servings.*

PAN-FRIED PORK & CABBAGE DUMPLINGS
(Gyoza Yaki)

For an evening of shared fun, invite several friends to participate in a dumpling-making party. But if you are on your own, the dumplings can be conveniently made ahead and frozen. Cook the dumplings, partially thawed.

Dumpling Sauce (page 101)
Pork & Cabbage Filling (see below)
1 (10-oz.) pkg. Japanese *gyoza*
    skins (about 54 skins)
1 tablespoon cornstarch mixed
    with 1 tablespoon water
4 tablespoons vegetable oil
About 1/2 cup chicken broth,
    bouillon or water

PORK & CABBAGE FILLING

1 cup minced cabbage, lightly
    salted 30 minutes, rinsed and
    drained

1 teaspoon salt
1 lb. lean ground pork or beef
3 tablespoons saké
3 tablespoons soy sauce
1 garlic clove, minced
1 teaspoon minced gingerroot
2 green onions, minced
1 teaspoon potato starch or
    cornstarch
1/4 teaspoon sesame oil
2 to 3 dashes ground black
    pepper
1/2 teaspoon sugar

◉ Prepare Dumpling Sauce; set aside. Prepare filling. Place 1 teaspoon filling in center of each *gyoza* skin. Paint edge with cornstarch mixture. Pleat top edges if desired, then fold skins over, forming semicircles. Press tightly to seal. Place on a tray; press bottoms to flatten slightly. Cover dumplings loosely with plastic wrap.

◉ In a large nonstick skillet, heat 2 tablespoons of the oil over medium-high heat. Fry 1/2 of dumplings until the dumpling bottoms are browned. Drizzle in 1/4 cup stock. Quickly cover skillet with a tight-fitting lid. If no lid is available, apply heavy foil wearing protective kitchen mitts. Steam 2 to 3 minutes, shaking pan occasionally. Remove cover; cook until liquid evaporates. Fry dumplings a few seconds longer to recrisp bottoms. Place dumplings on a serving platter, bottom sides up. Wipe skillet. Repeat process to make remaining dumplings. Serve with sauce.

◉ *Makes 6 to 8 servings.*

PORK & CABBAGE FILLING

◉ Prepare cabbage. After salted cabbage is rinsed and drained, mix well with remaining filling ingredients in a large bowl.

GRILLED CHICKEN SKEWERS
(Yakitori)

Yakitori is the Japanese specialty Americans love. It's a perfect party appetizer; the glaze and skewering can be done ahead for easy last-minute cooking. Better double the recipe for large groups. Pour the glaze into a tall narrow jar for dipping the skewers. The glaze is also good brushed on chicken livers, tofu, chicken parts or fish. In Japan, "grilled hormones" on a *yakitori-ya* menu refers to certain organ meats.

Yakitori Glaze (see below)
6 chicken thighs, skinned, boned,
    each cut into 8 cubes
2 bunches green onions, white
    parts only, cut into thirds
Seven-Spice Powder (page 228)

YAKITORI GLAZE
1/2 cup soy sauce
1/2 cup mirin
1/4 cup saké
1/4 cup sugar
1 garlic clove, crushed
1 (1/8-inch-thick) slice peeled
    gingerroot, crushed
1 tablespoon water
1 tablespoon cornstarch or
    potato starch

◉ Soak 16 (8- to 10-inch) bamboo skewers in water 30 minutes. Prepare Yakitori Glaze; set aside. Thread 3 chicken pieces alternately with 2 pieces green onion on each skewer.

◉ Preheat a portable tabletop grill or outdoor charcoal grill. Grill chicken skewers 2 to 3 minutes. Turn as necessary for even cooking. When almost done, begin basting chicken with glaze. Grill 2 minutes longer or until done. Baste 1 final time; remove from grill. Keep warm. Cook remaining skewers. Season with Seven-Spice Powder.

◉ *Makes 4 servings.*

YAKITORI GLAZE

◉ In a small saucepan, combine soy sauce, mirin, saké, sugar, garlic and gingerroot. Simmer over medium-high heat 3 to 4 minutes. In a small bowl, blend water and cornstarch. Pour mixture into pan; cook, stirring constantly, until thickened. Strain glaze. Will keep at room temperature 10 to 12 hours. Refrigerate leftover glaze; reheat gently on low heat before using.

◉ *Makes about 1 cup.*

DUMPLING SAUCE

This spicy sauce goes well with pan-fried, steamed or simmered dumplings. It's a wonderful dip for any Chinese-style dumplings or fried appetizer.

1/2 cup soy sauce	1 garlic clove, minced
1 to 2 tablespoons water or *dashi*	1/2 teaspoon sesame oil
2 teaspoons sugar	1 teaspoon toasted sesame seeds
2 tablespoons rice vinegar	Dried hot-red-pepper flakes
1 green onion, minced	to taste

◉ In a small bowl, combine all ingredients. Allow to stand at room temperature 30 minutes for the flavors to blend.

◉ *Makes 3/4 cup.*

SALT-GRILLED TROUT
(Shio Yaki)

Salting firms the fish, sealing in moisture as it is cooked. Salting also crisps the skin, drawing out the fat layer just underneath, helping keep the fish moist. In traditional Japanese cooking, the side of the fish to be presented is the first side to be placed on the hot grill. When served, the fish head should be on the diner's left. For oven-broiling, fillets with skin are cooked skin-side up (close to the heat source), then turned if necessary, to complete the broiling. Serve the fish skin-side up.

4 whole small trout, ready for cooking	1/4 cup fresh lemon juice (optional)
About 2 tablespoons kosher salt or sea salt	Finely shredded daikon radish
	Lemon wedges

◉ Rinse fish. Rinse cavity under cool water. Apply 1 generous teaspoon salt to each side of fish, adding an extra-thick layer on tails and fins. Spread open fins. Let stand at room temperature 30 minutes. Place fish on a flat surface with heads to the right. Insert a metal skewer into head of each fish behind eye. Bring skewer out near gills on same side. Do not pierce skin on the opposite side. Insert skewer again midway into side of fish. Bring it out near the tail. Tail and fins can be covered with foil to prevent burning, if necessary. Fish will appear to be in a swimming motion with head and tail up.

◉ Preheat a hibachi, portable tabletop grill or charcoal grill. Place fish on hot grill on the opposite, unskewered side. Cook 4 to 5 minutes; turn and cook 4 to 5 minutes more, depending on thickness of fish. Baste skin with a little lemon juice if desired. Serve on a bed of shredded daikon. Garnish with lemon wedges.

◉ *Makes 4 servings.*

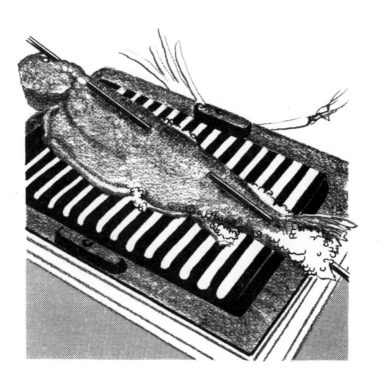

SPICY DAIKON DIPPING SAUCE

Daikon radish is always a good accompaniment for grilled foods, especially meats. It is thought to be an important aid in the digestion of fats.

1/2 cup soy sauce
1 cup Sea Vegetable & Bonito
   Stock (page 46)

Red Maple Radish (page 233)
   to taste

◙ In a small bowl, combine all ingredients.

◙ *Makes about 1 1/2 cups.*

SPICY MARINATED GRILLED MEAT

(Yakiniku)

This succulent meat is served at a *yakiniku-ya*, or Korean barbecue restaurant, on a sizzling, domed brass or iron shield. The subtle soy sauce taste is Japanese, but the garlic and hot chile are pure Korean.

Korean diners enjoy putting a small portion of meat on a tender lettuce leaf along with a spoonful of white rice and a dab of delicious Korean bean paste, or *kochu jang*. The lettuce is folded over into a neat package for eating. Serve Korean Winter Kim Chee (page 234) on the side.

1/3 cup soy sauce
2 tablespoons sugar
2 green onions, slivered
2 garlic cloves, minced
1 tablespoon saké
1 1/2 teaspoons toasted sesame
  seeds

1 teaspoon sesame oil
1/4 teaspoon ground red pepper,
  sansho pepper or ground
  black pepper
1 lb. beef rib eye or other tender
  beef, sliced 1/8 inch thick

◉ In a large bowl, combine all the ingredients except beef for a marinade. Dip slices of meat into marinade. Arrange attractively on a serving platter for cooking. Meat can be covered and refrigerated 30 minutes.

◉ Preheat a hibachi, portable tabletop grill or griddle. Gently shake excess marinade off each meat slice before cooking. Grill just until no longer pink, turning once or twice.

◉ *Makes 3 or 4 servings.*

SIZZLING SOY SAUCE STEAK
(Gyuniku Yaki)

This simple recipe demonstrates the "tastiness" of shoyu (soy sauce). "Tastiness" is a word coined in Japan to explain a special flavor component, based on amino acids. It is considered to be *umami,* or savory, the fifth primary taste in addition to salty, sweet, sour and bitter. For the Japanese this tastiness is also found in dried mushrooms, seaweed and dried bonito. The succulent flavor of this grilled steak is hard to beat. It is delicious dipped into the Sashimi Dipping Sauce (page 61), blended with grated daikon radish and minced green onion. It is also good with the Peanut Miso Sauce (page 219).

2 to 2 1/2 pounds top-grade beef sirloin steak	2 tablespoons saké
3 to 4 tablespoons soy sauce	2 tablespoons brown sugar
	1 large clove garlic, crushed

◉ Trim excess fat from meat. In a glass baking dish, combine remaining ingredients. Marinate meat at room temperature 30 minutes. Remove meat from marinade.

◉ Preheat a charcoal grill or large frying pan. Gently shake excess marinade off meat before cooking. Lightly oil grill top. Grill meat to medium rare or desired degree of doneness. Let the meat sit 5 minutes before cutting. Slice across the grain. Serve with dipping sauces.

◉ *Makes 5 or 6 servings.*

GLAZED SALMON FILLETS
(Sake Teri Yaki)

In the Imperial Court kitchens of medieval Japan, teriyaki cuisine was limited to seafood because of Buddhist edicts prohibiting the consumption of meat. Even today, fish immediately comes to mind when the Japanese think of teriyaki. Try this teriyaki glaze on a variety of seafood including shrimp, scallops, squid, trout or halibut. Yellowtail is a teriyaki favorite. Since yellowtail is oily, some Japanese cooks pour a little boiling water over pan-grilled fish, then pour it off before the teriyaki mixture is added.

1 lb. fresh salmon fillets, cut into 2-inch-square pieces	1 tablespoon soy sauce
3 tablespoons saké	Yakitori Glaze (page 100)

◉ Soak 8 to 10 (6- to 8-inch) bamboo skewers in water 30 minutes. Place salmon pieces in a small shallow pan. Pour saké and soy sauce over fish. Cover and refrigerate 15 minutes. Prepare Yakitori Glaze. Drain fish well. Insert 2 skewers, running parallel, through each piece of fish.

◉ Preheat a hibachi or portable tabletop grill. Grill fish 2 minutes, turning once. Brush both sides of skewered fish pieces with glaze. Continue grilling until fish barely flakes, 3 to 6 minutes, depending on the thickness. Watch carefully so fish does not overcook and become dry. Use skewers to turn fish. Brush with glaze. Serve warm or at room temperature. Push fish from skewer before eating.

◉ *Makes 4 or 5 servings.*

CRANBERRY TOFU MEATBALLS

(Cranberry Dofu Niku Dango)

Tofu adds extra nutrition to ground meat mixtures and keeps them moist and light.
The cranberry-orange glaze gives these meatballs a unique flavor. Skewered meatballs
are a popular inclusion in the Japanese box lunch. Serve these as appetizers
or as a side dish with rice.

1/2 lb. tofu (about 1 cup),
   rinsed and mashed
1 lb. lean ground pork, beef or
   chicken
1 small onion, finely minced
1 1/2 teaspoons finely minced
   gingerroot
1 garlic clove, finely minced
2 eggs
2 tablespoons soy sauce
1/4 teaspoon sesame oil

Salt and ground black pepper
   to taste
1/4 cup cornstarch
1 tablespoon vegetable oil
1 tablespoon unsalted butter or
   margarine
3/4 cup cranberry juice
1/4 cup fresh orange juice
1 teaspoon fresh grated
   orange peel
1 tablespoon toasted sesame seeds

◉ In a large bowl, combine tofu, meat, onion, gingerroot, garlic, eggs, soy sauce,
sesame oil, salt and pepper. Shape mixture into about 28 moist meatballs, using 1 tablespoon mixture per meatball. Dust with cornstarch. In a large skillet, heat oil and
butter over medium-high heat. Brown meatballs. Pour off fat if desired.

◉ Pour in juices and orange peel. Cover partially and simmer 20 minutes or until liquid is reduced and meatballs are well glazed. Shake pan occasionally. Place on a platter; garnish with sesame seeds.

◉ *Makes 8 appetizer or side dish servings.*

JAPANESE-STYLE PIZZA
(Okonomi Yaki)

My first taste of this unusual pancake was in Kyoto at a street festival. *Okonomi yaki*, created in Osaka in recent years, means the food is cooked "as you like it." The possible additions are limitless; try thinly sliced raw beef or ham, bean sprouts, carrot shreds, bacon bits, raw shrimp or cooked noodles. *Modan yaki* is another version made with eggs, grilled sunny-side up. *Okonomi yaki* is basted with spicy sauce, drizzled with mayonnaise, then sprinkled with *ao-noriko*—green seaweed flakes.

2 recipes Tonkatsu Sauce
  (page 157)
3 cups cake flour
1 3/4 cups water
6 medium-size eggs, lightly beaten
1/2 teaspoon salt
1 teaspoon baking powder
3 cups finely shredded cabbage
6 green onions
3/4 pound thinly sliced pork,
  cut into 1/8-inch strips

12 medium-size fresh shiitake
  mushrooms or round
  mushrooms, stemmed
Vegetable oil
Top-quality mayonnaise, in a
  squirt bottle
Ao-noriko
1/4 cup shredded red pickled
  ginger (*beni shōga*)

◉ Prepare Tonkatsu Sauce; set aside. In a bowl, whisk together cake flour, water, eggs, salt and baking powder. Divide batter among 6 medium-size bowls. Arrange cabbage, green onions, pork and mushrooms on a platter; place on the table for cooking. Every diner receives a bowl of batter. To each bowl, stir in 1/6 of the cabbage and green onions. Divide the meat and mushrooms in 6 portions. Heat an electric griddle on medium-high heat; add oil.

◉ For each pizza, place a small pile of meat on griddle. Turn once; grill until almost done. Cover each pile of meat with a bowl of batter. Cook on 1 side until set; flip and cook until done. Top with sauce, mayonnaise, *ao-noriko* and ginger. Serve at once.

◉ *Makes 6 servings.*

Steamed Foods, Simmered Foods & One-Pot Dishes

(Mushimono, Nimono & Nabémono)

Steamed Foods

Steaming is a popular and healthful cooking method throughout Japan. Foods are suspended over boiling water in a closed container, surrounded by intense moist heat. The advantages of steaming are many. It is a clean, quick and economical method of cooking which preserves natural flavors, colors and nutrients. Steamed foods are self-basting, so moisture is retained. For all these reasons, steaming is an excellent method for reheating leftovers. Saké-marinated chicken, fish and vegetables lend themselves well to steaming. Savory soup-custards, filled wheat buns and glutinous rice are among Japan's favorite foods for steaming. Steamed foods are valued for their warming effect upon the body during cold weather.

Steaming units are available in aluminum, stainless steel and bamboo. Sturdy metal steamers have a deep base with one or two perforated stacked trays and a tight-fitting lid. Aluminum steamers are recommended because metal is an excellent heat conductor. However, condensation can be a problem with metal steamers; dripping liquid will often ruin your food. If the food isn't covered inside the steamer, wrap a towel around the lid and secure the four corners at the top. The Chinese bamboo steamer is a handsome addition to the kitchen and will last for years with proper care. The tiers fit into a wok or other suitable pan filled with boiling water. Bamboo steamers should be used regularly to keep them moist, preventing cracking and splitting. The wood is extremely porous and will absorb condensation, preventing soggy foods.

If you don't own a steamer, improvise one. Round, perforated, metal steaming trays that fit inside a wok are available in Asian markets and cookware stores. Or try crossing two wooden slats or bamboo chopsticks in the bottom of a wok to improvise a tray for holding up the dish of food. This type of arrangement limits the space for water, but is an adequate substitute. A covered stockpot or roasting pan will serve as a substitute steamer. Place an inverted bowl or empty can inside for holding the plate of food out of the water. Be sure the can isn't too tall or it will prevent the lid from fitting securely in place. A slight adjustment in steaming time may be necessary, depending upon the type of steamer used and how close the food is to the water. All the recipes in this book were tested on the bottom tray of a bamboo steamer fitted inside a wok.

Simmered Foods

Simmered foods, prepared daily in Japan, are an important part of the Japanese meal. Seasonal vegetables, seafood, poultry and meats are cooked in flavorful seasoning liquids until tender and slightly glazed. There are several variations of the seasoning liquid as well as several techniques for simmering the foods. Sea Vegetable & Bonito Stock (page 46) or *dashi* is usually the primary seasoning liquid. Some cooks like to use Second-Quality Stock (page 46) or convenient instant dashi powder.

Vegetables may require a quick precooking or blanching in plain boiling water. Tough root vegetables are blanched to soften fibers and neutralize strong flavors. Green vegetables are blanched to bring out their bright color, then immediately dropped into an iced-water bath, or *irodashi* ("color giving"). Blanched vegetables absorb the flavor of the dashi seasoning liquid better than unblanched vegetables. Chicken and fish are blanched to remove odors.

Seasonings for the *dashi* might include saké, mirin, and/or sugar, salt, soy sauce, miso and gingerroot. There are several classic seasoning variations including: *miso-ni* (*dashi*, miso, mirin, soy sauce and ginger), *kara-ni* (half soy sauce and half saké) and *shoga-ni* (*dashi*, soy sauce and gingerroot).

Saké tenderizes and is excellent for fish and poultry dishes. Use sugar in moderation to add sweetness and to temper the acidity of foods. Many cooks burn off the alcohol in large amounts of mirin to enhance its true flavor.

Simmered foods might be cooked in two parts, first deep-fried or sautéed (agé-ni or itamé-ni), then simmered in the seasoning liquid. The latter method is used in the recipe Beef & Onion Rolls (page 125).

When simmering foods, an *otoshi-buta*, or drop lid, is placed on top. Immersing the foods in the flavorful liquid helps promote even cooking. Sometimes the components of a dish are simmered separately in a way that is best for each food, then combined during the final minutes of cooking. The resulting dish offers an exciting contrast of tastes and textures bound together by a unifying sauce. Sometimes the ingredients are cooked separately and not combined until they are carefully arranged together in individual serving bowls.

Most of these dishes can be made two to three days in advance and refrigerated until time to serve. They are good warm or at room temperature. Simmered foods are regularly part of the obentō and comprise a large portion of the special meal for New Year's Day. The cook can relax, enjoy the festivities and know that delicious foods can be served at a moment's notice. Simmered dishes may have a similar glazed appearance. Garnishes are the final appropriate touch. Sesame seeds, sliced green onions, herbs and bonito threads will add variety in appearance as well as in taste.

One-Pot Dishes

Nabémono includes a variety of country casserole-type dishes prepared by simmering foods in a pot of savory broth. Suki Yaki and Chicken Hot Pot are two of the most well known examples. In Japan, these are great wintertime favorites. The beauty of a *nabémono* dish is in the arrangement of the raw materials when presented to guests for cooking. The cooking is done at the table, which allows the guests to participate. As the foods are added to the pot, guests can help themselves. While there is no denying that *nabémono* dishes are delicious, part of their charm lies in the fact that guests will cook and eat together from the communal pot. The Japanese view this as an important time for relaxation and for bonding new and strengthening old friendships. In earlier years, it was believed that the personalities of people would instantly merge together when they touched food from a common pot with their chopsticks. Although frowned upon in polite society, the habit of using individual chopsticks in a common pot persisted, especially among families and close friends. Today it is accepted practice, except at formal meals. If your guests are adventurous, perhaps they will be willing to chance such a convivial experience to enjoy the delicious and dramatic culinary tradition of *nabémono*.

Sukiyaki is traditionally cooked in a suki yaki *nabé*, a heavy cast-iron pot with low sides. It is excellent for braising many foods. Treat it like your cast-iron skillet. After use, dry it well, oil lightly, then heat it over low heat for 2 to 3 minutes.

A *donabé* is an earthenware casserole glazed only on the inside. It is excellent for simmering *nabémono* dishes, such as Chicken Hot Pot. Soak the pot in water 1 hour before use. Drain and dry well. Add the stock. Place the pot over low heat, raising the temperature gradually so the pot will not crack. Never put an empty pot directly on the heat.

A *tetsunabé* is a cast-iron cooking pot with a curved handle and wooden lid for keeping foods warm after cooking. It is excellent for serving Savory Rice Porridge. These pots require the use of a portable burner for tabletop cooking and warming. A gas burner is found in most Japanese homes. They are available in Asian markets and by mail order (page 269).

STEAMED SAVORY CUSTARD WITH SEAFOOD

(Chawan Mushi)

This is traditionally cooked in *chawan mushi* cups. Substitute custard cups, china rice bowls or even Western teacups.

2 1/3 cups Sea Vegetable & Bonito Stock (page 46) or chicken stock
1 tablespoon light soy sauce (**usukuchi shoyu**)
1/2 teaspoon salt
1 tablespoon mirin
1 teaspoon sugar
1 teaspoon freshly grated lemon peel

4 large eggs
6 raw shrimp, peeled
4 chunks crabmeat
4 gingko nuts (*ginnan*) (optional)
1 small clump tree oyster mushrooms, blanched and separated
4 trefoil sprigs (*mitsuba*), each stem knotted, or 4 edible pea pods

◙ In a medium-size bowl, combine stock, soy sauce, salt, mirin, sugar and lemon peel. In a small bowl, slightly beat eggs. Gently stir eggs into stock mixture. Strain mixture through a fine strainer into a medium-size bowl. In a small saucepan, bring 1 cup water to a boil; reduce heat to low. Add shrimp to small saucepan; poach 30 seconds. Drain shrimp; set aside. In a wok or deep pot, bring about 4 cups water to a boil.

◉ Divide crabmeat and gingko nuts among 4 *chawan mushi* cups or custard cups. Pour stock mixture into cups; cover with lids or foil. Place on a steamer tray. Cover tray; place over boiling water. Reduce heat to medium. Steam 10 minutes. Uncover cups. Add 1 shrimp, 2 or 3 mushrooms and 1 knotted trefoil sprig or 1 pea pod to each custard; cover and steam 5 to 8 minutes longer. Custards are done when a small knife inserted off-center comes out clean. Serve custards with a pair of chopsticks and a small spoon.

◉ *Makes 4 servings.*

VARIATIONS

◉ Custard can be steamed in 8 to 10 Japanese teacups for appetizer servings. Increase seafood and other ingredients as necessary; divide among teacups.

Steaming Foods

To steam foods successfully, select a dish at least 1 inch smaller than the diameter of the steamer so the steam can circulate freely around the dish of food. Do not add the food until the water has come to a rolling boil over high heat. It will be necessary to reduce the heat to gently steam egg dishes and delicate custards. Simmer a kettle of water on the side to replenish the steamer during long periods of steaming. Several marbles in the bottom of the pan would be a noisy reminder that it is time to refill the pan!

Dumplings and buns can be placed directly on a steamer tray lined with dampened cheesecloth, lettuce leaves or cabbage leaves, depending on the type of filling to be steamed. Do not remove the lid while steaming is in progress unless indicated in a recipe. Remember that the food on the bottom steamer tray near the simmering water will cook faster than food in the upper trays. Remove the steamer from the heat before lifting a steamer tray. Lift the lid away from you to avoid scalding burns.

STUFFED PATTYPAN SQUASH

(Seiyo Uri No Buta Ebi Zumé)

Partial cutting of the squash before steaming makes eating with chopsticks a snap.

8 to 10 well-shaped pattypan
squash, rinsed

SHRIMP & PORK FILLING
4 medium-size raw shrimp,
peeled, deveined and chopped
1/4 pound lean ground pork
1 tablespoon saké
1 tablespoon mirin
1/2 teaspoon minced gingerroot
1 tablespoon light soy sauce
(*usukuchi shoyu*)
1/4 teaspoon sesame oil
1/4 teaspoon sugar
1/8 teaspoon salt (optional)

SHIITAKE MUSHROOM SAUCE
1 large dried shiitake mushroom
1/3 cup warm water
1 1/2 cups chicken broth
2 tablespoons soy sauce
2 teaspoons brown sugar
1 tablespoon saké
1/4 teaspoon *dashi-no-moto*
powder
1 tablespoon potato starch or
1 1/2 tablespoons cornstarch
1/2 teaspoon sesame oil

◉ Using a small sharp knife, cut off rounded blossom ends of squash. Reserve for caps. Scoop out insides, forming hollow shells. Trim a small piece off stem ends so squash will sit flat. Make a shallow 1/4-inch cut across stem end of each squash. Turn squash 90 degrees and make another cut. Do not cut all the way through or squash will fall apart. Prepare Shrimp & Pork Filling. Pat a small amount of filling into each hollowed squash.

◉ In a wok or deep pot, bring 4 cups water to a boil. Place stuffed squash and reserved caps in a shallow heatproof pan. Place pan on a steamer tray; cover tray. Place over boiling water; steam 15 minutes or until tender. While squash is steaming, prepare Shiitake Mushroom Sauce. If desired, stir drippings from cooking squash into sauce; strain before use. Place 2 squash on each serving plate; cover with mushroom sauce. If desired, place 1 cap at an angle on top of each stuffed squash.

Makes 4 or 5 servings.

SHRIMP & PORK FILLING

In a medium-size bowl, combine all ingredients.

SHIITAKE MUSHROOM SAUCE

Place mushroom in a small bowl; add warm water. Soak 30 minutes. Squeeze mushroom dry, reserving mushroom liquid. Discard tough stem. Slice mushroom into strips. In a small saucepan, combine chicken broth, soy sauce, brown sugar, saké and *dashi* powder over medium-high heat. In a small bowl, blend potato starch and reserved mushroom soaking liquid. Stir into sauce. Cook until thickened, stirring constantly. Stir in sesame oil and sliced mushroom.

Makes about 2 cups.

FANTAIL SHRIMP

(Sugata Ebi)

Shrimp tails will spread open into fan shapes.

Large or jumbo raw shrimp

Peel shrimp, leaving tails intact. Make a shallow cut lengthwise down back of each shrimp. Rinse out dark vein. Pull away strips of loose skin on each side of cut. Make a slit about 1 inch long through middle of deveined shrimp. Bend head backward through slit, pulling tail up into place. Secure with a wooden pick. Spread tail open into a fan. Poach shrimp in salted simmering water 1 minute. Remove wooden picks. Use shrimp as a garnish or as directed in recipes.

STEAMED SEAFOOD IN KELP BOATS

(Sakana No Konbu Buné)

Seafood forms its own delicious dipping sauce, enhanced by the natural flavor
boosters found in the sea vegetable *konbu*.

1/3 pound littleneck or cherrystone
clams (about 4 clams)

4 to 8 mussels

2 teaspoons salt

1 (3-oz.) pkg. good-quality wide
dashi konbu, cut into 4
(8 x 6-inch) pieces

8 (7-inch) dried-gourd strips
(*kampyo*), soaked in salted water

4 to 8 sea scallops, halved, or
1/4 pound baby scallops

8 to 12 medium-size raw shrimp,
peeled and deveined

2 or 3 fresh or thawed frozen
king crab legs (optional), cut
into 3-inch pieces

4 teaspoons saké

4 teaspoons light soy sauce
(*usukuchi shoyu*)

4 teaspoons unsalted butter

Scalloped Lemon Slices
(page 16)

◉ Using a stiff brush, scrub clams under cool running water. Discard any that do not
snap shut as you begin scrubbing. Scrub mussels under cool running water. If necessary, pull off beard or strands coming from shells. Make sure mussels are closed
tightly; discard any that are not. Refrigerate until needed. Place clams in a large bowl;
add salt and cover with cool water. Soak 3 to 4 hours.

◉ To soften dried *konbu,* dip pieces into a large bowl of warm water. Gently flex
pieces 1 minute or until they begin to soften. Do not soak too long or *konbu* softens,
losing its flavor in the water. Pat dry. Gather each end of a piece of *konbu;* tie with 2
strips of soaked gourd. Form *konbu* into a boat shape. Form 3 more boats with remaining *konbu* pieces and gourd strips. Into each boat, put 1 clam, 1 or 2 mussels, 4
half pieces of scallop or several baby scallops and 2 or 3 shrimp. Using kitchen scissors, snip open shell of each piece of crab leg; leave meat in shell. Add 1 or 2 pieces to
each boat.

■ In a wok or deep pot, bring about 4 cups water to a boil. Place seafood boats on a steamer tray. Add 1 teaspoon saké, 1 teaspoon soy sauce and 1 teaspoon butter to each boat. Cover tray. Place over boiling water; steam seafood 5 to 8 minutes or until clams and mussels have opened. Garnish with lemon slices. Serve immediately. Instruct diners to dip seafood into the delicious broth that has formed in bottom of boats.

■ *Makes 4 servings.*

SESAME SAUCE

(Goma Su)

This nutty-tasting sauce is good with any type of grilled beef, hot pot, cooked vegetables or noodles.

1/2 cup toasted sesame seeds	1/2 teaspoon salt
3 tablespoons soy sauce	1 teaspoon vegetable oil
1/4 cup rice vinegar	1 garlic clove (optional), minced
1 1/2 tablespoons sugar	1/2 teaspoon salt

■ Toast sesame seeds in a hot skillet, shaking constantly to prevent burning. In a grinding bowl or blender, grind toasted seeds to a paste. Blend in remaining ingredients until sauce is smooth. Pour into small individual bowls. Sauce can be made 1 to 2 days ahead and refrigerated.

■ *Makes about 1/2 cup.*

STEAMED BUNS WITH MISO PORK FILLING
(Miso Buta Manju)

In Japan, children often head for the corner market after school to buy one of these savory buns. Decorate the top of each bun by branding them with a small clean stamp or cutter dipped in red food coloring. Stamps can be found in Asian shops or stationery stores. Look for birds, flower designs or Japanese characters. Or stamp a flower design using a single drinking straw dipped in food coloring.

Miso Pork Filling (see below)
2 1/2 cups cake flour
1 tablespoon baking powder
1/2 cup sugar
1/2 teaspoon salt
1/4 cup butter or vegetable
   shortening, cut into small pieces
1/2 cup evaporated milk
Vegetable oil

MISO PORK FILLING
1 tablespoon vegetable oil
3 green onions, minced

1 teaspoon minced gingerroot
1 large garlic clove, minced
1/2 pound lean ground pork
3 to 4 dashes ground *sansho*
   pepper or regular black pepper
2 tablespoons red miso paste
1 tablespoon saké
1 tablespoon sugar
1 tablespoon soy sauce
1 teaspoon mirin

◉ Prepare Miso Pork Filling; cool completely, then set aside. In a medium-size bowl, sift flour, baking powder, sugar and salt. Rub butter into flour mixture until fine crumbs form. Pour evaporated milk over flour mixture; stir until blended. Dough will be soft. Scrape onto a lightly floured surface. Coat with flour, kneading lightly several seconds. Pat dough into a ball; rub lightly with oil. Cover with a small bowl; let dough rest 20 minutes.

◉ Divide dough in half. Gently roll each half into a sausage-shaped roll. Cut each roll into 6 equal-size pieces. With your fingers, press each piece into a circle 3 1/2 to 4 inches in diameter. Pat circles to make sure dough is well blended and smooth. Cracks could split during steaming. (This will not harm the bun except for appearance.) Place

1 heaping teaspoon of filling in center of each circle. Shape dough around filling. Pinch edges tightly closed to seal buns. Rub lightly with oil. Cut 12 squares of foil or waxed paper slightly larger than buns. Rub squares lightly with oil. Place 1 bun seam-side down on each square.

◉ In a wok or deep pot, bring about 4 cups water to a boil. Place buns on foil or waxed paper on a steamer tray, about 3/4 inch apart; cover. Place over boiling water. Reduce heat to medium-high; steam 10 to 12 minutes. Remove foil or paper from buns. Serve warm or at room temperature. Store leftover buns in an airtight plastic bag in the refrigerator. Reheat in a microwave oven or resteam.

◉ *Makes 12 filled buns.*

MISO PORK FILLING

◉ In a medium-size skillet, heat oil over medium-high heat. Add green onions, gingerroot and garlic; stir-fry until aromatic. Add pork; stir-fry until crumbly and no longer pink. Add *sansho* pepper. Reduce heat to medium. In a small bowl, stir together miso, saké, sugar, soy sauce and mirin. Add to meat mixture; cook 3 to 4 minutes, stirring often. Scrape mixture onto a plate; cool before using.

◉ *Makes about 1 cup.*

SIMMERED CHICKEN WITH DAIKON RADISH

(Tori No Kiriboshi Daikon)

My sister, Dee Bradney, learned to cook dried daikon from a neighbor when she lived in Misawa, Japan.

1 1/2 oz. shredded dried daikon radish (2 cups rehydrated)	1 1/2 cups water
2 tablespoons vegetable oil	1/2 teaspoon *dashi-no-moto* powder
2 green onions, slivered	2 tablespoons mirin
1 medium-size carrot, cut into matchstick strips	1 tablespoon sugar
1 chicken breast half, skinned, boned and diced	1/4 cup soy sauce
	1 tablespoon rice vinegar
	Hot-pepper sauce (optional)

◉ Place dried daikon in a medium-size bowl; add water to cover. Soak 1 hour. Rinse and drain daikon several times. Squeeze out excess water. Cut pieces once or twice to make shorter lengths. In a medium-size saucepan, heat oil over medium-high heat. Add green onions and carrot; stir-fry 1 minute. Add chicken; stir-fry 30 seconds. Add daikon; stir and toss mixture 30 seconds.

◉ In a medium-size bowl, combine the water, dashi powder, mirin, sugar and soy sauce. Pour over chicken and vegetables. Cover saucepan with a tight-fitting lid. Simmer over low heat 20 minutes. Remove lid; cook 2 to 5 minutes longer or until all liquid has evaporated. Stir in vinegar. Serve warm or at room temperature in small serving dishes. Serve with hot pepper sauce if desired.

◉ *Makes 3 or 4 servings.*

SPICY BRAISED GOBO

(Kimpira Gobo)

Mrs. Mieko Kaiede of Toki City, Japan, prepared a small bentō of this addictive dish for me as I left her home to return to America. This is a favorite New Year's dish and can be prepared several hours ahead.

2 (15- to 18-inch) pieces *gobo*
   (burdock root)
2 1/2 tablespoons soy sauce
2 tablespoons saké
1 tablespoon mirin
2 1/2 tablespoons sugar
1/2 teaspoon *dashi-no-moto*
   powder

2 tablespoons vegetable oil
Seven-Spice Powder (page 228)
   to taste
1 heaping tablespoon toasted
   sesame seeds

◉ Using a vegetable brush, scrub off earthy brown covering from each piece of *gobo*. Cut pieces in half; soak in a pan of cool water 10 minutes. Cut each piece into 2-inch lengths, then cut into matchstick strips. Return strips to pan of water.

◉ In a large skillet, boil *gobo* in 4 cups water over high heat 5 minutes; drain well and set aside. Dry skillet. Combine soy sauce, saké, mirin, sugar and *dashi* powder in a small bowl. In same skillet, heat vegetable oil over high heat. Add drained *gobo*; stir-fry 2 minutes. Reduce heat to medium-low. Pour in soy sauce mixture. Cook and stir until sauce has almost all evaporated. Add Seven-Spice Powder. Place braised *gobo* into a serving bowl. Sprinkle with sesame seeds.

◉ *Makes 5 or 6 servings.*

SEASONED SHIITAKE MUSHROOMS
(Shiitake No Nimono)

Seasoned shiitake can be served as a side dish or used as an ingredient in many dishes. *Kampyo,* or edible strips of gourd, can be minced for rice dishes, cut into strips for rolled sushi or used as an edible string. *Konnyaku,* a jellied paste made from devil's tongue, is served as a low-calorie side dish, and is good for the digestive system. It is often included in braised vegetable dishes. See variations below for cooking *kampyo* and *konnyaku.*

8 to 10 dried medium-size shiitake mushrooms	2 tablespoons sugar
1 cup mushroom soaking liquid, Sea Vegetable & Bonito Stock or Second-Quality Stock (page 46)	2 tablespoons mirin
	2 tablespoons saké
	2 tablespoons soy sauce

◉ Soak mushrooms in a bowl of warm water 30 minutes. Squeeze dry; cut off stems. In a medium-size saucepan, combine remaining ingredients over medium heat; stir to dissolve sugar. Add mushroom caps. Bring to a boil; reduce heat; simmer on low until sauce is reduced and mushrooms are well seasoned. Use a drop lid to press mushrooms into sauce, or occasionally stir liquid with a wooden spoon. Serve mushrooms warm or at room temperature. Spoon any remaining sauce over mushrooms, or use as a seasoning for rice and other dishes.

◉ *Makes 4 servings.*

VARIATIONS

SEASONED KAMPYO

◉ Soak 1 (3/4-oz.) pkg. dried gourd strips in 2 cups water with 1 teaspoon salt 20 minutes. Rinse well. Cut in desired lengths. Simmer in sauce as directed above. Use as directed in recipes.

SEASONED KONNYAKU

◉ Cut 1 block *konnayaku* into braids as described in the *tazuna* cut (page 259). Blanch in boiling water 2 to 3 minutes; drain well. Cook in sauce as directed above.

Serving One-Pot Dishes

One-pot dishes (*nimono*) are delicious placed over large bowls of steamed rice. Or they can be served separately. On the side, offer a salad such as Sweet & Sour Crab (page 172) along with warm saké, hot green tea or cold beer. Soft drinks and cold water are always welcomed and should be kept on hand for those who become extra thirsty from consuming soy sauce. End the meal with a refreshing dish of Strawberry Tofu Sherbet (page 244).

As a final thoughtful touch, provide steaming-hot perfumed towels. Soak small towels in water to which you have added a few drops of rose water or a favorite perfume. Squeeze towels; tightly roll up. Heat until steaming hot in the microwave or in a stovetop steamer. Guests can refresh themselves Japanese-style by wiping their hands and faces.

Suki Yaki

Suki yaki (pan-simmered beef and vegetables) is one of the most savory and robust of Japanese foods. The flavors of succulent meat and fresh vegetables are enhanced when simmered together in soy sauce. A complex yet delicious taste is created, one not to be found in other Japanese foods.

No one is exactly sure how suki yaki originated. One popular theory states that hungry peasants and farmers working in the fields caught small game and other animals to eat. Since eating meat was forbidden in the seventh century by the teachings of Zen Buddhism, the snared animals had to be consumed on the spot. They were cut up and grilled on spades or plows over an open fire. *Suki* means "plow or spade"; *yaki* means "to broil." Today, suki yaki is prepared using a combination of two cooking techniques: *nabémono* (one-pot cooking) and *nimono* (simmered in seasoned liquids).

Suki yaki, as we know it, was created during the Meiji period (1868–1912) as an attempt to encourage people to eat beef for its nutritional value. Today, some of the finest beef in the world is Japanese Kobe and Matsuzaka beef. Beer-fed and massaged, the pampered beef is so tender that the meat and fat seem homogenized into one. Traditionally not a beef-eating nation, Japan has produced the best. Unfortunately, it is so costly that only a privileged few can enjoy it.

Have your butcher slice partially-frozen beef for suki yaki or other dishes that require thinly sliced meats. For suki yaki, request the meat be sliced from 1/16 inch to 1/8 inch thick. Asian markets carry excellent meats, sliced especially for these dishes. Because of personal preference and a market's ethnic background, the thickness of meats might vary from market to market. Paper-thin slices of *shabu shabu* meat are too thin to be used in suki yaki. Korean *bulgogi* beef is slightly thicker than suki yaki beef.

Suki yaki is a highly individualized dish and can be changed to suit your tastes. Feel free to vary the suggested vegetable amounts or substitute other vegetables. All types of mushrooms, edible pea pods, bean sprouts and water chestnuts are good additions. However, be careful not to use too many vegetables at one time with a high water content such as celery, mushrooms, spinach and cabbage. The delicious sauce will be diluted considerably.

BEEF & ONION ROLLS

(Gyuniku No Negi Maki)

For an appetizer, each beef roll can be cut into 4 or 5 pieces and served with wooden picks.

1/4 cup soy sauce

2 tablespoons mirin

2 tablespoons sugar

1 pound beef rib eye, partially frozen for easier slicing, sliced 1/8 inch thick across the grain (about 16 slices)

About 1 tablespoon Wasabi (page 237)

2 (8 x 7 1/2-inch) sheets nori, cut into 16 (4 x 1 3/4-inch) strips

1 bunch green onions, white parts only, cut into 4-inch slivers

1/2 cup potato starch or cornstarch

Cooking Sauce (see below)

2 tablespoons vegetable oil

COOKING SAUCE

1/2 cup Sea Vegetable & Bonito Stock (page 46)

2 tablespoons soy sauce

2 tablespoons sugar

2 tablespoons mirin

◉ In a shallow dish, stir together soy sauce, mirin and sugar. Add beef slices; marinate 10 minutes. Remove a slice of beef from marinade; shake off excess liquid. Place on flat surface. Spread 1/4 teaspoon Wasabi over beef. Place a strip of nori on top of Wasabi. Place 2 or 3 slivers green onion at 1 end of beef slice. Beginning at end with green onion, roll up. Secure roll with wooden picks. Roll in potato starch. Place on a platter. Continue making beef rolls. Reserve remaining marinade.

◉ Prepare Cooking Sauce; combine with reserved marinade. In a medium-size nonstick skillet, heat oil over high heat. Add beef rolls; sauté on all sides 2 to 3 minutes. Reduce heat to low; pour in sauce mixture. Simmer rolls 8 to 10 minutes or until sauce becomes glazed. Remove wooden picks from beef rolls. Cut beef rolls in half; serve warm.

◉ *Makes 4 servings.*

COOKING SAUCE

◉ In a small bowl, combine all ingredients.

SUKI YAKI

Guests gather around the communal pot to share the tabletop cooking duties.

1 1/2 lbs. beef tenderloin or rib
   eye, partially frozen for easy
   slicing
1 bunch green onions, cut
   diagonally into 1 1/2-inch pieces
2 medium-size Bermuda onions,
   halved and thinly sliced
6 medium-size Scored Shiitake
   Mushrooms (page 18)
1 large carrot, cut diagonally
   into thin slices
1 (1-lb.) napa cabbage, cored
   and sliced
1 (15-oz.) can peeled straw
   mushrooms, drained
1/2 pound Grilled Tofu
   (page 139), cut into 1-inch
   cubes
1 bunch garland chrysanthemum
   leaves, rinsed and stems
   removed, or 1 bunch spinach,
   well rinsed

1/2 pound devil's-tongue-jelly
   noodles (*shirataki*) or 1 oz.
   dried bean thread noodles,
   soaked in hot water
Cooking Sauce (see below)
5 to 6 cups Basic Cooked Rice
   (page 194)
1 to 2 oz. beef suet or 3
   tablespoons vegetable oil

COOKING SAUCE
2 cups Sea Vegetable & Bonito
   Stock (page 46) or beef
   stock
1 cup soy sauce
1/3 to 1/2 cup sugar
1/4 cup saké

◉ Using a large sharp knife or an electric knife, slice meat across the grain as thinly as possible. Arrange meat attractively on a serving platter. Arrange green onions, Bermuda onions, shiitake mushrooms, carrot, cabbage, straw mushrooms, tofu and chrysanthemum on platter with meat, leaving room for noodles. Blanch noodles 1 minute in boiling water; drain. Add noodles to platter. Prepare Cooking Sauce. Serve bowls of rice.

◉ At the table, heat a *suki yaki-nabé* over a portable tabletop burner or an electric wok. Cook suet; discard when fat is rendered. Or heat oil.

● Add ingredients in thirds, beginning with the onions. As they become aromatic, add 1/3 of sliced meat. Add a portion of shiitake mushrooms, carrot, cabbage and straw mushrooms. Keep foods in separate piles in the pot. Pour in 1/3 of Cooking Sauce. When foods begin to simmer, add some tofu, chrysanthemum and noodles. These will require less cooking time. Simmer 4 to 5 minutes, turning foods as necessary. Guests can begin helping themselves from the pot. The cook should replenish pot halfway through first batch of Suki Yaki. Continue cooking as instructed above.

● *Makes 6 servings.*

COOKING SAUCE

● Blend ingredients in a medium-size saucepan over medium-low heat. Heat and stir until sugar is dissolved.

Note

In Japan, the cooked beef and vegetables are often dipped in beaten raw eggs as they are eaten.

SHABU SHABU

The name of this dish is onomatopoetic and is said to come from the soft swishing sound as the meat slices are washed in the broth. This dish is traditionally prepared in a *hokonabé*, a metal tabletop cooking pot with a chimney-like center. The Sesame Sauce is good with the vegetables and noodles. Serve plenty of rice on the side.

1 small head napa cabbage, sliced
1 large onion, cut into thin wedges
1 bunch green onions, cut
    diagonally into 2-inch pieces
1 large carrot, sliced thin
    diagonally
12 fresh shiitake mushrooms, sliced
1/2 pound spinach leaves, blanched
1 block Grilled Tofu (page 139),
    cut into 1-inch cubes
Sesame Sauce (page 117)
Lemon-Soy Dipping Sauce
    (page 65), with orange
    juice instead of lemon juice
8 oz. fresh udon or 1 recipe

Fresh Udon (page 188),
    cooked and rinsed
1 1/2 to 1 3/4 lbs. beef rib eye or
    sirloin, partially frozen, cut
    into paper-thin slices
6 cups Sea Vegetable & Bonito
    Stock (page 46) or beef
    stock

CONDIMENTS
Seven-Spice Powder (page 228)
1/3 cup grated daikon radish
3 or 4 green onions, minced
2 to 3 tablespoons grated
    gingerroot

◉ Arrange vegetables, sauces, udon and beef on large platters. Prepare stock. Prepare Condiments; place in separate bowls. Give each guest a pair of chopsticks, a small dish for meat and vegetables, a rice bowl, 2 small dipping-sauce bowls and a soup bowl. Pour stock into a Japanese hot pot (*hokonabé*), a soaked earthenware *donabé* with a tabletop burner or an electric wok or skillet. Bring stock to a boil. Begin cooking by adding some cabbage, onions, carrot and mushrooms to hot stock. After several minutes, invite diners to use their chopsticks and swish pieces of beef through stock until cooked to desired doneness. Meat will cook in seconds. Add spinach and tofu.

◉ Diners should help themselves to the pot as they cook. Stir small amounts of Condiments into individual bowls of Lemon-Soy Dipping Sauce for dipping meat and vegetables. Add more meat and vegetables to hot stock as needed.

When meat and vegetables have been cooked, add noodles to broth in pot and heat through. Divide noodles and broth among soup bowls for a soup course. Sprinkle soup with Seven-Spice Powder, salt and pepper. Any remaining Condiments or sauce can be stirred into broth as a seasoning.

Makes 6 servings.

SWEET SIMMERED SQUASH

(Kabocha No Nimono)

A favorite Japanese vegetable dish which can also be made with Hubbard, butternut squash or pumpkin.

1 small kabocha or acorn squash (about 1 1/2 lbs.), unpeeled	3 tablespoons sugar
1 1/2 cups Sea Vegetable & Bonito Stock (page 46)	1 tablespoon mirin
1 tablespoon soy sauce	1 tablespoon saké
	1 green onion, minced

Rinse and dry squash. Using a large sharp knife, cut in half; remove seeds. Cut squash into 1-inch pieces. Pour stock into a medium-size saucepan over medium-high heat. Stir in soy sauce, sugar, mirin and saké. Bring to a boil; stir to dissolve sugar. Add squash; reduce heat to low. Place a drop lid or small saucepan lid on top of squash; simmer 25 to 30 minutes. Liquid will reduce and squash will become slightly glazed. Garnish with green onion.

Makes 4 servings.

CHICKEN HOT POT

(Mizutaki)

I enjoyed this rich, delicious hot pot at an inn high in the snowy mountains of Kyoto.

6 cups Chicken Stock with Ginger
  (page 51)
1/4 cup red miso
2 tablespoons yellow miso
1/4 cup saké
1 tablespoon sugar
Salt to taste

HOT POT INGREDIENTS

1 (1-lb.) napa cabbage, cored
  and sliced
6 medium-size fresh shiitake
  mushrooms
2 medium-size carrots,
  diagonally sliced
1 medium-size onion, halved
  and thinly sliced
2 medium-size new potatoes,
  sliced 1/3 inch thick
3 small Japanese eggplants or
  1 small regular eggplant,
  cut into strips
1/2 pound Grilled Tofu
  (page 139), cubed, or
  1/2 pound firm tofu, rinsed
  and cubed

1 bunch green onions,
  diagonally sliced
3 chicken breast halves, skinned,
  boned and cut into
  1-inch cubes
1 small pkg. fresh *enokidaké*
  mushrooms, rinsed and
  drained
8 oz. fresh ramen noodles or
  1 recipe Chinese Egg Noodles
  (page 190)

CONDIMENTS

1/2 cup grated Red Maple
  Radish (page 233)
1 bunch small green onions,
  thinly sliced
1 lemon, cut into wedges
Soy sauce
Pickled *takuan* (daikon radish),
  sliced

◉ Heat stock until hot in a large stockpot over medium heat. Place red and yellow miso in a medium-size bowl; dilute with a small amount of hot stock; stir into remaining stock. Stir in saké, sugar and salt. Heat mixture over low heat; pour into a soaked earthenware *donabé* or heatproof casserole dish. At the table, place pot on a portable tabletop burner. Adjust heat so mixture simmers.

◉ Arrange Hot Pot Ingredients on platters. Arrange Condiments in small bowls. Provide each person with a pair of chopsticks and a bowl for the chicken and vegetables. Add some cabbage, shiitake mushrooms, carrots, onion and potato to simmering broth. As foods cook, add eggplant, tofu, green onions, chicken and *enokidaké* mushrooms. Invite diners to help themselves from the pot. Instruct them to season foods with small portions of Condiments. When chicken and vegetables have been eaten, add noodles to pot. Simmer until hot, then spoon noodles and broth into bowls for a soup course.

◉ *Makes 6 servings.*

STEAMED PORK &
RICE CHRYSANTHEMUMS
(Kiku Mushi Dango)

Delight your guests with a plate of colorful autumn "chrysanthemums." Savory pork patties are rolled in softly tinted rice, then steamed until they "blossom." Serve as appetizers or as part of a multicourse meal. Chrysanthemums are attractive served on a large black platter or in pairs on individual plates.

1 cup *mochi gomé*
   (sweet glutinous rice)
2 cups water
2 or 3 drops each red and
   yellow food coloring
1 pound ground pork
1 large egg
2 green onions, finely minced
2 teaspoons sesame oil

2 tablespoons soy sauce plus
   additional for dipping
2 tablespoons chicken broth
2 tablespoons saké
1/2 teaspoon salt
1 teaspoon grated gingerroot
1 large garlic clove, finely minced
Fresh chrysanthemum leaves
Soy sauce

◙ Place rice in a large bowl; fill with cool water. Swish your hand through the water; pour off water and add fresh. Repeat process until the water is fairly clear. Drain rice in a large strainer; tap gently to remove liquid. Divide between 2 medium-size bowls. Add 1 cup water to each bowl. Add red color to one bowl, yellow coloring to the other bowl. Soak 6 hours or overnight.

◙ In a large bowl, combine pork, egg, green onions, oil, soy sauce, broth, saké, salt, gingerroot and garlic. Drain each bowl of rice separately in a fine strainer; place on separate plates. Form 16 to 18 meat patties, approximately 2 inches in diameter and 3/4 inch thick. Press tops and sides of 1/2 of the patties into pink rice; the other 1/2 into yellow rice.

◙ In a wok or deep pot, bring water to boil. Line steamer tray with damp cheesecloth. Place patties on cloth, rice-side up. Cover and place over boiling water. Reduce heat to medium-high. Steam 20 minutes or until pork is no longer pink inside and rice is tender. Place 1 pink and 1 yellow rice chrysanthemum on each individual black plate. Garnish with chrysanthemum leaves. Serve with soy sauce.

◙ *Makes 8 to 10 servings.*

FLOUNDER SIMMERED IN GINGER SOY SAUCE

(Karei No Nimono)

Simmered foods are an important type of everyday home cooking in Japan. Spoon the fish with its delicious sauce into bowls of steaming cooked rice. The green onion shreds curl when dropped into iced water.

Basic Cooked Rice (page 194)
1/2 cup light soy sauce
   (*usukuchi shoyu*)
1/2 cup Sea Vegetable & Bonito
   Stock (page 46) or water
1/4 cup mirin

1/4 cup sugar
1 tablespoon saké
2 (1/4-inch) slices gingerroot
3 green onions
1 pound skinless flounder, sole
   or other white-fish fillets

◘ Prepare rice and keep warm. Combine soy sauce, stock, mirin, sugar, saké and gingerroot in a 10-inch skillet. Smash the green onion to flatten; add 1 to the skillet. Bring to a boil over medium-high heat; reduce heat to low. Simmer, uncovered, 10 minutes. Discard gingerroot and onion.

◘ Add fish fillets. Cover with a wooden drop lid or an oiled circle of parchment paper. Simmer 5 to 8 minutes or until fish changes from translucent to opaque.

◘ Meanwhile, use the sharp point of a knife to cut the remaining green onions into shreds. Drop into iced water.

◘ Remove fish from heat. Spoon sauce over fish. Cool 5 minutes. Spoon portions of fish and sauce over bowls of hot rice. Garnish with onion shreds.

◘ *Makes 4 servings.*

TOFU

Tofu is an inexpensive protein alternative to meat. Not only is it rich in vitamins, minerals and important amino acids, but it is low in calories—an 8-ounce piece contains less than 150 calories. Tofu is also 95 percent digestible and low in sodium and fat.

To produce this extraordinary food, soaked soybeans are ground with water to produce soy milk, a nutritious liquid in itself. After straining the milk, *okara*, a high-protein soybean pulp, remains. The soy milk is combined with a coagulating agent to produce curds and whey, similar to making cheese. The curds are pressed until firm, then covered with cool water until eaten. Instructions for making tofu are on page 136.

Historians believe that tofu, like so many other foods, was introduced to Japan by Buddhist clergy traveling from China. At first, tofu was the food of the nobility. Its use was expanded and refined in Buddhist monasteries when the consumption of animal-protein foods was forbidden. Tofu Treasure Balls and Monk's Tofu Loaf are examples of foods created during this period. When Buddhism spread throughout the land, so did the knowledge and use of tofu. Tofu-making shops sprang up all over the countryside; tofu evolved into the excellent-quality product we are familiar with today. Several varieties of tofu were invented, many of which are still in popular use.

Blocks of regular Japanese tofu (*momen-goshi*) and the soft or silken-style tofu (*kinu-goshi*) can be purchased in sealed tubs of water. Package weights from various manufacturers may vary a few ounces throughout the country. Regular Japanese tofu is also referred to as "cotton style" because it has an impression of the cotton cloth used to line the molding box during production. This type is firmer than silken tofu but softer than Chinese tofu. Regular Japanese tofu should be wrapped and pressed to remove liquid and firm up the texture for frying. Press the blocks whole or sliced, as directed in the recipes. Pressing times may vary, depending on the texture required. If time permits, tofu can be firmed up by wrapping it in two layers of clean kitchen towel, then refrigerating it overnight for the next day's use. Silken tofu has a softer, delicate consistency unsuitable for frying without long careful pressing. Better to take advantage of its silken texture and use it for making custards, dips, sauces and ice cream. Another brand of soft tofu custard or pudding is sold in refrigerator sections in small sealed containers. It is best used like silken tofu; the shelf life is six months. Packages of low-fat tofu are now available.

Tofu is available in other forms. Large thick blocks of deep-fried tofu called *atsu-agé* are prepared daily in Japan. Cut them into smaller pieces; add to soups and stews. Deep-fried, golden tofu puffs, or *abura-agé,* can be pulled open and stuffed with sushi rice, meat or vegetable mixtures; see Stuffed Tofu Puffs (page 70). Blanch tofu puffs in boiling water to remove excess frying oils. Blanching the puffs makes it easy to pull them apart for stuffing. Grilled tofu is called *yaki-dofu. Yuba,* the highly nutritious skin that forms on top of soybean milk, is dried into sheets, then used as a protein-rich meat substitute. It is available in sheets or coiled strips; soak before use.

Purchase fresh tofu at Asian markets or from large local supermarkets. Look for well-chilled packages with fresh clear packing water. Packages should be stamped with a pull date for quality control. Do not purchase tofu with an expired date. At home, rinse tofu and store it in a bowl of cool water. Refrigerate up to seven days, changing the water daily. Older, slightly sour tofu can be refreshed by blanching it for a few minutes. Older tofu is best used in dishes that require cooking. Some recipes call for crumbled tofu. Wrap and press the tofu first, then squeeze in cheesecloth to break up and remove any additional water.

Tofu can be frozen, but the consistency becomes spongy and porous after thawing. Squeeze out the liquid; shred this protein-packed food as a meat substitute in casseroles, sauces and stir-fry dishes. Freeze-drying is a traditional method of preserving tofu. The resulting *koya-dofu* is produced on a large scale today in Japan. In the West, it is referred to as textured vegetable protein. Soak in warm water before cooking with seasonings.

For a taste of tofu in its purest and finest

form, prepare Bubbling Tofu Hot Pot or Chilled Summer Tofu. To savor the taste of freshly made tofu, follow my directions and make your own. Japan's finest tofu is made with natural spring water and is eaten the day it is made. The Japanese ideal for preparing tofu is little or no cooking so its natural taste can be enjoyed to the fullest.

The Soybean Culture of Japan

From ancient times, soybeans have played an important role in Japanese cuisine. They have influenced the social, religious and economic aspects of daily life. Rich in proteins, soybeans are often re-ferred to as "the meat of the fields." They contain the eight essential amino acids of the twenty-one that form the protein building blocks of the body. The body is able to utilize the eight essential amino acids to produce the rest, qualifying soybeans as a complete protein food.

Soybeans in any form must always be cooked to inactivate the trypsin inhibitor that prevents the body from digesting protein. Whole dried soybeans are eaten simmered, roasted and deep-fried. Fresh green soybeans are simmered and popped out of the pod for eating. Soybeans are germinated into sprouts or used to make roasted flour (*kinako*) for confections.

Three ancient soybean foods form the foundation of the Japanese cuisine. They are miso paste, soy sauce and tofu.

TOFU

Making homemade tofu isn't really difficult; it just requires a little careful attention to detail. Use natural spring water for tofu with a pure clean taste. Nigari is the traditional coagulant used in Japan for making tofu.

1 lb. dried soybeans (2 1/2 cups)
Bottled natural spring water or
    tap water

4 teaspoons magnesium sulfate
    (Epsom salts), 3 teaspoons
    magnesium chloride (*nigari*)
    or 2 teaspoons calcium sulfate
    (gypsum)

◉ Rinse soybeans in cool water. Discard black, broken or discolored beans. Soak in 8 cups water 10 to 12 hours or overnight. Cut open a bean; the color should be the same throughout, indicating that beans have soaked long enough. Drain and rinse beans.

◉ In a blender or food processor fitted with a steel blade, grind beans in 5 (1 1/2-cup) batches. Add 1 cup boiling water to each batch; process 1 to 2 minutes. Beans will form a thick, slightly granular mixture. Add each batch to a 6- to 8-quart soup pot. Stir in 3 quarts water. Bring to a boil over medium-high heat; stir several times. Watch thick foam forming on top to make sure it does not boil over. Reduce heat to low; simmer 5 minutes. Remove from heat; cool slightly.

◉ Line a large metal colander with a dampened tofu-pressing sack, unbleached muslin or several layers of cheesecloth. Place lined colander in a large metal bowl. Pour in soybean mixture. Wearing insulated rubber gloves to protect your hands from the heat, gather edges of cloth; squeeze tightly to press out soy milk. Slightly open pouch. Pour 3 cups water into remaining soy pulp. Squeeze tightly to press out remaining milk. Wash soup pot; return soy milk to clean pot. Scrape soy pulp from pressing cloth; reserve for Sugar & Spice Okara (page 138) and other uses. Rinse out pressing cloth.

◉ Bring soy milk to a boil over medium-high heat. Reduce heat slightly; simmer 5 minutes. In a small bowl, combine 1 cup water and magnesium sulfate. Remove milk from heat. If a thick skin layer forms, skim it off. This is *yuba*, a delicious ingredient in Japanese cooking. Pour 1/3 of coagulating agent into hot milk. Using a wooden spoon, gently cut through milk 6 to 8 times. Let milk stand, undisturbed, 2 minutes so curdling action can begin. Add 1/2 of remaining coagulating agent; cut through milk 3 or 4 times.

◉ Check curds. If thick white curds are floating in clear yellow whey, curdling action is finished. If whey is milky and there is not a definite division between curds and whey, add remaining coagulating agent. Let mixture stand, undisturbed, 5 minutes. Too much coagulating agent could cause curds to become heavy and sink to the bottom, resulting in very firm tofu. Some people prefer their tofu this way. Curds may vary with each batch. Line a wooden tofu pressing box or another small perforated container with damp pressing cloth. A small round, square or rectangular perforated pan can be substituted for wooden pressing box. Tofu shape and thickness vary with shape of mold. Place lined box in the sink or in a pan if you wish to retain whey.

◉ Using a medium-size strainer, scoop curds out of whey. Drain off excess whey; tap curds into box. When box is filled with curds, smooth top. Smooth pressing cloth over top. Place pressing box lid on top. Use an appropriate-size saucer or a piece of trimmed plywood to fit your homemade pressing container. Add 2 to 3 pounds of weight; press 30 minutes. For firmer tofu, increase weight slightly; press as long as 2 hours for very firm tofu. Pressing weight must be increased gradually so tofu does not break up. Check curd occasionally to determine desired degree of firmness. Firm tofu gives a smaller yield but has a higher concentration of protein. For frying purposes, firm tofu is the best type to use. Carefully turn tofu out of pressing box into a pan of cool water. Refrigerate 7 to 10 days, changing water daily.

◉ *Makes 2 1/2 to 3 pounds regular-firm tofu or about 1 1/2 pounds extra-firm tofu.*

SUGAR & SPICE OKARA
(Ama Okara)

Okara is the nutritious soybean pulp you will have left over when you make tofu.
Sprinkle this sugar and spice version over hot cereal or muffin batter or
use for coating *mochi* or rice balls.

3 cups fresh soybean pulp (*okara*),
   left over from Tofu (page 136)
3/4 cup packed light brown sugar
1/2 teaspoon ground cinnamon
   or nutmeg

1/8 teaspoon salt
1 teaspoon vanilla extract

◉ Preheat oven to 325F (165C). Spread soybean pulp in a 15 x 10-inch jelly roll pan.
Dry in oven 25 to 30 minutes, stirring occasionally. Place dried pulp in a medium-size
bowl. Add brown sugar, cinnamon, salt and vanilla. Mix together with your hands.
Refrigerate in an airtight container up to 2 weeks, or freeze several months.

◉ *Makes about 3 cups.*

GRILLED TOFU
(yaki-dofu)

Prepare hard-to-find grilled tofu on a special cast iron skillet with ridges.

1 or 2 regular Japanese tofu blocks, rinsed and patted dry | Vegetable oil

◙ Cut tofu blocks in half horizontally or leave whole. Place between double layers of clean kitchen towels or several layers of paper towels. Place 1 to 2 pounds of weight on top to press and firm tofu for grilling. Press at least 1 hour, up to 4 hours. Change towels once. With your fingers, rub oil on both sides of tofu blocks.

◙ Add a small amount of oil to a medium-size heavy skillet or a seasoned cast-iron skillet with raised ridges for stovetop grilling. Wipe skillet evenly with oil. Place over medium-high heat. When hot, place 2 or 3 pieces tofu in skillet. Sear 1 to 2 minutes. If using ridged skillet, lift 1 end of tofu to check grill marks. When marks are medium golden brown, turn tofu over. Do not turn more than once or attractive grill marks from skillet will be uneven. Use tofu immediately, or cool, cover and refrigerate for use within 1 to 2 days. Grilled tofu will not fall apart when simmered in one-pot dishes.

◙ *Makes 6 to 8 servings.*

BUBBLING TOFU HOT POT
(Yu-dofu)

This is an example of the purest type of Kyoto temple cooking and is still popular in Japan today. The success of this dish depends on the quality of the tofu. Use homemade or the very freshest available.

6 cups water
Dipping Sauce (see below)
Condiments (see below)
1 (5-inch) square *dashi konbu* (kelp), wiped and pierced with 3 knife slits
2 (14- to 16-oz.) pkgs. silken or regular tofu, rinsed
1 large carrot slice, cut into a flower shape
Trefoil sprigs (*mitsuba*) or watercress, blanched and stems knotted

DIPPING SAUCE
1/3 cup soy sauce
1/3 cup Sea Vegetable & Bonito Stock (page 46)
1 tablespoon mirin

CONDIMENTS
2 to 3 tablespoons grated gingerroot
1 tablespoon Wasabi (page 237)
4 small green onions, thinly sliced
2 to 3 tablespoons grated daikon radish
2 tablespoons dried bonito thread shavings
1 tablespoon toasted sesame seeds

◉ One hour before cooking, soak a 2- to 2 1/2-quart earthenware *donabé* (Japanese pottery casserole) with water, or use a regular 2- to 2 1/2-quart stovetop casserole dish. Add the water to casserole. Prepare Dipping Sauce; pour into 4 small bowls for the table. Choose 3 or more Condiments; place in separate small dishes for guests to help themselves at the table.

◉ Add *konbu* to water in *donabé*. Heat 10 minutes over low heat; remove *konbu*. Cut tofu blocks in half; add to seasoned water. Adjust heat so water gently simmers. Tofu will be heated in 3 to 4 minutes. Do not boil or overcook or tofu will toughen. Garnish with carrot flower and trefoil. Bring *donabé* to the table. Place a block of tofu in a serving bowl for each diner. Serve with Dipping Sauce and Condiments. Makes 4 servings.

DIPPING SAUCE

◉ Combine all ingredients in a small bowl.

CHILLED SUMMER TOFU
(Hiya Yakko)

One of Japan's favorite ways to beat the summer heat.

Dipping Sauce and Condiments for Bubbling Tofu Hot Pot, page 140	Cold water
	Crushed ice or small ice cubes
	Lemon wedges
2 (14- to 16-oz.) pkgs. fresh silken or regular tofu, rinsed	

◉ Prepare Dipping Sauce ingredients; pour into 4 small bowls for the table. Prepare 3 or more Condiments; place in separate small dishes for guests to help themselves at the table. Cut 2 tofu blocks crosswise in half to make 4 blocks. Place each piece in an attractive glass serving dish. Add a small amount of cold water and crushed ice or small ice cubes around base of each piece of tofu. Serve with Dipping Sauce and Condiments.

◉ *Makes 4 servings.*

MONK'S TOFU LOAF
(Gisei-dofu)

Gisei-dofu is a vegetarian dish whose origin lies in Buddhist monasteries. The savory mixture is steamed, then pan-fried for a golden finish. If you prefer, the mixture can be baked first in a moderate oven 20 minutes or until set. I like to serve this with a mustard sauce. At other times, I make Shiitake Mushroom Sauce (page 114) to spoon over each serving.

2 (14- to 16-oz.) pkgs. regular tofu, rinsed
2 medium-size dried shiitake mushrooms
1 (5-inch) piece *gobo* (burdock) (optional)
1 tablespoon rice vinegar (optional)
3 large eggs
2 tablespoons mirin

1 tablespoon light soy sauce (*usukuchi shoyu*)
1 teaspoon salt
1 tablespoon sugar
4 tablespoons vegetable oil
2 teaspoons minced gingerroot
1/4 cup finely diced carrot
2 green onions, minced
1/4 cup frozen petit green peas, thawed

◙ Line an 8-inch-square baking pan with foil; grease foil. Cut tofu blocks in half horizontally. Place between double layers of clean kitchen towels or several layers of paper towels. Place 2 to 3 pounds of weight on top to press out excess liquid and firm tofu. Press 1 hour. Change towels once.

◙ Soak mushrooms in a bowl of warm water 30 minutes. Squeeze dry; cut off stems. Dice mushroom caps. Scrape and rinse *gobo*. Dice into small pieces. Place in a small bowl. Cover with water; add rice vinegar. Drain well before use.

◙ In a blender or food processor fitted with a steel blade, place tofu, eggs, mirin, soy sauce, salt and sugar; process until smooth. Scrape into a medium-size bowl; set aside. In a medium-size skillet, heat 2 tablespoons of the oil over medium-high heat. Add mushrooms, *gobo,* gingerroot, carrot and green onions; cook, stirring occasionally, 1 to 2 minutes. Add peas. Cook 30 seconds; cool. Stir vegetables into tofu mixture. Pour into prepared pan; cover with foil.

◉ In a wok or deep pot, bring about 4 cups water to a boil over high heat. Place pan on a steamer tray. Cover tray; place over boiling water. Reduce heat to medium. Steam over simmering water 20 minutes or until set. Test mixture by inserting a small knife in center; it should come out clean. Remove tray. Cool to room temperature. Turn out of pan; pull off foil. Cut in half, then into 1-inch strips. Add 1 tablespoon oil to a medium-size heavy skillet over medium-high heat. Add 1/2 of tofu cake and cook 1 to 2 minutes, turning, until golden brown. Add remaining oil; cook remaining loaf. Serve warm or at room temperature. Refrigerate leftovers up to 5 days; reheat in skillet.

◉ *Makes 8 servings.*

SILKEN PEACH TOFU
(Momo-dofu)

Celebrate Hina Matsuri, the Peach Blossom Festival, on March 3 with this soft peach and tofu *kanten*. For a special touch, prepare the kiwi and strawberry variations. Arrange a diamond-shaped piece of each flavor on each guest's serving plate. The three colors and the diamond shape are traditional for this happy occasion.

1 (0.25-oz.) stick white agar-agar
    (*kanten*)
1 cup water
About 2 cups fresh, peeled
    peach chunks
1/2 lb. silken tofu, rinsed

2 tablespoons fresh lemon juice
1/8 teaspoon salt
1/2 teaspoon pure almond
    extract
1/2 cup sugar
Mint leaves

◙ Tear agar-agar stick into 4 pieces. Place with water in a medium-size saucepan. Press into water several seconds to soften. Shred pieces with your fingers. Soak 30 minutes. In a blender or food processor fitted with a steel blade, puree peach chunks. Scrape puree into a small bowl. Measure 1 cup puree; add back to blender or food processor bowl. Add tofu; process until mixture is smooth. Add lemon juice, salt and almond extract. Process until blended; scrape into a medium-size bowl.

◙ Simmer agar-agar and water over very low heat until dissolved, 10 to 12 minutes. Stir once or twice while simmering. When dissolved, add sugar; simmer 2 minutes longer. Remove from heat. Strain hot agar-agar into peach-tofu puree through a fine strainer. Scrape agar-agar from bottom of strainer into bowl. Quickly stir to blend. Rinse an 8-inch-square pan with cold water. Quickly pour mixture into damp pan. Mixture will set at room temperature or can be chilled until serving time. Cut into 8 or 9 square, diamond or flower shapes. Garnish with mint leaves.

◙ *Makes 8 or 9 servings.*

VARIATIONS

SILKEN KIWIFRUIT TOFU (KIWI-DOFU)

◉ Substitute 1 cup kiwifruit puree for peach puree. Garnish with fresh mint leaves if desired.

SILKEN STRAWBERRY TOFU (ICHIGO-DOFU)

◉ Substitute 1 cup strawberry puree for peach puree and 1/2 teaspoon vanilla extract for almond extract.

PEANUT TOFU
(Jimami-dofu)

Jimami means "earth bean." This version was adapted from a
popular Okinawan snack.

1 (0.25-oz.) stick white agar-agar
  (*kanten*)
2 cups water
1 cup unsalted cocktail peanuts
1 (14- to 16-oz.) pkg. regular tofu,
  rinsed and patted dry
1 tablespoon light brown sugar
1/4 teaspoon salt

DIPPING SAUCE
1/2 cup Sea Vegetable & Bonito
  Stock (page 46)

2 tablespoons light soy sauce
  (*usukuchi shoyu*)

CONDIMENTS
1/2 cup dried bonito thread
  shavings
1/3 cup grated daikon radish
2 tablespoons grated gingerroot
6 green onions, minced
1 tablespoon Wasabi (page 237)
1/4 cup unsalted cocktail
  peanuts, finely chopped

◙ Tear agar-agar stick into 4 pieces. Place with water in a medium-size saucepan. Press
pieces into water several seconds to soften. Shred with your fingers. Soak 30 minutes.
In a blender or food processor fitted with a steel blade, chop 1 cup peanuts until finely
ground. Add tofu to peanuts; process until as smooth as possible. Blend in sugar and
salt; set aside. Simmer agar-agar and water over very low heat until dissolved, 10 to 12
minutes. Stir once or twice while simmering. When dissolved, remove pan from heat.

◙ Scrape tofu-peanut mixture into agar-agar; blend with a whisk. Strain mixture into
a medium-size bowl through a fine strainer. Scrape mixture from bottom of strainer
into bowl. Quickly stir to blend. Rinse an 8-inch-square pan with cold water. Working
quickly, pour tofu-peanut mixture into damp pan. Mixture will set at room temperature or can be chilled until serving time.

◙ Prepare Dipping Sauce; pour into 8 or 9 small bowls for the table. Place Condiments in separate small dishes for guests to help themselves at the table. Cut tofu into
8 or 9 squares. Place 1 square on each serving dish. Season tofu with Dipping Sauce
and Condiments.

◙ *Makes 8 or 9 servings.*

◉ Combine all ingredients in a small bowl.

CRISPY FRIED
TOFU NUGGETS
(Agédashi-dofu)

Tofu is high in protein and calcium. Cucumbers are not a traditional Japanese
accompaniment for fried tofu, but they provide a wonderful taste
and textural contrast.

1 Japanese cucumber or 1/2
    European cucumber
1 cup Sea Vegetable & Bonito
    Stock (page 46)
1/4 cup light soy sauce
    (*usukuchi shoyu*)
3 tablespoons mirin
2 small green onions, thinly sliced

2 tablespoons grated gingerroot
2 tablespoons grated daikon
1 (16- to 20-oz.) pkg. regular
    Japanese or firm Chinese
    tofu, rinsed
4 cups peanut or vegetable oil
1/2 cup potato starch or
    cornstarch

◉ Cut cucumber in half lengthwise. Cut halves crosswise into 1/4-inch-thick slices.
Spread cucumber slices over a serving platter. Set aside.

◉ Combine stock, soy sauce and mirin in a bowl or cup. Pour into 4 or 5 small serving bowls. Arrange onions, gingerroot and daikon in small bowls or on a serving plate.

◉ Cut tofu in half horizontally. Place slices between double layers of clean kitchen
towels; press 10 minutes. Heat oil to 360F (180C). Cut tofu into 1-inch cubes. Coat
well with potato starch. Fry tofu in several batches until golden brown and crispy.
Drain on a wire rack. Spread tofu over cucumber. Offer small plates and bowls of dipping sauce. Season dipping sauce as desired with onions, gingerroot and daikon.

◉ *Makes 4 or 5 servings.*

TOFU TREASURE BALLS

(Hirousu)

This Kyoto specialty can be eaten warm with soy sauce or Mustard Miso Sauce (page 161) or added to soups and stews. Mountain yam is a traditional binder; if available, use 1 tablespoon in place of cornstarch.

1 (14- to 16-oz.) pkg. regular
    tofu, rinsed
1 medium-size dried shiitake
    mushroom
2 (1/8-inch-thick) slices gingerroot
4 small green onions
1/2 medium-size carrot
1 (4-inch) piece *gobo* (burdock)
    (optional)
1 tablespoon rice vinegar
    (optional)

1 tablespoon vegetable oil
2 tablespoons toasted sesame
    seeds
2 teaspoons soy sauce
1/2 teaspoon salt
2 teaspoons mirin
1 tablespoon cornstarch or
    grated mountain yam
About 4 cups peanut oil or
    vegetable oil

◙ Cut tofu horizontally into 3 slices. Place between double layers of clean kitchen towels or several layers of paper towels. Place 2 to 3 pounds of weight on top to press out excess liquid and firm tofu. Press 3 to 4 hours. Change towels once. Soak mushroom in a bowl of warm water 30 minutes. Squeeze dry; cut off stem. Mince mushroom cap, gingerroot and green onions. Shred carrot. Scrape, rinse and shred *gobo*. Place in a small bowl. Cover with water; add rice vinegar. Drain well before use.

◙ In a small skillet, heat 1 tablespoon oil over medium-high heat. Add mushroom, gingerroot, green onions, carrot and *gobo*. Stir-fry 1 to 2 minutes; cool. In a grinding bowl or other medium-size bowl, mash tofu. Mix in vegetables. Add sesame seeds, soy sauce, salt, mirin and cornstarch. If not using a grinding bowl, blend with your hands. Use at once, or cover and refrigerate up to 2 hours. Using a tablespoon, shape mixture into balls. In a wok or shallow saucepan, heat oil over medium heat to 350F (175C). Fry several balls at a time, 3 to 5 minutes or until slightly puffed and golden brown. Turn for even browning. Drain on paper towels. Serve warm or at room temperature. Balls can be recrisped with a second frying; heat oil to 370F (190C). Fry 1 to 2 minutes.

◙ *Makes about 15 balls.*

DEEP-FRIED FOODS

(Agémono)

◉

The Japanese excel at deep-frying. No other cuisine can consistently match the high quality of the crisp, grease-free fried foods of Japan. In the mid-sixteenth century Japan had its first contact with the West. Portuguese missionaries introduced their native method for deep-frying seafood. The Japanese refined their techniques, elevating deep-frying to a fine art.

Tempura is an example of the batter-frying technique called *koromo-agé*. In small tempura shops throughout Japan, piping-hot pieces of batter-coated seafood and vegetables are plucked from hot oil and passed directly over the counters for immediate consumption. Tokyo chefs like to season their secret oil blends with a little sesame oil, resulting in a rich golden batter. Kyoto chefs use a lighter blend, preferring a snowy-white batter. Soba shops prepare a slightly thicker batter which will hold up well in broth-based dishes like *tempura-soba*. Whatever the variation, the high quality of the finished product is always the same.

The Japanese chef is a master at deep-frying. I witnessed this skill in a Japanese *robata yaki* restaurant. With lightning speed the chef deep-fried a batter-coated ice cream ball, then passed it to me across the counter on a paddle before the first drop had melted! The ice cream was sizzling hot yet icy cold at the same time; truly a culinary paradox.

Other types of unusual coatings for fried foods are collectively referred to as *kawari-agé*: *Su-agé* are firm-textured foods fried without any coating. The natural shapes and colors are retained. *Kara-agé* are foods lightly dusted with starch before frying. *Kuzu* starch, potato starch and cornstarch are the favored coatings. *Tatsuta-agé* are pieces of food marinated in soy sauce, then dusted with starch before frying. *Matsuba-agé* are foods dipped in egg, then coated with pieces of green-tea soba for frying. This gives the appearance of green pine needles. *Harusamé-agé* is a similar technique, except foods are coated with snipped pieces of *harusamé,* or bean thread noodles. When deep-fried, *harusamé* expands, forming an attractive puffed-noodle coating.

Japanese cooks use top-quality oil for deep frying. It must be light and have a neutral taste to allow natural food flavors to come through. Peanut oil, corn oil and safflower oil are good choices. Never use butter or olive oil. Many chefs combine oils to produce a special blend. Tempura chefs may add around 20 percent sesame oil to their regular oils.

Japanese cooks rely on instinct and familiar signs to gauge oil temperatures. It may help inexperienced cooks to use a deep-fat frying thermometer, or dip a pair of wooden cooking chopsticks into the hot oil; bubbling activity around the chopsticks indicates the oil has reached about 360F (180C). You can test the oil by frying a small cube of bread. The bread will sink to the bottom of the pan, then bob right back to the top after a few seconds if the oil is in the 350F (175C) range.

Never add foods to hot oil by tossing them in. Hot splashing oil can cause serious burns. Lower the foods to just above the oil level, then allow them to gently glide in. Maintain correct oil temperatures for greaseless fried foods. Do not overcrowd the pan because this reduces the oil temperature. Skim oil with a fine-mesh strainer several times to remove fried batter. Do not overheat oil; rapid deterioration allows foods to absorb excess oil.

If the oil is light after one use, it can be used again. Skim the surface, then filter through a strainer lined with several layers of cheesecloth. Store the oil a short time in a cool dark place to prevent rancidity. Fry a slice of gingerroot in the recycled oil to neutralize odors that might cling to foods during frying. Discard oil after second use; it begins to darken and break down, developing a low smoking point.

The deep-frying pot should be sturdy with a wide surface and deep enough to comfortably hold 2 to 3 inches of oil. A small Chinese flat-bottomed iron wok works fine for deep-frying. Swift heat conduction produces quick and even browning. The wok requires less oil for deep-frying because of its unique bowl shape.

Secrets of Making Tempura

One secret for making good tempura lies within the batter, or *koromo*, which means "clothing." The "clothing" on the tempura should be transparent as a woman's veil.

Prepare the batter in the final moment just before cooking. The water must be ice-cold. When a batter-coated food hits the hot oil, it is immediately sealed. The resulting steam inside the food helps it cook quickly. Under-mix the batter; leave flour around the bowl. The tiny lumps of unmixed flour will puff up in the hot oil.

Another secret is to be able to judge the cooking time and prevent overcooking. The professional chef determines doneness through sound as well as sight. As foods are slipped into the sizzling oil, he begins to listen, recognizing changes as the sizzling sound deepens to a lower pitch. Far better to slightly undercook tempura. The ingredients should be so fresh, they can be eaten raw.

Pass bowls of miso soup as you fry your first batch. Good tempura waits for no one. Serve it hot and crispy, straight from the oil. For each place setting, provide a pair of chopsticks and a small basket or plate lined with a folded piece of special absorbent paper known as *shiki-shi*. Napkins or folded pieces of coated white kitchen paper work well. Fresh cooked rice and a side dish of pickles completes the meal. Serve warm saké, hot green tea or cold beer.

TEMPURA

In the sixteenth century, Portuguese Jesuits introduced batter-fried fish to southern Japan. After seclusion edicts were imposed in 1639, the Jesuits were expelled but the fried dish remained. Considered *namban ryōri,* "barbarian cuisine," the Japanese adapted the dish to suit their taste and renamed it tempura. By the nineteenth century, tempura shops had sprung up throughout old Edo. Tempura evolved into the light, grease-free battered food we associate with Japanese cooking today. Many foods can be cooked as tempura, including scallops, squid, tofu, bell pepper, eggplant, carrots, strawberries and banana.

Daikon Dipping Sauce (page 153)
1 lb. large raw shrimp, peeled,
    with tails left intact (16 to 18)
1/2 lb. fish fillets, cut into 1-inch
    pieces
5 medium-size fresh shiitake
    mushrooms, stems trimmed
2 small onions, halved and sliced
    1/3 inch thick (secure slices
    with wooden pick)
1 medium-size sweet potato,
    peeled and cut into thin slices
12 small fresh green beans,
    ends trimmed

About 5 1/2 cups peanut oil or
    vegetable oil
All-purpose flour

TEMPURA BATTER
1 cup cake flour or *tempurako*
1/4 cup potato starch or
    cornstarch
1/2 teaspoon baking powder
1 large egg white
About 1 cup ice-cold sparkling
    water or tap water
Additional flour if necessary

◙ Prepare Daikon Dipping Sauce; keep warm. Slit shrimp backs open lengthwise, 3/4 of the way through; do not cut into tail sections. Remove veins. Place on a flat surface, cut-sides down. Lightly pound 2 or 3 times to flatten.

◙ Arrange shrimp, fish and vegetables on a serving platter. At the table, heat oil in a *tempura-nabé* or electric wok to 360F (180C). Prepare Tempura Batter as needed. Coat 4 or 5 shrimp with flour; dip into batter. Lower into hot oil, holding tails above oil a few seconds to help set the shape. Fry 2 minutes or until crisp. Coat, dip and fry a few of the other ingredients at a time. Cooking times may vary with each ingredient.

Drain Tempura on a wire rack. Serve at once with rice and dipping sauce.

◉ *Makes 4 to 5 servings.*

TEMPURA BATTER

◉ In a medium-size bowl, combine cake flour, potato starch and baking powder. In a small bowl, use chopsticks to mix egg white and water. Stir into dry ingredients with chopsticks, leaving batter lumpy and undermixed. Set bowl of batter in a larger pan of iced water. If batter becomes too smooth, stir in extra flour. Add a few tablespoons water if too thick. Experiment to find the consistency you like best.

◉ *Makes 2 1/4 cups.*

DAIKON DIPPING SAUCE
(Tentsuyu)

Serve small bowls of this warm dipping sauce with any type of fried tempura.
Tempura tastes best lightly dipped into the sauce, then immediately eaten.

1/3 cup light soy sauce (*usukuchi shoyu*)	1/3 cup mirin
1 1/4 cups Sea Vegetable & Bonito Stock (page 46)	1/2 to 3/4 cup grated daikon radish, to taste
	2 tablespoons grated gingerroot

◉ In a medium-size saucepan, heat soy sauce, stock and mirin over low heat; keep warm until needed. Prepare daikon and gingerroot; place in separate small dishes. At serving time, divide sauce among 4 or 5 medium-size bowls. Pass daikon and ginger-root at the table for mixing into dipping sauce.

◉ *Makes about 2 cups.*

AUTUMN LEAF TEMPURA

(Aki No Ha Tempura)

This exquisite vegetarian tempura represents Kyo-ryōri, the elegant cuisine of Kyoto.
Autumn Chestnut Rice (page 198) is a colorful seasonal accompaniment.

Daikon Dipping Sauce (page 153)
   or Lemon Ginger Sauce
   (opposite)
1 cup cooked spaghetti squash
   (from 3/4 lb. raw squash),
   chopped into short lengths
18 fresh shiso leaves
1 (20-oz.) pkg. firm fresh tofu,
   rinsed
1 (1-lb.) yam, peeled and cut
   into 1/8-inch-thick slices
18 canned, drained ginkgo nuts
   (*ginnan*), skewered on
   6 wooden picks

2 (8 x 7 1/2-inch) sheets nori, cut
   into 12 (4 x 2 1/2-inch) pieces
1 firm ripe Japanese persimmon,
   sliced
About 4 cups peanut oil or
   vegetable oil
Tempura Batter (page 152),
   prepared as needed
All-purpose flour

◉ Prepare Daikon Dipping Sauce. Place squash in a small bowl. Rinse shiso leaves; pat
dry. Slice tofu horizontally into 1/4-inch-thick slices. Place between double layers of
clean kitchen towels or layers of paper towels. Press with 1-pound weight, 15 minutes,
to firm up. With a metal cookie cutter, cut into 2 1/2-inch scalloped flower shapes, or
cut into 1-inch cubes. Cut yam slices into leaf shapes with a metal cutter or small knife,
or leave in slices. Place in cool water. With scissors, cut a stack of nori into oval leaf
shapes, or leave in strips.

◉ At serving time, drain yam slices; dry on paper towels. Arrange with vegetables,
nori and persimmon on a serving platter. At the table, heat oil in a *tempura-nabé* or
electric wok to 360F (180C). Prepare Tempura Batter. Pour 1/3 of batter into bowl of
squash; mix with chopsticks. Spread 1 tablespoon squash mixture over underside of
each shiso leaf. Dip squash-coated leaf into remaining batter. Fry in hot oil 25 seconds
or until crisp. Coat remaining foods lightly with flour; dip in batter and fry. Drain on
a wire rack. Serve on flat paper-covered baskets with dipping sauce.

◉ *Makes 6 servings.*

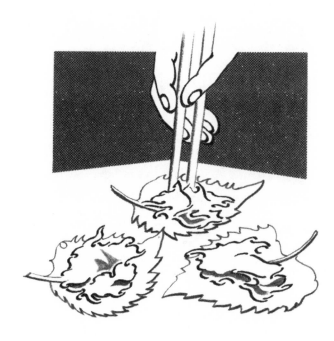

LEMON GINGER SAUCE

(Lemon Shōga Sōsu)

This amber sauce is good with the fried foods in Autumn Leaf Tempura (opposite). It also complements the taste of fried shrimp, chicken or zucchini.

3/4 cup chicken broth	1/4 teaspoon grated gingerroot
3 tablespoons fresh lemon juice	1 tablespoon mirin
1/4 cup sugar	2 teaspoons cornstarch
2 teaspoons light soy sauce	1/8 teaspoon sesame oil
(*usukuchi shoyu*)	Pinch of salt (optional)

◙ In a small saucepan, combine chicken broth, lemon juice, sugar, soy sauce, gingerroot and mirin. In a small bowl, dissolve cornstarch in a small amount of chicken broth mixture. Stir into mixture in saucepan. Cook over medium-high heat, stirring constantly, until thickened. Strain sauce into a small bowl through a fine strainer. Stir in sesame oil and salt.

◙ *Makes about 3/4 cup.*

CRISPY FRIED PORK CUTLETS
(Tonkatsu)

Tonkatsu is everyone's favorite! According to the Japanese newspaper *Asahi Shimbun, tonkatsu* first appeared on a Japanese menu in 1932 at a Tokyo restaurant called Rakuten. *Tonkatsu* and another version, *katsudon* (pork cutlet in a bowl of rice), are now considered celebration food, often served on the day of a tournament or contest. The word katsu means "to win." The cabbage looks and tastes best when shredded very finely.

Tonkatsu Sauce (opposite)
1 lb. pork tenderloin or pork loin, sliced 1/2 inch thick
Salt and ground pepper to taste
1/2 cup all-purpose flour
1 egg, slightly beaten
2 tablespoons milk

1 cup Japanese-style bread crumbs (*panko*), more if needed
6 cups peanut oil or vegetable oil
1 medium-size green or red cabbage or half of each
Tomato wedges

◉ Prepare Tonkatsu Sauce; set aside. Lightly pound pork; sprinkle with salt and pepper. Coat with flour. In a shallow pan, combine egg and milk. Place bread crumbs in a second shallow pan. Dip pork slices into egg mixture, then coat both sides with bread crumbs. Set aside on a platter.

◉ In a wok or shallow heavy saucepan, heat oil to 360F (180C). Fry 2 or 3 slices at a time, 6 to 8 minutes or until golden brown and done inside. Pork loin may need slightly longer frying time. Turn once or twice for even cooking. Drain on paper towels. Skim oil to remove pieces of fried coating. Keep fried pork warm in a 150F (65C) oven while slicing cabbage. Cut cabbage in quarter wedges. Slice each piece across the leaves into very fine shreds. Mound a large pile of cabbage on each plate. Slice pork cutlets into 1/2-inch strips. Lift pork pieces, in their original shapes, and arrange on plates. Garnish with tomato; nap with sauce.

◉ *Makes 4 servings.*

TONKATSU SAUCE
(Tonkatsu Sōsu)

Serve this piquant sauce with *tonkatsu*, Japanese pizza, fried oysters or your favorite grilled steak.

1 cup ketchup	1 tablespoon Worcestershire
1/4 cup soy sauce	sauce
2 tablespoons sugar	1 teaspoon minced gingerroot
2 tablespoons mirin	1 large garlic clove, minced

◉ In a small bowl, combine all ingredients; mix well. Cover and let stand 30 minutes for flavors to develop.

◉ *Makes 1 1/2 cups.*

FISH CAKE TEMPURA
(Satsuma-age)

These pleasantly chewy fish cakes are made like those from Kagoshima Prefecture in southern Japan. Satsuma is the old name for Kagoshima. The fish cakes are prepared like *kamaboko* (steamed fish loaf), except deep-fried. If you use frozen fish, you may have to increase the cornstarch by 1 or 2 tablespoons. Add slices of fish cake to soups, noodle dishes, salads, stews. Or just dip a slice into soy sauce for a wonderful snack.

1/2 lb. fresh fish fillets, skinned (halibut, flounder, scrod, haddock)	1 tablespoon salt
1 tablespoon saké	1 (2-inch) piece *gobo* root (burdock), if available
1/2 cup sugar	1/2 medium-size carrot, shredded
1 cup water	1 green onion, minced
1 cup cornstarch	About 4 cups peanut oil or vegetable oil
1 large egg	

◉ Cut fish into 1-inch pieces. In a blender or food processor fitted with a steel blade, grind fish to a paste. Add saké, sugar, water, cornstarch, egg and salt. Process until smooth. If used, scrape, rinse and shred *gobo*. Swish in a small bowl of water with 1 tablespoon vinegar. Drain; add to fish paste with carrot and green onion. Blend 5 seconds. Scrape paste into a medium-size bowl. Cover and refrigerate 30 minutes.

◉ In a wok or shallow heavy saucepan, heat oil to 350F (175C). Spread 1/3 cup paste on a 2 1/2-inch-wide wooden rice paddle or spatula; smooth paste with a knife to fit shape of paddle. Fish cake should be 3/4 inch thick. Hold paddle to edge of hot oil. Using a knife, scrape fish cake off paddle upside down into hot oil. Form 2 or 3 more fish cakes. Fry slowly 15 to 18 minutes or until puffy and golden brown. Drain on paper towels. Fish cakes deflate slightly upon cooling. Do not fry too fast or they brown too quickly, remaining uncooked in the center. Cook remaining fish paste. Serve warm or cold.

◉ *Makes 7 fish cakes.*

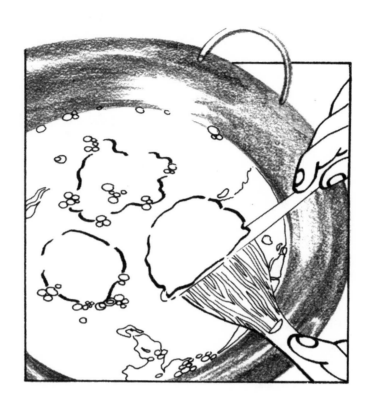

CRISPY CHICKEN, EGGPLANT & MUSHROOM SKEWERS

(Kushi-agé)

These savory morsels can be served as part of a meal or as a party appetizer. The coating stays crisp 2 or 3 hours. Darker chicken thighs are economical and stay moist and tender during frying. Serve with a fruity dipping sauce, soy sauce, Tonkatsu Sauce (page 157) or Mustard Miso Sauce (opposite).

4 chicken thighs, skinned, boned and cut into 1-inch cubes
1 tablespoon mirin
1 tablespoon soy sauce
1 teaspoon minced gingerroot
2 Japanese eggplants, cut into small wedges
8 small whole round mushrooms
6 cups peanut oil
2 cups Japanese-style bread crumbs (*panko*)

CURRY-FLAVORED BATTER
    1/3 cup cake flour or *tempurako*
    1/3 cup potato starch or cornstarch
    1/2 teaspoon curry powder (optional)
    1/2 teaspoon baking powder
    3/4 teaspoon salt
    1/2 cup plus 2 tablespoons sparkling water or tap water
    1 teaspoon vegetable oil

◙ In a large bowl, combine chicken, mirin, soy sauce and gingerroot. Marinate 30 minutes; drain well. Lace pieces of chicken, eggplant and mushrooms alternately on 6-inch skewers. Prepare Curry-Flavored Batter; pour into shallow pan. In a wok or shallow pan, heat oil to 360F (180C). Dip chicken skewers into batter; coat with bread crumbs. Fry 2 or 3 at a time 3 minutes. Turn often, until crisp and golden brown. Drain on wire rack. Serve with dipping sauce of choice.

◙ *Makes 6 servings.*

CURRY-FLAVORED BATTER

◉ Whisk all ingredients together in a medium-size bowl.

◉ *Makes about 1 cup.*

MUSTARD MISO SAUCE
(Karashi Miso Sōsu)

A tasty sauce for Crispy Chicken, Eggplant & Mushroom Skewers (opposite), fried
tofu, spring rolls, grilled chicken or fish.

2 tablespoons toasted sesame seeds	1 teaspoon mirin
1/2 cup imported Dijon mustard	1 teaspoon sugar
1/2 teaspoon sesame oil	1 generous tablespoon sweet white miso
1 teaspoon soy sauce	Hot red-pepper sauce to taste

◉ In a grinding bowl or small electric spice grinder, process sesame seeds until powdery. Pour into a small bowl; blend in remaining ingredients.

◉ *Makes about 1/2 cup.*

KAMABOKO FRITTERS
(Kamaboko No Agé)

The fish cake *kamaboko* is chewier than fresh fish. This is because of the development of the protein actomyosin, which results in the formation of ashi. Ashi means elasticity, the characteristic resilience found in *kamaboko*. Strong ashi is desirable in Japan. American *kamaboko* has less ashi than its Japanese counterpart. California *kamaboko* manufacturer Frank Kawana explains that fish species caught off the California coast don't have the characteristics to make Japanese-style *kamaboko*. Japanese Americans consider products from Japan to be too rubbery. Whichever you use, *kamaboko* is delicious. Enjoy these crispy fritters as they are fried; leftovers are delicious, too. *Agédama,* the golden crispy bits of fried leftover batter, are delicious added to soba noodles in hot broth or Japanese-Style Pizza (page 108).

6 ounces *kamaboko*, thinly sliced and cut into 1/4-inch strips, or *surimi* crab or lobster, or 20 raw large shrimp, peeled and each cut into 4 pieces

1 medium-size onion, quartered and thinly sliced

1/2 medium-size carrot, thinly sliced diagonally and cut into 1-inch matchstick strips

1 small red or green bell pepper, cut into 1-inch julienne strips

1 large egg

1 cup sparkling water or tap water

1 cup cake flour

1/2 teaspoon baking powder

1/2 teaspoon salt

6 cups peanut oil or vegetable oil

Soy sauce

◉ In a medium-size bowl, combine *kamaboko,* onion, carrot and bell pepper. In another medium-size bowl, use chopsticks to slightly beat egg. Stir in water, flour, baking powder and salt until just blended, then stir in fish mixture.

◉ In a wok or heavy shallow saucepan, heat oil to 360F (180C). Fry tablespoons of batter, turning occasionally, 3 to 4 minutes or until crispy and golden brown. Drain on wire rack. Serve with soy sauce.

◉ *Makes 6 servings.*

SALADS OR VINEGARED & DRESSED FOODS

(Sunomono & Aemono)

●

The Western concept of salad does not exist in traditional Japanese cuisine. The Japanese dishes *sunomono,* "vinegared things," and *aemono,* "dressed things," are the equivalent. Today, Western-style salads have gained tremendous popularity in Japan, thanks to young Japanese women who are becoming more health conscious. Concerns for fitness and health in America have inspired us to experiment with traditional Japanese cooking methods and ingredients to enhance the nutritional values of our own salads.

Sunomono are made with any combination of raw or cooked vegetables, fruit, seafood or poultry. They are coated with a thin tangy dressing based on rice vinegar, Sea Vegetable & Bonito Stock (page 46) or *dashi,* soy sauce and sugar. Fresh lemon juice, plum vinegar, mirin, ginger, daikon radish, fresh herbs, *wasabi,* red peppers, sesame seeds and mustard are optional flavor boosters. Mild rice vinegar enhances food flavors, keeping them fresh tasting. *Dashi* adds depth to combined flavors. Sugar enriches the flavor of rice vinegar and softens the acidity.

The dressing for *aemono* is usually thicker than for *sunomono*. The base ingredient might be miso, ground sesame seeds, preserved plum paste, tofu, egg yolk, soybean pulp (*okara*) or fermented soybeans (*natto*). Vinegar may be used as a flavoring agent. Dried fruits, especially persimmons and apricots, are tasty additions. Japanese-style salads taste as delicious as they look; flavor is never sacrificed for beauty.

Fresh fish, shellfish and chicken can be poached, steamed or grilled. Raw vegetables often benefit from a short salting period or from quick blanching in boiling water or stock to intensify colors and flavors. Blanching softens vegetable fibers, making them more digestible. Crisp the blanched vegetables in an iced-water bath. Pat dry and refrigerate until needed.

Western-style tossed salads are noteworthy because they often resemble small sculpted flower gardens within a bowl. Pieces of fresh fruit, slivers of raw fish, vegetable flowers or real flowers are arranged upon beds of delicate lettuce or finely shredded cabbage.

Ohitashi refers to a method of quick boiling usually reserved for spinach, but other seasonal vegetables or even edible flowers such as chrysanthemum leaves will benefit. After quick boiling, the vegetable is briefly soaked in a liquid seasoning. Vegetables prepared for *ohitashi* are served as a *sunomono* course.

MARINATED SPINACH SALAD

(Hōrenso No Mariné Salada)

This spunky Korean-style spinach dish goes nicely with barbecued meats and poultry.

2 (1/2-lb.) bunches fresh spinach
1 garlic clove, finely minced
2 green onions, finely minced
1/2 teaspoon *kochu* (Korean
   ground red pepper), or to
   taste

1/4 cup rice vinegar
1 tablespoon soy sauce
1 teaspoon sesame seed oil
1/4 teaspoon salt, or to taste
1 tablespoon toasted sesame
   seeds

◉ Cook spinach in a large pot of boiling water, about 1 minute or until wilted and bright green. Drain spinach in a colander. Rinse with cool water. Gently press out water. On a cutting board, cut spinach into small pieces.

◉ Whisk together all remaining ingredients except sesame seeds in a large bowl. Add spinach; combine well with vinegar mixture. Cover and chill until serving time. Serve in small dishes; garnish with sesame seeds.

◉ *Makes 4 or 5 servings.*

BEEF TATAKI WITH WASABI CREAM
(Gyūniku Tataki)

This recipe is prepared in the style of *bonito tataki*. Bonito is passed quickly over a hot fire to sear the outside, then chilled in iced water and pounded with seasonings. A similar method has become popular for beef. The meat can be seared quickly in a heavy skillet or over a hot charcoal fire. Inside, the beef should be rare. The meat is sliced and served much like beef tartare. The degree of doneness can vary to suit personal tastes.

2 pounds beef tenderloin, trimmed
2 tablespoons soy sauce
1 tablespoon mirin
1 tablespoon fresh lemon juice
2 teaspoons grated gingerroot
1 garlic clove, minced
1 green onion, thinly sliced
Salt and freshly ground black
    pepper to taste
Red-leaf lettuce leaves
6 fresh shiso leaves or basil
    leaves, rolled and
    finely shredded

2 tablespoons toasted sesame
    seeds
1 1/2 cups crème fraîche or
    sour cream
1 to 3 teaspoons Wasabi
    (page 237), to taste
2 tablespoons snipped fresh
    chives
6 Lemon Cups (page 16)

◉ Preheat oven to 400F (205C). Place meat in a heavy roasting pan. Roast until a meat thermometer inserted in center registers 135F (50C) for rare or 140F (60C) for medium-rare. Remove from oven. Plunge into iced water. When chilled, remove and pat completely dry.

◉ In a medium-size deep bowl, combine soy sauce, mirin, lemon juice, gingerroot, garlic and onion. Add salt and pepper. Coat meat in mixture; marinate several hours or overnight, turning often. Pat meat dry; cut into very thin slices. Cut slices in half.

◉ Place lettuce on 6 chilled serving plates. Arrange slices of beef on lettuce. Garnish with shiso and sesame seeds. Combine crème fraîche, Wasabi and chives in a small bowl. Spoon mixture into Lemon Cups; place 1 on each serving plate. Or drizzle dressing over each serving.

◉ *Makes 6 servings.*

MUSTARD GREENS OHITASHI

Southern greens never tasted so good as this dish seasoned Japanese-style!

1/2 pound fresh mustard greens
    or collards, stems trimmed,
    well rinsed
	3 tablespoons plum vinegar
	    (*umé su*)
	Dash hot-pepper sauce to taste

1 teaspoon sugar	Bonito thread shavings (optional)

◉ Bring about 2 quarts water to boil in a large pot. Add mustard greens; boil 10 minutes or until tender. Drain greens; liquid can be saved for soups. Refresh greens in cool water. Drain well. Press out excess water. Cut greens into small pieces. Place in a medium-size bowl. In a small bowl, whisk together sugar, vinegar and hot-pepper sauce. Pour over greens; toss well. Serve at room temperature or chilled. Arrange mounds of the marinated greens on serving plates. Garnish with bonito shavings.

◉ *Makes 6 servings.*

VARIATION

◉ The greens are delicious served southern-style in a bowl of the warm pot liquor (cooking water). Season each portion with a small amount of the tangy dressing.

WAKAMÉ SEA SALAD WITH GINGER SESAME DRESSING

(Wakamé No Shōga-zu)

Wakamé, or lobe leaf, is a tender, naturally sweet sea vegetable. It is rich in iron and vitamin A, and calories are almost nonexistent. Generally, soak packaged wakamé in warm water about 20 minutes. Soak fresh spring *wakamé* in cool water to remove packing salt.

Look for a plastic package of 5-gram packets of small dark tangles. Dipped into hot water, the tender pieces expand almost instantly. *Wakamé* can also be added to soups during the last minute of heating.

1 ounce dried *wakamé*	2 teaspoons grated gingerroot
1/4 cup rice vinegar	1/2 teaspoon sesame seed oil
2 tablespoons mirin	1/4 teaspoon salt (optional)
1 tablespoon soy sauce	2 teaspoons toasted sesame
2 teaspoons sugar	seeds

◉ Place *wakamé* into a large bowl of warm water; soak 20 minutes or until it expands 6 or 7 times and is tender. Trim off any tough parts; cut into smaller pieces. Rinse well; pat dry thoroughly. In a small bowl, combine remaining ingredients. Pour over *wakamé;* mix well. Serve chilled.

◉ *Makes 4 servings.*

VARIATION

◉ Add a small amount of paper-thin cucumber or daikon slices to this salad.

TURNIP ROSE SUNOMONO

(Bara Sunomono)

Invite your guests to use their chopsticks and pluck the tasty petals from this exquisite rose.

1 (1/2-lb.) well-shaped round turnip	1/4 cup sugar
2 tablespoons rice vinegar	1/2 teaspoon salt
2 tablespoons fresh lemon juice	Fresh shiso leaves or fresh rose leaves (optional)

◙ Peel turnip, keeping shape as rounded as possible. Using a Benriner cutter, a French mandoline or a large sharp chef's knife, cut into paper-thin slices, about 1/16 inch thick. Cook turnip slices 30 seconds in boiling water; drain. Rinse in cool water; drain again. Place in a small bowl with vinegar, lemon juice, sugar and salt. Cover and refrigerate at least 30 minutes, up to 6 hours. Slices will become very soft and flexible.

◙ At serving time, drain turnip slices. Make a cut on 1 slice from center to edge. Overlap cut edges tightly, forming a cone shape. Mold 5 or 6 turnip slices around turnip cone. Set the flower upright or on its side on a small serving dish. Mold remaining turnip slices around it to resemble a rose in full bloom. Gently bend back tops of slices to resemble rose petals. Garnish with shiso leaves. Serve immediately.

◙ *Makes 1 rose.*

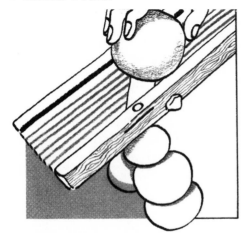

SOMEN, CRABMEAT & ASPARAGUS WITH SESAME DRESSING

(Somen, Kani To Asparagus No Goma-zu)

Somen is always served chilled. Prevent the noodles from overcooking by using a favorite cooking technique called *sashimizu*, which means to add water while the noodles are cooking.

1 tablespoon toasted sesame seeds
4 tablespoons safflower oil or sunflower oil
1/4 cup rice vinegar
1 1/2 tablespoons sugar
1 1/2 tablespoons light soy sauce (*usukuchi shoyu*)
1/2 teaspoon salt
3 fresh shiitake mushrooms, stemmed and shredded
1 packed cup shredded napa cabbage

1/4 pound thin fresh asparagus, trimmed, blanched and chilled
1 small carrot, cut in matchstick strips
1/2 pound lump crabmeat, cooked clams or squid, cut into thin strips
3 green onions, thinly sliced
6 fresh shiso leaves or basil leaves, finely shredded
2 (3-oz.) bundles somen

◉ In a small bowl, combine sesame seeds, 3 tablespoons of the oil, vinegar, sugar, soy sauce and salt; set aside. Heat remaining 1 tablespoon oil in a small skillet. Stir-fry mushrooms 30 seconds; add cabbage and cook 30 seconds more. Cool completely.

◉ Cut asparagus into thin diagonal pieces. Arrange all ingredients except dressing and somen on a platter; set aside. In a large pot, bring 1 quart water to a boil. Add somen. When water returns to the boil, add 1 cup cold water. When water returns to the boil again, add another cup of water. Somen should be soft and pliant. If not, cook only seconds longer. Pour into a fine strainer. Rinse well; drain completely. Place in a large bowl with salad ingredients. Add dressing; toss well. Divide salad among serving plates.

◉ *Makes 4 to 6 servings.*

LEMON & PINE NUT SUSHI

Tangy sushi salad is served on tender lettuce leaves, then wrapped for eating. Serve as a salad or appetizer course. The rice can be cooked and seasoned 3 or 4 hours ahead; leave at room temperature. Just before serving, toss in the chilled shrimp and vegetables.

1 recipe Sushi Rice (page 72), seasoned as directed below
2 tablespoons white vinegar
1 tablespoon sugar
1 tablespoon saké
1/2 teaspoon salt
2 teaspoons grated lemon peel
1/2 pound medium-size cooked shrimp, chopped, or cooked clams
1 Japanese cucumber or 1/2 European cucumber, seeded if necessary and diced

3 tablespoons toasted pine nuts
1/4 cup frozen petit green peas, thawed
2 small green onions, thinly sliced
2 tablespoons pink pickled gingerroot (amazu shōga), shredded
12 Boston lettuce leaves

◉ Cook the rice. As the rice cooks, combine vinegar, sugar, saké, salt and lemon peel in a small saucepan. Simmer over low heat 1 minute, stirring to dissolve sugar. Remove from heat. Scoop hot rice into an odorless, damp wooden bowl or glass bowl. Drizzle dressing over rice; lightly cut through and turn rice with a damp rice paddle or large wooden spoon. As you work, fan the rice so that it cools quickly and becomes glossy.

◉ When the rice is completely cool, mix in remaining ingredients except lettuce. To serve, spoon a small portion of rice mixture onto a lettuce leaf. Fold the sides of the lettuce over to enclose rice. Eat the packet out of hand. Rice can also be eaten with chopsticks or a fork.

◉ *Makes 4 servings.*

Sweet & Sour Crab

(Kani Amazu)

Why not try poached squid strips, shrimp or chicken in this refreshing salad?

Sweet & Sour Sauce (see below)
2 small white onions, sliced
    paper-thin crosswise
3 celery stalks, trimmed and
    halved lengthwise
2 Japanese cucumbers or
    1 European cucumber
1/2 lb. chunk crabmeat
1 or 2 clementine tangerines,
    peeled and segmented, or
    1 (11-oz.) can mandarin
    orange segments, drained
1 tablespoon toasted sesame seeds

SWEET & SOUR SAUCE

1/2 cup chicken stock
3 tablespoons sugar
2 tablespoons light soy sauce
    (*usukuchi shoyu*)
5 tablespoons rice vinegar
1/4 teaspoon salt
1 teaspoon sesame oil
1/2 cup unsweetened pineapple
    juice
2 tablespoons cornstarch

◙ Prepare Sweet & Sour Sauce. Soak sliced onions in iced water 15 minutes to crisp; drain well. Place in a medium-size bowl. Cut celery strips into 1/4-inch-thick diagonal slices. Add to onions. Cut cucumbers in halves lengthwise. Cut diagonally into 1/4-inch pieces. Add cucumber to onions and celery. Cover and refrigerate until needed.

◙ At serving time, toss together crabmeat, vegetables, tangerines and sauce. Serve on a platter or small serving dishes. Sprinkle with sesame seeds. Salad can be assembled 2 hours ahead of serving time; keep refrigerated.

◙ *Makes 6 to 8 servings.*

SWEET & SOUR SAUCE

◙ In a small saucepan, combine stock, sugar, soy sauce, vinegar, salt and sesame oil over medium-high heat. Blend pineapple juice and cornstarch in a small bowl. When sauce mixture boils, stir in cornstarch mixture. Cook, stirring, until thickened. Cool; refrigerate until needed.

Green Beans with Sesame Miso Dressing

(Saya Ingen Goma-Aé)

The nutty sesame dressing is delicious over other cooked vegetables including cauliflower, broccoli and zucchini.

1 pound small green beans, rinsed
Sesame Miso Dressing (see below)
1 tablespoon toasted sesame seeds

SESAME MISO DRESSING
2 tablespoons toasted sesame seeds
2 tablespoons white miso

1 tablespoon sugar
2 tablespoons mirin
1 teaspoon fresh lemon juice
1/2 teaspoon soy sauce

◉ Trim the ends from the beans; remove any strings. Spread 1/2 of the beans evenly on a microwave-safe dinner plate. Sprinkle with a few drops of water. Cover tightly with plastic wrap. Microwave on high (100 percent power) 3 minutes. Beans should be crisp-tender and still bright green. Remove from oven; spread out to cool. Microwave remaining beans; cool. Cut beans diagonally into 2-inch lengths. Beans can be refrigerated up to 2 hours.

◉ Prepare dressing. Gently mix dressing with beans. Divide salad among serving dishes. Sprinkle with additional sesame seeds.

◉ *Makes 8 small servings.*

SESAME MISO DRESSING

◉ Grind sesame seeds in a Japanese grinding bowl until a paste is formed. Scrape into a small bowl; mix in remaining ingredients. Use immediately or refrigerate until needed.

SHRIMP & BROCCOLI WITH DAIKON SAUCE

(Ebi To Broccoli No Daikon Oroshi Aé)

Hisamichi Fujimura is the executive chef of the magnificent Nippon Center Yagoto in Greenville, South Carolina. The complex was built in the Shoin Zukuri style, which first appeared in the Muromachi period (1333–1568). Japanese craftsmen built the interior without nails; master gardeners from Japan created a replica of Ryoan-ji, the famous rock garden in Kyoto. Here is one of Chef Fujimura's recipes.

1/2 pound broccoli flowerets, stems trimmed
1/4 pound fresh small shrimp, cooked and peeled
2 tablespoons top-quality mayonnaise

1 teaspoon soy sauce
2 tablespoons grated daikon radish
1 teaspoon fresh lemon juice
Salt and black pepper to taste

◉ Cook broccoli in boiling water 1 minute. Drain and cool in iced water. Drain and pat dry. Place broccoli and shrimp in separate bowls. Cover and refrigerate until serving time. In a medium-size bowl, combine mayonnaise, soy sauce, grated daikon and lemon juice. Add salt and pepper. Cover tightly and chill until serving time.

◉ To serve, divide portions of shrimp and broccoli among small attractive dishes. Drizzle with daikon sauce. Serve at once.

◉ *Makes 4 or 5 servings.*

KIWI & ASIAN PEAR IN LEMON SAUCE

(Kiwi To Nashi No Lemon Aé)

This refreshing salad features the tangy kiwi and the Asian pear (*nashi*), which has the juiciness and texture of jicama and the flavor of a ripe pear. If unavailable, substitute a crisp Anjou pear. Cut all the fruits and vegetables exactly the same size, for an attractive presentation.

Lemon Sauce (see below)
2 kiwifruit, peeled, sliced and cut
   into matchstick strips
1 crisp Asian pear, peeled, sliced
   and cut into matchstick strips
1/2 yellow or red bell pepper,
   cut into matchstick strips
1/2 European cucumber, halved,
   seeded and cut into
   matchstick strips
1 tablespoon lightly toasted
   black sesame seeds

LEMON SAUCE

Freshly grated peel of 1 small
   lemon
1/4 cup fresh lemon juice
2 tablespoons sugar
1/4 teaspoon salt
1/2 teaspoon sesame oil

◉ Prepare sauce. Add fruits and vegetables to sauce in bowl; toss well. Cover and refrigerate 1 hour. Small portions are pretty served in blue and white Japanese dishes. Garnish with sesame seeds.

◉ *Makes 5 or 6 servings.*

LEMON SAUCE

◉ In a large bowl, whisk together all ingredients.

Japanese Cooking in the Microwave

The microwave is an excellent tool for preparing crisp vegetables for Japanese salads. The water content of many vegetables seems to be just enough for cooking; water-soluble vitamins and minerals are retained and not washed down the drain. A small amount of *dashi* or water may be needed for fibrous vegetables. Vegetables keep that fresh-picked flavor; colors stay bright. Ordinary vegetables become extraordinary.

Vegetables cook best on high (100 percent power). Microwave about 5 minutes per pound. Covered with plastic wrap, vegetables stay moist, and cooking is so quick, color change does not occur. In Japan, vegetables are often microwaved in plastic cooking bags or even wrapped in plastic wrap. Loosen the wrap after vegetables come from the oven. If too crisp, continue cooking in 30-second periods. Undercook slightly, allowing a standing time of 2 to 3 minutes. Vegetables continue softening, but this method allows them to become tender without losing texture. Beware of overcooking; microwaved vegetables can dehydrate quickly.

Cut vegetable pieces in similar sizes. Pay attention to the arrangement of foods in the cooking dish. Arrange shapes like broccoli and asparagus like the spokes of a wheel, with the broccoli flowerets and asparagus tips placed toward the center of the dish. Many well-rinsed vegetables can be cooked in their natural form. Small Japanese eggplants, yams and potatoes should be of a uniform size and arranged in a circular pattern. For irregular-shaped vegetables, place the smaller ends pointing toward the center of the oven.

The texture of raw salad vegetables benefits from a 30-second to 1-minute cooking period in the microwave. Chill quickly in iced water, drain and pat dry. The microwave can save time by softening vegetables before they are cut and skewered for the grill. If salt is added, dissolve in *dashi* or water. Salt added directly to vegetables dehydrates them. It also interferes with the microwave cooking pattern and causes brown "freckles" to appear.

NOODLES

(Menrui)

◉

Noodles, a Japanese passion, are the "fast food" of Japan. Inexpensive and tasty, they are ideal for a quick lunch or snack. Noodles were introduced from the eighth-century Chinese Tang dynasty by Buddhist priests. Two of Japan's most popular noodles—soba and udon—are made from buckwheat flour and soft white wheat flour. Somewhat different in taste and texture from European noodles, most Asian noodles are cut and not extruded.

The first mention of buckwheat (soba) in extant written records came from Shoku Nippon Shoki. An imperial edict in 722 demanded that farmers cultivate buckwheat because drought had destroyed the annual rice crop. Fast-growing buckwheat would thrive on barren soil. During the Kamakura era (1185–1333), people ate buckwheat in the form of starchy whole grain dumplings. Historical records show soba noodles were popularized by temple priests during the sixteenth or seventeenth century. During the Edo period (Tokyo before 1868) they were made with boiling water and sticky mountain yam (*yama-no-imo*). Similar, slightly chewy noodles are still made today.

Soba made from *uchiko*, dark 100 percent buckwheat flour, has a certain roughness, not unlike whole grain breads. The textures of different soba noodles depend on the grade of buckwheat flour used and the ratio of wheat flour added.

Buckwheat flour contains no gluten. It is better for noodle-making if a portion of wheat flour is mixed in to add cohesiveness and elasticity. Japanese soba is usually 40 to 60 percent buckwheat flour. American natural-food companies import an 80 percent buckwheat flour noodle. *Ito-soba* (40 percent buckwheat) and *jinenjo-* (mountain potato) *soba* are more tender and are excellent for frying as well as for broth.

Two varieties of soba are *yabu soba* and *sarashina soba*. *Yabu soba* is made from the outer portion of the whole grain. The buff-colored noodle evolved from the original-style rustic soba, popular with the Edokko ("child of the city"). *Sarashina-soba* is made from expensive white buckwheat flour, milled from the center of the grain. This special, light noodle is sometimes colored with green tea, black sesame seeds, poppy seeds, *yuzu* (golden Japanese citron), or the herbs *yomogi* (mugwort) and shiso (perilla).

You can easily create variations for basic Soba Shop Noodles (noodles in hot broth). Raccoon soba, or *tanuki soba*, calls for a topping of crispy fried bits of tempura or fritter batter. *Tempura-soba* is wildly popular. Drop an egg into a bowl of udon and broth and create tsukimi udon, or moon-viewing noodles. Add any topping you can think of including sliced cooked poultry, cooked seafood, seafood fritters, fried tofu or cooked vegetables.

Zaru-soba, or Soba in a Bamboo Basket, is topped with black nori and served with a chilled broth for dipping. *Mori*-style soba is the same except it comes without the nori topping. *Tenzaru-soba* includes a dish of tempura on the side. Except for the fragile-flavored soba and pure buckwheat soba, these hearty noodles hold up well in stir-fries.

Noodle connoisseurs prefer the simple taste of plain noodles, perhaps moistened with a little broth. The soba master is judged by his broth as well as handmade noodles. Mild sweet broth is favored in the western Kansai region around Kyoto; stronger broth is preferred in the Kanto, or Tokyo, region. The finest soba shops serve a simple soup appetizer called *nuki*. The quality of *nuki* reflects the skill of the soba master. *Nuki* is fortified with *soba yu*, the mineral-rich cooking water from the soba pot. Save your soba water to cook vegetables and enrich noodle sauces, soups and breads.

Soba has a rich heritage and has contributed to the customs and folklore of Japan. It is a symbol of good fortune and longevity. At midnight on December 31, the new year is welcomed with a bowl of *toshi-koshi-soba*, meaning "from one year to another." *Hikkoshi soba* is the customary gift presented to new neighbors when moving into a new house.

The forerunner of the wheat noodle, udon, was a dumpling made in the Nara period (710–84). Udon-making techniques were introduced from China during the Heian era (794–1185). Udon is often eaten in broth or added to a hot pot with a variety of ingredients. Fox Noodles, or *kitsuné-udon,* has a topping of fried bean curd, spinach and green onion. Fried noodles, or *yaki-udon,* are everyone's favorite. Udon and soba are interchangeable in recipes.

Ramen, a Chinese-style wheat noodle, is often packaged with different names, sometimes indicating a method of preparation. *Yaki-soba,* available fresh or fresh-frozen, is used for stir-fried noodle dishes. *Miso-ramen* means ramen in miso soup. *Chuka-soba* is precooked and dried; use for soup, stir-fries and cold noodle dishes. Look for a clear package of tan wavy noodles. When attached to ramen noodles, the name "soba" does not refer to buckwheat.

Instant ramen was the brainchild of Momofuku Ando, founder of Nissan Food Products. On August 16, 1945 (the first day of peace), he came up with the idea for instant noodles and felt the concept would contribute to rebuilding his country. Chicken ramen was first marketed in 1958; by 1990 export figures ran more than $15 billion. Instant ramen's appeal is its quick preparation time, a boon for the working person and the student.

Ramen noodles are interchangeable, but cooking times can vary among the different types. Instant ramen requires minimal, careful cooking.

Other popular noodles include *hiyamugi,* a thin, white wheat noodle, and somen, a thinner version, both usually eaten chilled. *Kishimen* is a flat wheat noodle like udon;

harusamé, wiry dried bean threads, and *saifun,* wiry Japanese rice pasta. Refer to the glossary for additional information.

In Japan, noodles are eaten quickly and with great gusto. Proper etiquette dictates that noodles be eaten and sucked up with a slurping sound. A meal of noodles might not be quite as tasty for some Japanese diners if eaten in silence. It would be like serving a food and omitting the final, most important seasoning of all!

Cooking Japanese Noodles

Japanese noodles should be cooked slightly al dente. Some noodles like somen need to cook a bit past this stage. The Japanese refer to overcooked noodles as "stretched" noodles because they have lost their firmness. Have cold water on hand to pour into the boiling pot if you think your noodles are in danger of overcooking.

To cook 1 pound of noodles, bring at least 4 quarts of unsalted water to boil in a large pot over high heat. Slowly add noodles. Stir with chopsticks to prevent sticking. Test noodles after 2 minutes by removing one from the pan. It should be slightly chewy and the same color throughout. Fresh ramen or *yaki-soba* will cook in 2 to 3 minutes, fresh soba and fresh udon in 3 to 4 minutes. Dried noodles need more time. Dried somen cooks in 2 to 3 minutes, dried soba in 4 to 5 minutes, dried *chuka-soba* in 2 to 3 minutes. Thick, dried udon requires the longest time, 6 to 8 minutes. Cooking times vary depending on the thickness of the noodles.

Drain the cooked noodles; immediately pour into a large colander set into a large bowl. Reserve cooking water for noodle broth or soup, if you wish; otherwise, discard. Rinse noodles under water to cool and remove excess starch. Drain completely; coat with a tablespoon of safflower oil if noodles are not to be used at once. If to be served hot, quickly dip them into hot water just before serving.

A favorite method for cooking dried soba, udon or somen is called *sashimizu*, which means to add water while cooking. Japanese cooks believe noodles cook more evenly with this method. One cup cold water is added to the pot when the water returns to a boil after the noodles have been added. Repeat the process once. Reduce heat slightly and cook 1 to 3 minutes or until noodles are al dente. Sometimes noodles are removed from the heat after the second cup of water is added. The pan is covered, and the noodles are allowed to steep to perfection for 2 to 4 minutes.

GREEN-TEA NOODLES WITH SESAME GINGER DRESSING

(Matcha Soba Salada)

These pretty green noodles are flavored with green tea. The gingery dressing tastes best if made several hours ahead. If you like, toss in 1/2 cup cooked seafood, shredded chicken or duck.

1/4 cup rice vinegar

2 tablespoons safflower oil

2 teaspoons light soy sauce (*usukuchi shoyu*)

2 teaspoons grated gingerroot

1 teaspoon sugar

2 teaspoons toasted sesame seeds

Salt and ground black pepper, to taste

1/2 pound green-tea noodles or other favorite soba

1 cup fresh sugar snap peas, blanched 5 seconds and chilled in iced water

1 small red bell pepper, cut into matchstick strips

1/4 cup thinly sliced green onions

2 to 3 tablespoons shredded shiso leaves, mint leaves or cilantro leaves

1 sheet nori, cut into matchstick strips

◙ To prepare dressing, whisk together vinegar, oil, soy sauce, gingerroot, sugar and sesame seeds in a medium-size bowl. Add salt and pepper. Set aside.

◙ Bring 2 quarts water to boil in a large pot; add noodles. When the water returns to a boil, add 1 cup cold water. When water boils again, add another cup cold water. When water boils a third time, test noodles. They should be tender yet slightly firm to the bite. Cook 1 to 2 minutes longer if necessary. Rinse under cool water; drain well. Place noodles into a large bowl. Add peas, bell pepper, green onions and shiso; mix with noodles. Coat noodle mixture with dressing. Garnish with nori.

◙ *Makes 6 servings.*

SOBA SHOP NOODLES
(Kake-soba)

A classic method for serving soba is to pile it in a deep bowl and ladle on the rich hot broth called *kaké-jiru*, "soup for pouring on." During the seventeenth century, soba in tepid broth was a cheap, filling, countrified "fast food" for the lower class.

During the nineteenth century, soba shops began to resemble elegant teahouses, frequented by the upper class, who socialized, drank and ate soba. Skilled soba masters make their soup daily with fresh *dashi* and a portion of aged seasoning base made of shoyu, mirin and sugar. The hot noodle soup isn't seasoned as strongly as the chilled mixture used for dipping. The flavorful soup is equally good with udon.

1 recipe Sea Vegetable & Bonito Stock (page 46), about 4 cups	1 tablespoon sugar
3/4 cup *tamari shoyu* or soy sauce	1 pound dried soba or 1 1/4 pounds fresh noodles
3 tablespoons mirin	4 thin green onions, finely sliced
	2 tablespoons grated gingerroot

◙ Prepare stock; combine with shoyu, mirin and sugar over medium heat. Simmer 1 to 2 minutes or until sugar dissolves. Reduce heat; keep soup warm.

◙ Bring at least 4 quarts water to a boil in a large pot; add soba. When the water returns to a boil, add 1 cup cold water. When water boils again, add another cup cold water. When water boils a third time, test soba. They should be tender yet firm to the bite. Cook 1 to 2 minutes longer if necessary. Drain soba; reserve cooking water if desired. Rinse soba under cool water. Reheat by dipping into hot water. Divide among 4 or *5 domburi* or large deep bowls. Pour 1 cup hot soup into each bowl. Garnish with onion and gingerroot. Soba will soften further; eat at once.

◙ *Makes 4 or 5 servings.*

SOBA IN A BAMBOO BASKET

(Zaru Soba)

The tradition of eating soba in a basket reaches back to a time when pure buckwheat flour noodles wouldn't hold together when boiled. Noodle makers steamed and served soba in bamboo baskets. The unique serving custom has been retained. *Tsuké-jiru,* or dipping broth, is made with ample dark soy sauce and complements the rustic, whole-grain, *yabu*-style soba, favored in the soba capital, Tokyo. Toasted sesame seeds, walnuts or poppy seeds could be used in place of, or in addition to, *nori.* To toast the *nori,* pass the shiny side two or three times over the flame of a gas stove or electric burner on high heat.

1/2 recipe Sea Vegetable & Bonito
    Stock (page 46), about 2 cups
1/2 cup tamari shoyu or soy sauce
3 tablespoons mirin
1 tablespoon sugar
1 pound dried soba or 1 1/4
    pounds fresh soba

1 sheet toasted *nori,* in
    matchstick shreds
1 tablespoon Wasabi (page 237)
4 thin green onions, thinly sliced
1/4 cup grated daikon radish

◉ Prepare stock; combine with shoyu, mirin and sugar in a saucepan over medium heat. Simmer 2 minutes or until sugar dissolves. Remove from heat; cool to room temperature. Refrigerate until serving time or up to 24 hours, then use as a dipping sauce.

◉ Bring at least 4 quarts water to boil in a large pot; add noodles. When the water boils, add 1 cup cold water. When water boils again, add another cup cold water. When water boils a third time, test noodles. They should be tender yet slightly firm to the bite. Cook 1 to 2 minutes longer if necessary. Rinse under cool water; drain well. Divide noodles among 4 or 5 bamboo, lacquer or pottery plates. Garnish with nori. Pour dipping sauce into 4 or 5 *choko* or small deep bowls. Arrange Wasabi, onion and radish on a serving dish. At the table, mix small amounts of each into sauce. Lift small portions of noodles with chopsticks and dip into sauce before eating.

◉ *Makes 4 or 5 servings.*

FOX NOODLES
(Kitsuné-udon)

At the Inari Shrine in Kyoto, hundreds of stone foxes stand guard wearing colorful bibs. They are on the lookout to sneak a bite of their favorite tofu snack, *abura-agé*. You can susbstitute soba to make *kitsuné-soba,* a similar version of this dish. When you enjoy your next bowl of udon and broth, try one or two of these toppings: sliced mushrooms, sliced bamboo shoots, grilled pieces of *mochi,* fried tofu or chunks of cooked chicken or seafood.

Seasoned Abura-agé (see below)
1 1/2 recipes Sea Vegetable &
    Bonito Stock (page 46)
    (about 6 cups)
3/4 cup *tamari shoyu* or soy sauce
3 tablespoons mirin
1 tablespoon sugar
1/2 pound dried udon or *kishimen*
    or 1 recipe Nama Udon
    (page 188)
About 3/4 cup small fresh
    spinach leaves, rinsed
8 thin slices pinwheel fish loaf
    (*narutomaki*) or 1 cup crab
    surimi

2 green onions, thinly sliced
Red pickled ginger shreds
    (*beni shōga*)

SEASONED ABURA-AGÈ
8 to 10 pieces *abura-agé*
    (tofu puffs)
1 1/2 cups Sea Vegetable &
    Bonito Stock (from the above)
1/4 cup sugar
2 tablespoons light soy sauce
    (*usukuchi shoyu*)
1 tablespoon mirin

◉ Prepare Seasoned Abura-agé using 1 1/2 cups of the 6 cups stock. In a large pot, combine remaining 4 1/2 cups stock, shoyu, mirin and sugar over medium heat. Simmer 1 to 2 minutes or until sugar dissolves. Reduce heat; keep warm.

◉ Bring 4 quarts water to boil in a large pot; add udon. When the water returns to a boil, add 1 cup cold water. When water boils again, add another cup cold water. When water boils a third time, cook 4 to 5 minutes or until tender yet firm to the bite. Drain udon. Rinse to remove starch; drain well. Divide among 4 *domburi* or deep bowls. Divide *abura-agé,* spinach and fish loaf among the bowls. To each, add 1 cup hot broth. Garnish with onion and gingerroot. Serve at once.

◉ *Makes 4 servings.*

SEASONED ABURA-AGÉ

◉ Bring a large pot of water to a boil. Add *abura-agé* and cook 15 seconds to remove oil. Use a drop lid to hold under water or press with a wooden spoon. Drain and cool. Press out excess water. Bring remaining ingredients to a boil. Add *abura-agé;* reduce heat. Simmer 12 to 15 minutes, using a drop lid, until liquid is reduced by half. Cool *abura-agé;* cut into triangles.

FRIED NOODLES
(Yaki-soba)

Yaki-soba is popular throughout Japan. It isn't made with soba at all, but with a thin
noodle similar to ramen. Meat, fish and vegetables are fried together Chinese-style in
a large pan or on a grill. On Okinawa, I've eaten it with pork and vegetables, and in
Nagoya, with squid and octopus tentacles. My version includes fish cake tempura,
popular in Kyushu. You can substitute shrimp, ham, beef, pork or chicken.
For a satisfying meal, serve with a platter of Pan-Fried Pork &
Cabbage Dumplings (page 98).

2 to 3 medium-size dried shiitake
    mushrooms
8 ounces fresh ramen, 1 recipe
    Chinese Egg Noodles
    (page 190) or 6 ounces
    dried noodles
3 tablespoons vegetable oil
2 pieces Fish Cake Tempura
    (page 158)
1 small to medium-size onion,
    chopped

2 teaspoons minced gingerroot
2 cups coarsely chopped green
    cabbage leaves
1 tablespoon mirin
2 to 3 teaspoons soy sauce
2 to 3 dashes ground *sansho*
    pepper or black pepper
2 green onions, minced
Salt to taste

◉ Soak mushrooms in a bowl of warm water 30 minutes. Squeeze dry; cut off stems.
Slice mushrooms thinly. Bring 3 quarts water to a boil in a large pot; add ramen. Cook
1 to 2 minutes or until tender yet firm to the bite. Rinse ramen quickly; drain well. Toss
with 1 tablespoon of the oil; set aside.

◉ Cut fish cakes in half, then into thin strips. Heat remaining 2 tablespoons oil in a
wok or large skillet over medium-high heat. Add onion and gingerroot and stir-fry 2
minutes. Add cabbage and mushrooms; stir-fry 3 minutes. Add fish strips. Sprinkle
with mirin. Stir-fry 1 minute more. Add ramen; toss until hot. Season with soy sauce,
pepper, onions and salt.

◉ *Makes 2 or 3 servings.*

LU CHU POT ROAST NOODLES

Lu Chu is the Old Chinese name for the Ryukyu Islands, an island chain south of Kyūshū. Once under Chinese rule, the islands have a rich culture apart from their Japanese heritage. They produce some of the finest textiles and lacquer in the world. The Okinawans love pork and noodles. This hearty braised dish is served like Japanese *domburi*, or a "meal in a bowl." *Konbu* is a natural, healthful source of amino acids and will enrich the flavor of the delicious sauce.

1 tablespoon vegetable oil
1 (3 1/2- to 4-lb.) boneless pork
    shoulder roast, tied
2 green onions, cut in half
1 (1/4-inch-thick) slice gingerroot,
    crushed
2 large garlic cloves, crushed
6 cups Chicken Stock with
    Ginger (page 51)
1 (5-inch-square) piece *dashi
    konbu* (kelp), lightly wiped

1/4 cup red miso or *hatcho-miso*
    paste
2 to 4 tablespoons dark soy
    sauce
1/2 pound fresh ramen, 1 recipe
    Chinese Egg Noodles
    (page 190) or 6 ounces
    Chūka-soba
1/2 pound fresh young spinach
    leaves, rinsed

◉ Heat oil in a Dutch oven; add pork and cook until browned, turning. Add onions, gingerroot and garlic; cook 1 minute. Add stock; bring to a boil. Reduce heat. Add *konbu*; simmer 5 minutes. Remove from stock. With kitchen scissors, cut *konbu* into 5 strips. Knot each piece; drop back into stock.

◉ Partially cover and simmer 1 1/2 to 2 hours or until pork is tender. Stir in miso and soy sauce; simmer 5 minutes. Remove pork; cut off strings. Slice pork into small chunks.

◉ Bring 4 quarts water to a boil in a large pot; add ramen. Cook 1 to 2 minutes or until tender yet firm to the bite. Rinse ramen quickly; drain well. Divide among 4 deep serving bowls. Spoon pork, spinach and cooking liquid over ramen. Serve at once.

◉ *Makes 4 or 5 servings.*

Fresh Udon
(Nama Udon)

Té-uchi udon, or handmade noodles, are a substantial wheat noodle. The simple flavor of the thick, white, chewy noodle is a Japanese favorite. You might be able to find a special udon flour (*té-uchi udon senyo komugiko*) from a Japanese market. It is a blend of unbleached white flours. Knead the dough a minimum of 10 minutes to achieve the special texture. In Japan, the stiff dough is traditionally kneaded by foot!

The version given here is not completely handmade, but takes advantage of laborsaving devices such as the food processor and pasta machine. The noodles differ slightly from 100 percent handmade, but are delicious nonetheless. Serve noodles in soup, with dipping sauce or in one-pot dishes.

2 cups unbleached all-purpose flour	1/2 cup water
2 teaspoons salt	

◉ Place flour in a food processor fitted with a steel blade. In a small bowl, dissolve salt in water. Add to flour. Process until dough forms a ball; continue processing 30 seconds. Turn out dough on a flour-dusted surface; knead 8 to 10 minutes. Divide dough in half. Cover with a bowl; let rest 2 hours.

◉ Press 1/2 the dough into a flat oval shape. Pass through the widest roller setting of a pasta machine (number 1). Fold ends of dough to meet. Feed through roller, beginning at an unfolded side. Repeat rolling and folding process 2 times. Turn the notch on the pasta machine to the next setting (number 2). Feed dough through roller, unfolded. Continue process, changing the notch each time to narrow the roller setting. The final roll should be on the second to the last setting (number 5) for a noodle sheet 1/8 inch thick. Roll remaining dough.

◉ Dry dough sheets 10 minutes. Dust lightly with flour. Feed through the wide cutting blade to form a wide noodle, about 1/4 inch wide. (For thinner round noodles use the thin cutting blade.) Dust with flour.

◉ In a large pot, bring 4 quarts water to a rolling boil; add noodles. Stir noodles; bring to a boil. Pour in 1 cup cold water. Bring back to a boil; add another cup cold water. Continue cooking 6 to 8 minutes or until noodles are tender yet slightly firm to the bite. Drain well; rinse under cool water. If noodles cooked ahead need reheating, place in a large strainer and dip into a large pot of boiling water. Refrigerate uncooked noodles up to 3 days, or store in the freezer.

◉ *Makes about 10 ounces noodles.*

VARIATION

HAND-CUT UDON

◉ Prepare dough as directed above. Dust dough pieces with flour. With a long thin rolling pin, gently roll and stretch each ball into a rectangular shape, about 1/8 inch thick. Turn several times while rolling; dust with flour. Fold dough into 4 layers, accordion-style. Dust sharp knife with flour; cut into strips from 1/8 inch to 3/8 inch wide, depending on personal preference. Lift and shake out noodles; dust again lightly with flour. Cook as directed above.

CHINESE EGG NOODLES

If you can't find fresh ramen or Chinese noodles, try your hand at making the homemade kind. These light-colored, silky noodles are far superior to the dried Chinese noodles. Use when recipes call for ramen, *yaki-soba* or *chūka-soba*.

Double dough for about 1 pound of noodles.

1 1/2 cups all-purpose flour	4 tablespoons water
1/2 teaspoon salt	Cornstarch
1 large egg	1 teaspoon vegetable oil

◉ In a food processor fitted with a steel blade, add flour, salt and egg. With the motor running, slowly pour in water as needed, processing until dough begins to form into a ball. On a cornstarch-dusted surface, gather dough and knead together 1 minute to form a smooth ball. Divide into 4 pieces. Rub with oil. Cover; let rest 30 minutes.

◉ Roll 1 piece into a flat oval shape. Pass through the widest roller setting of a pasta machine (number 1). Fold ends of dough to meet. Feed through the roller, beginning at the unfolded side. Repeat rolling and folding process 3 times. Turn the notch on the pasta machine to the next setting (number 2). Feed through roller, unfolded. Continue process, changing the notch each time to narrow the roller setting. The final roll should be on the second to the last setting (number 5) for a noodle sheet 1/8 inch thick. (For a very thin noodle, go to number 6.)

◉ Dry dough sheets 10 minutes. Coat with cornstarch. Feed through the narrow cutting blade to form a thin round noodle similar to spaghettini. In a large pot, bring 3 quarts water to a rolling boil; add noodles. Cook about 1 minute or until tender yet firm to the bite. Drain well, rinse under cool water. Drain again. Serve in deep bowls with sauce or broth, or use in fried noodle dishes.

◉ *Makes about 8 ounces noodles.*

VARIATION

CHINESE WATER DOUGH

◉ Prepare the basic recipe, omitting the egg. Increase water to 6 to 8 tablespoons. Prepare as directed above.

RICE

(Gohan)

Rice is the foundation for the existence of the Japanese people given to them by the
Sun Goddess, Amaterasu Omikami, from her love of mankind.

—TSURUSHIRO SATO IN *JINYAKU SHINRAN*

◉

Rice, or *okome,* plays a central role in the lives of the Japanese people. According to archaeological findings, rice may have come to Japan from China around 2,000 years ago. Considered a gift from the gods, rice became the basis of ancient Japan's economy. The wealth of the feudal lord, or *daimyo,* was determined by the yield of his rice acreage each year. Farmers paid land taxes with rice. Today rice is used in the production of foods like saké, mirin, vinegar, miso paste and rice crackers. Even by-products of the rice harvest are useful. Dried rice stalks are stuffed into tatami mats and are used in fertilizers and building construction. Rice straw is used to make traditional raincoats, thatched roofs and ropes.

Gohan, cooked white rice, is the heart and soul of the Japanese cuisine. Rice is regarded with such reverence, the name for cooked rice is synonymous with the word "meal." *"Gohan desu!"* ("Let's eat rice") is a familiar cry at mealtime. If there is no rice, the meal is declared *"nandaka mono tari-nai,"* or incomplete!

In Japan, cooked, short-grain white rice is the table rice of choice. In the United States, Japanese people eat medium- and short-grain white rices, grown primarily in California.

Short- and medium-grain rices contain the protein amylopectin, a starchy substance that causes cohesion. The soft, moist grains have a special flavor and aroma. This kind of rice is perfect for eating with chopsticks.

Before milling was industrialized, only the upper class could afford polished white rice. Farmers ate buckwheat, barley and millet. *Genmai,* or brown rice, has never been popular in Japan. Today it is mostly eaten by practicing macrobiotics. White rice is revered, in part, because of tradition, digestibility and the elegant refinement of its pure white color.

Fresh rice is preferred at every meal in Japan, but leftover rice is put to good use. After breakfast, warm rice is shaped into *Onigiri,* or Rice Balls (page 222), for lunches or afternoon snacks. If *obasan* (grandmother) isn't feeling too well, she might eat a bowlful of the warm rice stew *zosui,* made with leftover rice, stock and vegetables. For lunch, Chinese-style fried rice is a family favorite, utilizing leftover rice. For a satisfying late-night snack, hot tea might be poured over a bowl of rice to make the simple dish *ocha-zuké.* Rice is never wasted; not even *okogé*—the crusty, browned rice that often forms in the bottom of the rice pot. *Okogé* can be added to soups or boiled with a little water in the rice pot to make a tea-like beverage. Chunks of *okogé* can be oven-dried on low heat, then deep-fried, to make a crunchy snack.

Rice at mealtime is usually served unseasoned and unadorned. Occasionally, rice is combined with other grains or red beans. Some cooks add a little barley or millet to the breakfast rice. You might enjoy rice embellished with one of the following: cooked green peas, fine shreds of shiso, edible flower petals or sesame seeds. Finely shredded ginger can be added to the cooking water. An infusion of *sencha* tea or jasmine tea in the cooking water will give the rice an elusive, pleasant flavor.

Rice is considered ceremonial food at festival time. *Mochi gomé,* used to make Steamed Sweet Rice, is another type of short-grain rice even more cohesive than regular short-grain rice. Deliciously sticky, this rice is used for Mochi and Sweet Peanut Mochi. *Mochitsuki,* or "rice-cake making," is an integral part of the New Year's celebration. *Mochi* is displayed at religious ceremonies and offered with prayers for good luck in the new year. Duplicate the traditional New Year's soup, *ozoni,* by adding Grilled Mochi to a rich vegetable soup made with the soup stock *dashi.* Considered a source of strength and vitality, *mochi* is eaten to ensure that one will possess the same qualities in the new year.

Trilling songbird . . .

Croaking frog and buzzing insect

Rice paddy music . . .

in three-part harmony

—Susan Fuller Slack

Preparing Rice

Rinsing Rice

According to the American rice industry, it is not necessary to pre-rinse domestic rice.

Thanks to modern agricultural technology, rice is cleaner and more uniform than ever. Plus, vitamins are added to topical coatings and would be lost during rinsing. However, rinsing is an ancient ritual stemming from a time, not too long ago, when rice wasn't enriched and might be mixed with dust, insects, rice hulls or tiny stones. Long-standing customs have prevailed: Japanese cooks continue to rinse. A quick soak in the cooking water does tenderize the grain. Alternately, rinsed rice can stand in a strainer 1 hour before water is added for cooking. In a country like Japan where individual food flavors stand on their own merit, the clean fresh taste of unseasoned rice is especially appreciated.

Cooking Rice

Cook rice in a solid flat-bottomed pot with a tight-fitting lid. Use the appropriate-size pot to prevent undercooked, burned or mushy rice. For example, a medium (3-quart) saucepan is ideal for cooking 2 cups raw rice. In Japan, the automatic rice cooker has simplified life considerably. The important daily job of preparing cooked rice has been entrusted to this marvelous machine. It produces perfectly cooked rice every time. After the rice is cooked, a thermostatic control turns the heat unit off. A new high-tech, state-of-the-art rice cooker by Zojirushi features a built-in computer that continually monitors the cooking time, temperature, removal of excess moisture and proper texture. Cooking options include settings for firmer rice, softer rice porridge and glutinous rice. A digital timer allows presetting the cooking time up to 13 hours in advance. Other brands have models that keep rice warm for hours as well as the time-delay cooking feature so that fresh, hot rice will be ready for breakfast.

BASIC COOKED RICE

(Gohan)

Japan is sometimes called *mizuho-no-kuni*, "land of the ripe rice ears." Rice has always been prepared in the same respectful way. The daily ritual of rice-rinsing is a prelude to meal preparation.

The water measurements given here are for California-grown medium- or short-grain, storage-crop rice, available January to late September. By midsummer, the rice may require 2 to 3 more tablespoons of water during cooking. For new-crop rice, available October through December, reduce the suggested water amounts by 2 to 3 tablespoons.

2 cups short- or medium-grain rice	2 1/3 cups bottled spring water or tap water

◉ Place rice in a large bowl in the sink. Add a large amount of cool water. Swish your hand through the water. Pour off milky water, or reserve for cooking vegetables. Add fresh water; repeat the process until the water is fairly clear. Drain rice in a mesh strainer; tap gently to remove liquid. Inspect rice for impurities; most domestic brands have few or none.

◉ In a 3-quart saucepan, combine rice with the water; soak 15 minutes. Bring to a rolling boil. Reduce heat to low. Cover saucepan with a tight-fitting lid. Simmer 15 minutes or until liquid is absorbed. Remove from heat. Let rice stand, covered and undisturbed, 15 minutes. Gently fluff cooked rice with a damp rice paddle or spatula. Remove, as needed, to a Japanese rice serving tub or other serving bowl. Before adding the lid, cover remaining rice with a cloth towel to prevent condensation from falling into the pot, making the rice too moist.

◉ *Makes about 3 1/2 cups.*

VARIATION

◉ To cook 1 cup rinsed rice, use 1 1/4 cups water. Smaller amounts are too difficult to cook.

STEAMED SWEET RICE

(Mochi Gomé)

The pearly oval grains of this short-grain rice cook into a rich, sticky rice, excellent for *mochi*, steamed rice dishes, puddings and traditional Japanese sweets.

This rice is always prepared by steaming.

1 1/2 cups sweet glutinous rice (*mochi gomé*)	Water as needed

◙ Place rice in a medium-size bowl. Rinse thoroughly in cool water, rubbing grains gently between your hands. Pour off milky water; add fresh water. Continue rinsing until water is clear. Drain rice and return to bowl; add 3 cups water. Soak 6 hours or overnight. Drain well. Spread rice evenly in a round, 8- or 9-inch, shallow baking pan. Add 1/3 cup water. In a wok, bring about 4 cups water to a boil over medium-high heat. Place a steamer tray in wok. Cover pan of rice and place on tray over boiling water. Steam 30 minutes. If rice is not tender, sprinkle with 2 or 3 tablespoons water; steam 5 minutes more. When tender, remove steamer tray from wok.

◙ *Makes about 3 cups.*

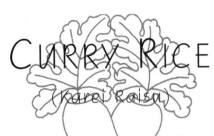

CURRY RICE
(Karei Raisu)

Curry was introduced to Japan from England. In Oriental markets, you can purchase dark Japanese curry paste in the shape of oversize chocolate bars. Resembling a chunky stew, Japanese curry is poured over rice on a plate and eaten with a spoon. It is also delicious ladled into a bowl of *kishimen* or ramen noodles.

Curry is always accompanied by tiny pickled onions (*rakkyō*), pickled red ginger (*beni shōga*) and *fuku-jin-zuké*, a seven-pickle blend named after the seven gods of good fortune.

2 tablespoons butter
1 tablespoon vegetable oil
1 pound boneless lean pork, cut into 1/2-inch cubes
1 large onion, diced
2 carrots, cut into chunks
1 small green or red bell pepper, cubed
4 cups Chicken Stock with Ginger (page 51)

1 1/2 to 2 tablespoons Japanese curry powder
1 medium-size potato, peeled and cubed
Salt and ground black pepper to taste
1/2 cup half-and-half
3 tablespoons potato starch or cornstarch

◉ Heat 1 tablespoon of the butter and oil in a large saucepan over medium-high heat. Add pork and cook until browned, stirring occasionally. Add onion, carrots and bell pepper; cook 3 minutes, stirring often. Add stock. When stock boils, reduce heat to low. Cover pan; simmer 35 minutes or until meat is tender.

◉ In a small pan, heat remaining 1 tablespoon butter; add curry powder and cook 30 seconds. Add to pork mixture. Rinse pan with 2 or 3 tablespoons water; pour into stew. Add potatoes; cook 10 minutes or until tender. Season to taste. Blend half-and-half with starch. Increase heat to boil stew. Add starch mixture; cook, stirring constantly, 1 minute or until thickened. Serve over rice with condiments on the side.

◉ *Makes 4 or 5 servings.*

GENMAI
(Brown Rice)

The old Japanese proverb "Ears of rice bow deeply as they ripen" was a word of counsel to the elite samurai class to display a demeanor of humility like the mature rice stalks of autumn, bent low from the weight of their heavy ears. Japan's cultural preference has long been for polished white rice. The bran is fed to animals or used for pickling vegetables. Nutty-tasting brown rice, sometimes preferred by the ill or the elderly, is slightly more nutritious than enriched white rice. It has more fiber and is rich in vitamin E and magnesium. However, enriched white rice is higher in iron and thiamin, necessary for the prevention of beriberi.

1 cup short- or medium-grain brown rice	2 1/2 cups water

◉ Rinse rice in a large bowl until the water is clear. Drain well in a fine strainer. Place rice and the water in a medium-size saucepan over medium-high heat. Bring to a rolling boil. Reduce heat to low. Cover saucepan with a tight-fitting lid. Simmer 45 to 50 minutes. Remove from heat.

◉ Let rice stand, covered and undisturbed, 15 minutes. Gently fluff rice with a damp rice paddle or spatula. Remove as needed to a serving bowl. Before adding the lid, place a cloth towel over the remaining rice to prevent condensation from making the rice too moist.

◉ *Makes 3 to 4 cups.*

AUTUMN CHESTNUT RICE

(Kuri Gohan)

Typhoons and red dragonflies are harbingers of Japanese autumn. So are burnished red maple leaves and *shinmai,* the first rice of the season. Celebrate the majesty of fall and serve this bountiful rice dish, with chestnuts, sweet potato and shiitake mushrooms.

2 medium-size dried shiitake mushrooms	1 small sweet potato, peeled and diced
2 cups rinsed short- or medium-grain rice, preferably *shinmai*	1 teaspoon salt
	2 tablespoons light soy sauce (*usukuchi shoyu*)
2 1/3 cups water (use 3 tablespoons less water if using *shinmai*)	2 tablespoons mirin
	1 tablespoon toasted sesame seeds
1 (7-oz.) jar chestnuts in heavy syrup, drained	Radish sprouts (*kaiwari daikon*) (optional)

◉ Soak mushrooms in a bowl of warm water 30 minutes. Squeeze dry; cut off stems. Dice mushrooms. In a 3-quart saucepan, combine rinsed rice and water; soak 15 minutes. Rinse chestnuts to remove syrup. Drain well; cut into quarters. Add mushrooms, chestnuts, sweet potato, salt, soy sauce and mirin to saucepan with rice; stir. Bring to a boil. Reduce heat to low. Cover saucepan with a tight-fitting lid. Simmer 15 minutes. Remove from heat.

◉ Let stand, covered and undisturbed, 10 minutes. Carefully break up rice mixture with a dampened wooden rice paddle or spatula. Spoon rice mixture into serving bowls. Sprinkle with sesame seeds and radish sprouts.

◉ *Makes 3 or 4 servings.*

◉ For a special occasion, cut the sweet potato in 1/4-inch slices, then make ginkgo leaves, maple leaves or fall flower shapes with small Japanese vegetable cutters. Simmer in a little *dashi*, separately from the rice; gently toss "leaves" or "flowers" with the cooked rice. If you don't have these cutters, use small metal canapé or sugar paste leaf cutters.

RICE WITH GREEN TEA & PICKLES

(Tsukémono Ocha-zuké)

Ocha-zuké, hot tea poured over rice, is the quintessential Japanese comfort food. Here it is seasoned with tasty pickles. *Ocha-zuké* is a favorite late-night snack or quick pick-me-up. Japan offers such a wealth of pickle varieties that there are restaurants that serve nothing but endless variations of *ocha-zuké*. Small pieces of grilled, salted fish are also a satisfying addition.

2 to 3 cups Basic Cooked Rice
   (page 194)
2 to 3 cups hot green tea
3 to 4 tablespoons Japanese pickles,
   chopped into small pieces

1 sheet nori, toasted and
   shredded

◉ Prepare rice or use leftover rice, preferably warm. Divide rice among 3 or 4 rice bowls. Pour tea over rice. Divide pickles over rice; garnish with nori. Serve at once with chopsticks.

◉ *Makes 3 or 4 servings.*

CELEBRATION RICE
(sekihan)

"Let's have *sekihan*!" This means there's a celebration in the air. *Azuki* beans stain the rice a reddish color, representing felicity and happy occasions. *Sekihan* is traditionally served on birthdays or at other festive celebrations. I first tasted this dish at Petit Pois, a charming little French restaurant in Hakoné. It was served in a beautiful black lacquer box in honor of our visit. Begin this dish 2 or 3 days in advance. It can be reheated in a steamer or microwave.

1/3 cup *azuki* beans or other
   small dried red beans, rinsed
2 cups sweet rice (*mochi gomé*),
   well rinsed and drained
1 (7-oz.) jar chestnuts in syrup
   (optional), drained and halved

2 teaspoons black toasted sesame
   seeds mixed with 1 teaspoon
   sea salt
Fresh kinomé leaves or
   watercress leaves

◉ In a medium-size saucepan, combine beans with about 3 1/2 cups water; bring to a boil. Reduce heat to low; simmer 45 minutes to 1 hour or until beans are soft yet not completely cooked. Cool. Drain bean liquid into a medium-size bowl. Place cooked beans in a small bowl with a few teaspoons water; cover and refrigerate overnight.

◉ Stir rice into bean liquid. Add more water if necessary, to cover rice. Soak in the refrigerator overnight. Drain, reserving soaking liquid. In a wok or deep pot, bring 4 cups water to a boil. Spread a piece of dampened unbleached muslin or several layers of cheesecloth over a steamer tray. Combine rice and beans; spread over dampened cloth. With your finger, poke holes in rice mixture. Sprinkle with reserved soaking liquid. Cover tray; place over boiling water. Steam 45 minutes or until beans are tender. Do not overcook or beans will split. Sprinkle additional soaking liquid over mixture every 15 minutes. During last 10 minutes, add chestnuts. Spoon mixture into a serving dish. Sprinkle with 1 teaspoon sesame-salt mixture. Garnish with kinomé leaves. Pass remaining sesame salt.

◉ *Makes 6 to 8 servings.*

SWEET CHEWY RICE CAKES
(Omochi)

Mochi is the quintessential Japanese food. One of winter's most pleasurable sounds is the cadence of the *mochi* maker's mallet as he pounds rice to make New Year's *mochi*. If fresh *mochi* isn't available, try this simplified version. It captures the essence of this satisfying snack.

1 cup sweet glutinous-rice flour (*mochiko*)	1 tablespoon sugar
	1/2 cup water
1/4 teaspoon salt	Potato starch or cornstarch

◉ In a medium-size bowl, combine rice flour, salt and sugar. Stir in the water to form a soft dough. Lightly knead 30 seconds. In a wok or deep pot, bring 4 cups water to a boil. Spread a piece of dampened unbleached muslin or several layers of cheesecloth over a steamer tray. Spread dough evenly over cloth, about 1/2 inch thick. Cover tray; place over boiling water. Steam 20 minutes.

◉ Remove tray from pan. Lift out cloth with dough. Pull cloth away from dough, letting dough fall onto a flat surface dusted with potato starch or cornstarch. Cool 2 minutes. Knead 1 minute or until smooth and shiny. Roll dough into an 8-inch-long sausage roll. Cut into 8 equal pieces. Dust lightly with potato starch or cornstarch to prevent sticking. Form into smooth round shapes. Cakes will flatten on the bottom when placed on a flat surface. Serve the same day while fresh. Well wrapped, *mochi* keeps 2 days; freeze several months.

◉ *Makes 8 rice cakes.*

VARIATIONS

GRILLED MOCHI

◉ Place *mochi* on a baking sheet; cook under a broiler several minutes until puffy and golden on both sides, turning frequently.

DEEP-FRIED MOCHI

◙ Cut leftover *mochi* into small pieces. Heat vegetable oil to 360F (180C). Deep-fry until crisp. Serve with soy sauce or add to soups.

BOILED MOCHI

◙ Simmer hard, leftover *mochi* in broth 1 minute to soften.

PAN-FRIED MOCHI

◙ Place *mochi* in a dry skillet over medium-low heat. Turn frequently until golden brown on both sides. Brush with soy sauce.

JASMINE TEA RICE WITH SHIMEJI MUSHROOMS

(Shimeji Gohan)

This dish is classified as *mazé-gohan*: cooked rice mixed with other ingredients. The rice is infused with the essence of jasmine tea, then embellished with sautéed tree oyster mushrooms. Try other mushrooms such as shiitake, chanterelles or *enokidaké*. This dish is a delicious companion to Beef & Onion Rolls (page 125).

1 1/4 cups water
1 tablespoon loose-leaf jasmine tea
1 cup rinsed short- or
    medium-grain rice, drained
8 ounces tree oyster mushrooms
    (*shimejitaké*), ends trimmed,
    separated

1 tablespoon vegetable oil
2 green onions, minced
1 teaspoon light soy sauce
    (*usukuchi shoyu*)
1/4 teaspoon salt
1 tablespoon toasted sesame
    seeds

◙ Bring water to a boil in a 2-quart saucepan. Remove from heat; add tea. Steep 1 minute for a delicate infusion. Strain into a bowl; discard tea leaves. Return tea water to saucepan. Cool, then add rice. Soak 20 minutes. Bring water and rice to a boil. Reduce heat to low. Cover pan with a tight-fitting lid. Simmer 15 minutes. Turn off heat. Let stand, covered and undisturbed, 15 minutes. Keep warm.

◙ Briefly rinse mushrooms under cool water. Gently press out water; pat dry on paper towels. In a large skillet, heat oil over high heat. Stir-fry mushrooms and green onions 1 to 2 minutes. Remove from heat. Stir in soy sauce and salt. Lightly toss mushroom mixture with warm rice. Serve in small bowls. Sprinkle with sesame seeds.

◙ *Makes 3 to 4 servings.*

SWEET PEANUT MOCHI

(Rakkase No Mochi)

If you find plain *mochi* too bland, try this honey-coated version. Roasted soybean powder has a wonderfully nutty flavor and aroma. If unavailable, substitute finely ground roasted pecans or walnuts.

1 cup sweet glutinous-rice flour
   (*mochiko*)
1/4 teaspoon salt
1/4 cup packed light brown sugar
1/3 cup unsalted cocktail peanuts
1/2 cup water

Potato starch or cornstarch
Orange blossom honey, rice
   syrup or molasses
1/2 cup roasted soybean powder
   (*kinako*) (optional)

◙ In a medium-size bowl, combine rice flour, salt and brown sugar. In a blender or food processor fitted with a steel blade, grind peanuts until they form a paste. Add the water; process until blended, scraping sides of container once or twice. Pour peanut mixture into rice-flour mixture. Stir to form a stiff dough. Lightly knead dough about 30 seconds.

◙ Steam and shape dough as directed in the recipe for Sweet Chewy Rice Cakes (page 201). Drizzle shaped rice cakes with honey. Roll in soybean powder. Serve each guest 1 piece *mochi* on a small plate with a cup of hot green tea.

◙ *Makes 8 rice cakes.*

VARIATION

COCONUT MOCHI

◙ Omit peanuts. Substitute 1/2 cup rich coconut milk for water. Roll honey-coated rice cakes in finely shredded coconut.

FLOWER PETAL CUISINE

From ancient times, Asian cooks have scented foods and teas with flower petals. In Japan, cherry blossoms are picked in the spring, then salt-pickled in huge crocks. They are used for cherry blossom soup, a treat served during the Doll Festival. *Sakura-yu* is tea made from the salted blossoms and served at weddings and special occasions. Two entwined blossoms unfold as they steep in a cup of boiling water, symbolizing family unity and happiness for the new couple. The salted blossoms are used to garnish rice balls and are tossed with hot rice. The famous confectionery shop Kimuraya tucks preserved blossoms inside baked buns stuffed with bean paste.

The perennial garland chrysanthemum, *shinguku,* blooms in the fall. It is eaten in sukiyaki and tempura. In Western markets, the leaves are sometimes called "chop suey greens." Japanese cooks like to "capture the season" and preserve the mild-tasting yellow flowers. They are blanched in salted water, then put up in jars of sweet vinegar dressing. The fresh petals are added to rice and other dishes.

When adding flowers to foods, take care to avoid poisonous ones. If in doubt, check with a horticulture society, perhaps one affiliated with a local university. Do not use flowers from the florist or nurseries that are sprayed with pesticides. Edible flowers may be available in larger markets and specialty shops. Check Asian shops and natural-food stores. Your best source for flowers is in your own backyard. Refer to the mail-order section (page 269) for a potpourri of edible flower seeds.

Select bright-colored flower heads in full bloom. Mist the flowers to remove dust and insects. Blot dry; refrigerate in an airtight bag. Gently tear off petals; mix into cooked rice, salads, soups or sweets. Whole, perfect blossoms may be used.

Experiment with plum blossoms, orange blossoms, marigold leaves, nasturtiums, garden pea blossoms (not sweet peas), violets and daylilies. All parts of the daylily plant are edible.

RICE & BEAN SPROUTS WITH SESAME SEEDS
(Moyashi Gohan)

Korean food is popular in Japan; both cultures enjoy similar foods. The common denominator of the cuisines is a bowl filled with cooked white rice. In this recipe, shared by a Korean friend who lives in Japan, the rice is embellished with sprouts and sesame seeds. It becomes a quick, satisfying meal with a side dish of Korean Winter Kim Chee (page 234).

1 cup rinsed short- or
    medium-grain rice
1 1/3 cups water
1 tablespoon vegetable oil
1 large garlic clove, finely
    minced
2 green onions, finely minced

1 tablespoon finely minced
    gingerroot
1 cup fresh bean sprouts
1 teaspoon medium soy sauce
1 teaspoon salt, or to taste
2 tablespoons toasted sesame
    seeds

◉ Place rice and water in a 2-quart saucepan. Soak 15 minutes. In a small skillet, heat oil over medium-high heat. Stir-fry garlic, green onions and gingerroot 15 seconds; add bean sprouts. Cook 30 seconds or just long enough to coat bean sprouts in oil. Add mixture to rice and water. Stir in soy sauce and salt. Bring to a boil over high heat. Reduce heat to a low simmer; cover pan and cook 15 minutes.

◉ Remove pan from heat; allow rice to sit covered and undisturbed for 15 minutes. Remove lid; fluff rice with a dampened rice paddle or spatula. Spoon rice into bowls; sprinkle with sesame seeds. Recipe can be doubled; increase water by 1 cup.

◉ *Makes 2 or 3 servings.*

KADENA COUNTRY CASSEROLE

In any country, casserole dishes are popular family fare. I was given this hearty dish from a Chinese friend who lived in Kadena-cho, on the island of Okinawa. It's an interesting blend of the two cuisines. Great for making ahead, this casserole tastes even better the next day.

4 medium-size dried shiitake
    mushrooms
2 tablespoons saké
1/4 cup light soy sauce
    (*usukuchi shoyu*)
1 1/2 cups chicken broth,
    more if needed
3 tablespoons vegetable oil
1 medium-size onion, chopped
1 tablespoon finely minced
    gingerroot
2 large garlic cloves, finely
    minced

1/2 pound lean ground pork
    or beef
2 cups coarsely chopped tender
    cabbage leaves
1 medium-size carrot, shredded
1/4 lb. fresh young green beans,
    trimmed and slivered
1 1/2 cups medium- or
    long-grain rice
1/2 teaspoon black pepper
1 medium-size zucchini, shredded
3 green onions, minced
Salt to taste

◉ Soak mushrooms in a bowl of warm water 30 minutes. Squeeze dry; cut off stems. Mince mushrooms. Reserve 1/4 cup soaking liquid; add to a bowl with saké, soy sauce and chicken broth. In a wok or electric skillet, heat oil over medium-high heat. When the oil is hot, add onion, gingerroot and garlic. Stir-fry 30 seconds; add pork. Cook pork, stirring, until browned; mix in cabbage, carrot, green beans and mushrooms. Cook 2 or 3 minutes. Stir in rice. Add pepper. Pour in broth mixture. Cover pan tightly. Reduce heat; simmer 20 minutes or until rice is almost done. If needed, add a little more mushroom liquid or broth. Stir in zucchini; cook 5 minutes more or until rice is dry and tender. Stir in green onions; add salt to taste.

◉ *Makes 6 servings.*

BENTŌ

In America, the box lunch means all too often a disposable carton of fast food such as fried chicken or cheeseburgers and fries. The Japanese obentō or bentō gives the term "box lunch" entirely new meaning. Packed in attractive compartmentalized containers, the bentō features a generous portion of cooked rice with a variety of side dishes such as seafood, meat, braised vegetables, sweet omelet and pickles. The rice might be molded in fancy shapes or shaped into rice balls. It may be made into sushi or a casserole dish called *kamameshi*—a mixture of rice, meat or seafood, and vegetables. Western and Chinese bentō foods are available, but with a distinct Japanese touch.

Portable bentō are purchased daily at markets, carryout shops, office buildings, roadside stands, temples, restaurants, train stations and even at rest stops on highways. They are eaten at work, school, in the park,

Nara period (710–84). When combined with another character, the word *hako* becomes *bako*, as in *bentō bako*, or box lunch. Japanese bentō boxes, prized for their beauty as well as utilitarian value, are made from a variety of materials such as lacquer, wood and pottery. Even the colorful disposable containers of paper or aluminum are eye-catching and worthy of recycling. Bentō are often wrapped like a treasured gift in colorful paper or fine cloth.

Edo-period nobility (1600–1868) dined on delicacies packed in *jubako*, or tiered, lacquered boxes. Some precious boxes were decorated with mother-of-pearl and pure gold and silver powders (*maki-é*), then sealed with lacquer. Today, lacquer and porcelain *jubako* are packed with exquisite foods and served during the first three days of the new year. Conveniently prepared in advance, the bite-size foods are symbolically arranged in each layer. The first layer might include traditional good-luck foods such as glazed anchovies (tazukuri), herring roe (kazunoko), sweetened black beans and *kamaboko* (steamed fish cake). The second layer contains heartier protein foods such as grilled fish or chicken. The third layer might include light, vinegared tidbits such as pickled vegetables or fish. The New Year's meal is served with *Ozoni* (page 58), a festive soup brimming with vegetables and a rice cake.

The lacquered Makunouchi ("between curtains") bentō was originally served at the kabuki theater during intermission. This type of box is often used in Japanese restaurants in the West. The *sagé jubako* is a beautiful lacquered case fitted with tiered boxes for food plus a compartment for saké.

at the theater or during travel. Always fresh and of the highest quality, bentō lunches must be sold within 3 or 4 hours.

Department-store restaurants often specialize in bentō foods. They are served in handsome lacquered boxes with a bowl of miso soup on the side. Magazines and cookbooks challenge housewives with creative bentō recipes. Japanese mothers spend hours making elaborate, specialized children's bentō to amuse their little ones and whet their appetites. Often resembling art, the delicious Japanese bentō reflects Japan's appreciation of beauty.

The bentō was created from humble origins. Farmers and travelers carried rice balls wrapped in seaweed or sweet potatoes wrapped in a bamboo-shoot sheath for quick sustenance. During the turbulent sixteenth century, feudal warlord Oda Nobunaga issued spartan rations of rice and pickles to his troops. Cease-fires came; the troops have long been gone, but the custom of bentō remains.

Boxes (*hako*) first appeared during the

The "rising-sun box lunch," or *hinomaru bentō*, consists of rice in a single compartment with a single *uméboshi* (pickled plum) in the center. It resembles the Japanese flag.

When cherry blossoms bloom in the spring, picnickers pack up special tiered bentō boxes, or *hanami jyu,* for cherry blossom viewing. The Shokado bentō, a square lacquered box divided into four sections, was named after the humble residence of artist-priest Nakanuma Shojo, who named his home Shokado Shoko, or Pine Blossom Hall.

The pleasures of Japanese train travel are directly linked to the pleasures of eating *ekiben* ("station bentō"), available at railway stations throughout Japan. The first *ekiben* appeared during the Meiji era (1868–1912) and consisted of rice balls (*onigiri*) and pickles wrapped in bamboo. Filled with specialty foods from each region, *ekiben* containers are often highly collectible. Each has its own special character. Over 1,600 varieties are now being sold throughout Japan.

Hiroshima Station sells bentō boxes shaped like a *shamoji* (rice paddle) and filled with rice and fried oysters, the local specialty. *Unagi bentō,* from the castle town of Hamamatsu, features teriyaki-glazed eel and rice packed in a long wooden box. An adorable children's version is available. *Togé-no-kamameshi bentō*, from Gumma Prefecture, offers *kamameshi* (rice cooked with chicken, chestnuts and vegetables) packed in rustic, earthy Mashiko pottery shaped like a caldron. *Saké meshi,* from Fukushima Prefecture, features pickled salmon and rice packed in fish-shaped Seto pottery. Other containers are shaped like fans, baskets, golf balls and tennis rackets. Kids are tempted with con-tainers resembling *kokeshi* dolls or the *daruma* doll, a symbol of good luck.

If you don't own traditional bentō containers, create your own for picnics, luncheons, suppers, cocktail parties or your next road trip. Arrange the foods in pretty, decorated baskets or plain white boxes. Folded pieces of handcrafted *washi* paper (see mail-order section, page 269) or paper lace can serve as lines and dividers. For picnics and special occasions, the boxes can be covered with *washi* paper. Or wrap them Japanese-style in a *furoshiki* made from a square piece of material such as silk crepe or soft cotton, with the corners drawn up and knotted at the top in a makeshift handle. A large bandanna or scarf will work quite well. Copy the Japanese and surprise your family and friends with bentō tied with pretty cords or ribbons. Tuck in a pair of chopsticks and a strip of paper with a handwritten poem in attractive script.

Bentō are a celebration of the seasons. Look through this book and select favorite recipes for creating your own. Many are delicious served at room temperature, which makes them perfect bentō fare.

Bentō Menus

PLUM BLOSSOM PARTY

February plum blossoms, a favorite of Heian-period aristocrats, are the first seasonal marker of spring. Known as *risshun*, or the "establishment of spring," this period is actually a time of gray skies and bitter cold. The tempting menu will remind you that spring is on the way.

Spicy Grilled Beef Sushi

Plum Blossom Pork Rolls*

Kamaboko Butterflies

Pickled Ginger Slices

Somen, Crabmeat & Asparagus with
Sesame Dressing

Plum Wine Jelly

TAILGATE PICNIC

This menu is perfect for tailgating events, especially when the weather becomes cool and the foliage turns from green to burnished red and gold.

Stuffed Tofu Puffs

Ramen with Peanut Miso Sauce

Picnic Box Stuffed Chicken Rolls*

Marinated Radish Mums

Honey Ginger Katsutera

Assorted Fresh Fruits

PEACH BLOSSOM FESTIVAL

Also known as the Doll Festival, this March 3 celebration springs from ancient Chinese origins. Families with daughters decorate their homes with pink peach blossoms and an elaborate doll display called *hina ningyo*. The girls show off their dolls and entertain friends with a special party. The menu might include rice balls molded into flower shapes and clam soup, a symbol of marital happiness.

Pork & Cabbage Dumplings

Kokeshi Doll Sushi

Silken Peach Tofu

Vegetable Flowers with Vinegar Lemon
Dressing*

Sweet Rice Saké

MOON-VIEWING SUPPER

Celebrate the beautiful harvest moon around August or September with a moon-viewing party, or *tsukimi*. Enjoy the evening with poetry readings, stories, delicious autumn fare and a flask of heated saké. A display of rice balls, taro root and silvery pampas grass offers a silent prayer to the moon for a successful harvest.

Savory Miso Soup

Autumn Leaf Tempura

Autumn Chestnut Rice

Deep-Fried Ginger Oysters*

Persimmon & Daikon Salad

Red Bean Macadamia Jelly

SUMMER EVENING BY THE POOL

Fireflies and purple wisteria represent *shoman,* the balmy summer season in Japan which falls around the end of May. Served on bamboo trays, this refreshing menu exudes coolness, the essence of summertime hospitality.

Yakitori

Kansai-Style Scattered Sushi

Grilled Fruit Kebobs with Plum
Wine Sauce

Chilled Summer Tofu
Banana-Orange Tofu Sherbet

WELCOME THE NEW YEAR

Osechi ryōri, or food for the New Year's festivities, is arranged in exquisite lacquer boxes called *jubako.* It is important to serve as many foods as possible that represent symbols of good luck to ensure prosperity in the coming year. The menu always includes sweetened black beans, vegetables simmered in *dashi,* sliced fish cake, Sweet Omelet Roll and fish roe. Add any of these to the menu below.

Savory Miso Soup with Grilled Mochi
Sashimi Roses
Sushi Canapés
Beef & Onion Rolls
Ham & Cheese Pinwheels with Shiso*
Kayoko's Smoked Salmon & Daikon Rolls
Persimmon & Daikon Salad*
Spicy Braised Gobo

*Recipes in this chapter. See index for other dishes.

SWEET OMELET ROLL
(Daté Maki Tamago)

This slightly sweet omelet can be sliced into 1/2-inch strips for rolled sushi or tucked into the bentō as a sweet course. The technique is simple, though it may take some practice to make a perfect roll. A rectangular *tamago* pan is really handy for this dish. If you can't locate one, refer to the mail-order section (page 269). Until you find one, make the roll in a small skillet. Or for a slightly different version, steam the egg mixture 5 to 6 minutes in a glass loaf pan.

4 large eggs
1 tablespoon light soy sauce
   (*usukuchi shoyu*)
1/4 teaspoon salt
1 tablespoon mirin
4 tablespoons Sea Vegetable &
   Bonito Stock (page 46)

1 teaspoon sugar
Vegetable oil
Additional soy sauce (optional)
Finely shredded daikon radish
   (optional)

In a medium-size bowl, lightly whisk eggs. In a small pan, heat 1 tablespoon soy sauce, salt, mirin, stock and sugar just until sugar dissolves. Remove from heat; cool. Blend into eggs. Line a bamboo sushi mat with foil or plastic wrap; set aside.

Heat a well-seasoned, rectangular 6 1/2 x 5-inch *tamago nabé* or small skillet over medium heat. Use a brush or a folded piece of paper towel to wipe pan with oil. Pour 1/4 of egg mixture into hot pan. Cook egg sheet 1 minute or until almost set. Adjust heat if necessary, to prevent browning.

Beginning at back of pan, use a spatula to fold up egg sheet toward you, into a narrow flat roll. Carefully push roll to back of pan. If pan is properly seasoned, roll will slide easily. Wipe front of pan with more oil. Pour in another 1/4 of egg mixture. Lift edge of roll in back of pan so egg mixture can run underneath, forming a layer. Cook egg sheet until almost set. Start rolling the folded egg sheet toward you, enclosing it in the flat egg sheet. Again, push multilayered roll to back of pan. Oil pan and continue, forming 2 more egg-sheet layers around large roll.

When finished, tilt the roll out of pan into lined bamboo sushi mat. Enclose roll securely inside mat; cool in mat 30 minutes. Remove; cut roll into slices. Serve with soy sauce mixed with daikon if desired, or cut into l/2-inch-wide strips to use in rolled sushi.

Makes 4 or 5 servings.

PERSIMMON & DAIKON SALAD

(Kaki To Daikon Namasu)

Fresh persimmons and dried persimmons are featured in this pretty salad. If persimmons are not in season, prepare this New Year's favorite with shredded carrot.

1 firm yet ripe Japanese persimmon or 1 medium-size carrot	1 1/2 tablespoons sugar
1/2 lb. daikon radish, peeled	1 tablespoon mirin
3 to 4 tablespoons slivered dried persimmon or apricots	1/2 teaspoon freshly grated lemon peel
3 tablespoons rice vinegar	1/4 teaspoon salt

◉ Peel persimmon; coarsely shred. Place in a medium-size bowl. Grate daikon into large shreds; gently squeeze out excess liquid. Add to bowl along with dried persimmon. In a small bowl, combine vinegar, sugar, mirin, lemon peel and salt; stir to dissolve sugar. Pour over persimmon mixture; toss well. Cover and refrigerate 30 minutes or until chilled. Using a slotted spoon, lightly press scoops of mixture against side of bowl to remove excess liquid. Spoon into small serving dishes.

◉ *Makes 6 servings.*

PLUM BLOSSOM PORK ROLLS
(Ume Buta Maki)

The sliced ends of the crispy pork rolls present an attractive pinwheel appearance from the circular layers of pork, cherry-pink plum paste and black nori. These delicious pork bites can be served as a first course, a side dish for rice or as a snack with saké or beer. If too salty, soak plums in 2 cups water a few hours before mashing. Ready-made plum paste is available in small jars in Asian markets.

1/4 cup soy sauce
2 tablespoons mirin
2 tablespoons sugar
1 lb. *shabu shabu* pork (pork butt), sliced 1/8 inch thick (about 14 pieces)
12 to 14 small pickled plums (*uméboshi*), halved and pitted
1 large egg, slightly beaten
1/2 cup all-purpose flour

About 2 cups Japanese-style bread crumbs (*panko*)
2 (8 x 7 1/2-inch) sheets nori, cut into 16 (4 x 1 3/4-inch) strips
About 4 cups peanut oil or vegetable oil
Spicy Mustard (page 227) (optional)

◉ In a shallow pan, mix soy sauce, mirin and sugar until sugar dissolves. Add pork slices and marinate 10 minutes. In a small dish, use a fork to mash plums into a paste. Place egg, flour and bread crumbs in separate shallow pans. Remove 1 slice pork from marinade; shake off excess liquid. Place on a flat surface. Spread about 1/2 teaspoon plum paste over pork. Place a nori strip over plum paste. Roll up pork slice, beginning at shortest side; secure with wooden picks. Roll in flour, then dip in beaten egg. Press pork roll into bread crumbs, covering all sides. Set aside. Repeat with remaining pork slices.

◉ In a wok or shallow heavy saucepan, heat oil to 350F (175C). Fry 3 pork rolls at a time, 3 to 4 minutes or until brown and crispy. Turn several times for even browning. If necessary, check cooking time by cutting into a roll to see if pork is done. Drain on a wire rack. Remove picks. Slice rolls diagonally in half, or cut each roll into 4 or 5 pieces for appetizer or snack servings. Serve with mustard.

◉ *Makes 6 servings.*

DEEP-FRIED GINGER OYSTERS
(Kàkì Nò Shōgà Agé)

Oysters are served dozens of ways at the famous floating oyster boat restaurants in Hiroshima. These oysters have a delicate, crispy coating from the special dried Japanese bread crumbs called *panko*. They taste wonderful seasoned with spicy Tonkatsu Sauce (page 157).

24 fresh oysters, shucked, shells
   reserved
2 teaspoons grated gingerroot
2 tablespoons saké
1/2 cup potato starch or
   cornstarch
2 or 3 dashes ground *sansho*
   pepper
2 eggs, slightly beaten
1/3 cup milk

2 cups Japanese-style bread
   crumbs (*panko*)
About 6 cups peanut oil or
   vegetable oil
1 1/2 to 2 cups finely shredded
   cabbage
1 medium-size carrot, shredded
2 large tomatoes, cut into wedges
1 lemon, thinly sliced
Watercress or parsley

◉ Wash and scrub 1/2 of the oyster shells. Rinse well and set aside. Marinate oysters with gingerroot and saké 10 minutes. In a shallow pan, mix potato starch and *sansho* pepper. In a second shallow pan, blend eggs and milk. Place bread crumbs in a third shallow pan.

◉ In a wok or shallow heavy saucepan, heat oil to 365F (185C). Drain oysters. Roll 3 or 4 oysters in potato starch, then dip into egg mixture. Press oysters in bread crumbs until well coated. Fry 3 to 4 minutes or until golden brown and crisp. Turn several times. Drain on paper towels. Prepare remaining oysters. Arrange oysters on reserved half shells. Mound cabbage and carrot in the center of 1 or 2 platters. Arrange oysters around cabbage. Garnish with tomato, lemon and watercress.

◉ *Makes 5 or 6 servings.*

VEGETABLE FLOWERS WITH VINEGAR LEMON DRESSING

(Yasai Sunomono)

Vary the vegetable shapes by cutting them into matchstick strips or shreds.

Vinegar Lemon Dressing
  (see below)
1/2 European cucumber or
  1 small regular cucumber
2 small turnips, thinly sliced
  crosswise
1 large carrot, thinly sliced
  crosswise
2 teaspoons toasted black
  sesame seeds

VINEGAR LEMON
DRESSING
  1/4 cup sugar
  1/2 cup rice vinegar
  1/4 teaspoon sesame oil
  1/4 teaspoon salt
  1 teaspoon grated fresh lemon
    peel

◉ Prepare dressing; set aside. Cut off and discard ends from cucumber. Cut in half lengthwise. Using a small spoon, scrape out seeds. Cut cucumber halves crosswise into 1/4-inch-thick pieces. Place in a medium-size bowl. Using a medium, metal, flower-shaped cutter, cut flower shapes from turnip slices. Place in bowl with cucumber pieces. Blanch carrot slices 1 minute in boiling water; drain. Place in iced water to chill; drain. Using a small cutter, cut carrot slices into flower shapes. Add to vegetables in bowl.

◉ Add dressing; toss to mix. Cover and refrigerate 30 minutes or up to 2 hours. Using a slotted spoon, place vegetables in small serving dishes. Sprinkle with sesame seeds.

◉ *Makes 6 to 8 servings.*

VINEGAR LEMON DRESSING

◉ In a small bowl, combine all ingredients.

RAMEN WITH PEANUT MISO SAUCE
(Hiyashi Chūka No Peanut Miso Aé)

A spicy blend of protein-rich peanut butter and miso paste dresses this tumble of golden noodles. The calcium-rich sea grass *hijiki* adds a sweet, pleasant taste to this dish. Other ingredients that can be added include strips of Seasoned Abura-agé (page 184), sliced shiitake mushrooms, shredded ham or carrots.

Peanut Miso Sauce (opposite)
1/4 cup dried *hijiki* or *aramé*
1/4 packed cup torn, fresh
   cilantro leaves
1 small red bell pepper, cut into
   matchstick strips
4 thin green onions, slivered
2 to 3 tablespoons finely
   chopped unsalted peanuts

3/4 pound fresh Chinese egg
   noodles, 1 recipe Chinese Egg
   Noodles (page 190), 1/2 lb.
   chūka-soba or 1/2 lb. thin
   spaghetti
1 tablespoon vegetable oil

◉ Prepare Peanut Miso Sauce; set aside. Rinse *hijiki;* cover with warm water. Soak 20 minutes. Place in a fine strainer; rinse well under cool water. Press out water. Cut into 1-inch lengths. Place *hijiki,* cilantro, bell pepper, onions and peanuts on a platter.

◉ Bring 4 quarts water to a boil in a large pot; add noodles. Cook 2 minutes or just until tender yet firm to the bite. Rinse under cool water; drain well. Toss with oil. Place noodles in a large bowl. Toss with vegetables. Divide among 5 or 6 large bowls. Garnish with peanuts. At the table, pass the Peanut Miso Sauce.

◉ *Makes 6 servings.*

PEANUT MISO SAUCE

This sauce has a strong Chinese influence. It can be mixed with any favorite cooked
noodle. It is a fine dipping sauce for grilled vegetables, tofu or steak.

2 tablespoons unsalted cocktail
   peanuts
1 (1/8-inch-thick) slice peeled
   gingerroot
2 tablespoons red miso or
   hatcho-miso
2 tablespoons mirin

2 tablespoons sugar
2 dashes ground *sansho* pepper
   or black pepper
2 tablespoons rice vinegar
2 teaspoons soy sauce
1 cup safflower or canola oil
Hot-pepper sauce (optional)

◉ In a blender or food processor fitted with a steel blade, process peanuts and gingerroot to a paste. Add miso, mirin, sugar, pepper, vinegar and soy sauce; process until
blended. With motor running, pour oil through feed tube in a steady stream. Stop processing when blended; sauce will not be thick like mayonnaise. Add hot-pepper sauce,
if desired. Use immediately or refrigerate until needed. If not used at once, whisk before serving to blend ingredients.

◉ *Makes about 2 cups.*

HAM & CHEESE PINWHEELS WITH SHISO

(Chikuwa no Shiso Maki)

Create a pleasing taste combination by rolling ham, cheese and fragrant shiso leaves
in thin sheets of fish cake. If shiso is unavailable, used toasted strips of nori
or even fresh basil leaves.

5 or 6 small hollow fish rolls
(*chikuwa*)
2 (1/8-inch-thick) slices Monterey
Jack or Swiss cheese
2 (1/8-inch-thick) slices cooked
ham

10 or 12 shiso leaves
1 tablespoon Wasabi
(page 237)
Soy sauce

◉ Using a small sharp knife, make a cut from top to bottom on 1 side of each fish roll.
When spread open, each roll will be a rectangle. Cut cheese and ham slices into narrow strips to fit rectangular pieces of fish roll. Place 2 shiso leaves on the inside white
portion of a rectangle. Place a strip of cheese and a strip of ham on top of each. Spread
a small amount of Wasabi over ham layer.

◉ Beginning at short end, roll up layers into a cylinder. Secure with 3 evenly spaced
attractive picks. Repeat with remaining ingredients. Cut each cylinder into 3 pinwheel
slices between wooden picks. Each slice will be secured with a pick. Arrange pinwheel
slices on a serving platter. Serve with soy sauce for dipping.

◉ *Makes 15 to 18 appetizers.*

KAYOKO'S SMOKED SALMON & DAIKON ROLLS

Japanese scholars believe that vinegared raw fish was eaten over 1,000 years ago, the same as it is today. Kayoko Tazoe, a nutritionist from Osaka, prepared these marinated smoked salmon and daikon pinwheels for a New Year's party I attended. Kayoko is a culinary artist, trained in the tea ceremony and flower arranging. She and her husband, an international business executive, temporarily reside in South Carolina.

1 piece daikon radish, about
   2 x by 5 inches
1 teaspoon salt
About 5 ounces smoked salmon,
   sliced paper-thin

1/3 cup rice vinegar
1 tablespoon sugar

◉ Peel radish. With a large sharp knife, cut at least 12 thin strips of radish, no more than 1/8 inch thick. Place strips in a shallow pan; barely cover with water. Add salt. Soak until pliable, about 10 minutes. Drain strips; cover each with a piece of smoked salmon. Carefully roll up radish and salmon into a log. Secure with wooden picks. Mix vinegar and sugar in a shallow dish. Add salmon rolls and marinate in the refrigerator at least 1 hour, up to 2 days. Remove from marinade; cut each roll in half. Pieces can be secured with a pick if necessary.

◉ *Makes 24 pieces.*

RICE BALLS

(onigiri)

The Japanese eat rice balls (*onigiri* or *omusubi*) as often as Americans eat
sandwiches. They are the perfect bentō food and have been eaten in one form or
another for 1,000 years. Rice balls were picnic fare during ancient Imperial Court
outings in Kyoto. They have secured a firm niche among the picnic-style foods served
for children's snacks, train travel (*ekiben*) and all outdoor activities. Making *onigiri*
is a great activity for your kids. I often serve an assortment of rice balls for a
Japanese-style lunch or casual supper in a leaf-lined handmade basket.

Basic Cooked Rice (page 194)

MIXERS
Minced herbs (shiso, parsley, dill)
Toasted sesame seeds
Sesame Salt (page 239)

FILLINGS
A single *uméboshi*
Salted, grilled salmon flakes
Pickled chopped vegetables
Seasoned Shiitake Mushrooms
(page 122), diced

COATINGS
Toasted black or white sesame
seeds
Sesame Salt (page 239)
Ao-noriko (sea vegetable)

WRAPPERS
Nori sheets, cut into 1/4-inch
strips

Fresh shiso leaves
Strips of Egg Crepes (page 23)
Tender small lettuce leaves
Thin slices ham or roast beef
Thin slices smoked salmon

TOPPINGS
Lumpfish caviar
1 large cooked shrimp per
rice ball
Sautéed mushrooms
Salmon-roe caviar (*ikura*)
Finely chopped pickled
vegetables
Shredded shiso
Shredded Egg Crepes
(page 23)

◉ Cook the rice. Prepare Mixers, Fillings, Coatings, Wrappers and Toppings as desired. If you are using one of the Mixers, lightly toss rice with it.

◉ Dip your hands into lightly salted water and measure 1/3 to 1/2 cup rice, depending on the desired size of the ball. Pat rice into a round ball. When you shape plain rice into *onigiri,* you can stuff them with one of the Fillings. Press a small amount of Filling into the center of a rice ball; press rice over the opening to close it. The rice balls can be sprinkled with one of the Coatings if desired. Or slightly flatten the top and spoon on a small amount of Topping. Rice balls can be eaten at once or packed in containers for later. Don't refrigerate; the rice becomes too hard.

◉ *Makes 6 or 7 rice balls.*

VARIATIONS

◉ *Onigiri* can be formed into triangles and cylinders by hand or with wood or plastic rice molds. They can be grilled on an open fire or deep-fried until golden brown. For a delicious flavor, lightly spread rice balls with miso paste before grilling. Children's *onigiri* are often whimsical and appealing. They are crafted into doll heads, robots, sea creatures and animals.

◉ Using deep, metal rice molds with pushers, *onigiri* can be cut into fans, gourds, butterflies, bamboo and flower shapes. Large, deep, metal cookie cutters are a fair substitute. One type of Japanese rice mold has five connecting cavities for shaping rice into cylinders. You can use small custard cups, metal gelatin molds or small decorative cake pans in various shapes and sizes. Dip the molds briefly in cold water before packing them with rice.

Picnic Box Stuffed Chicken Rolls

(Maki Dori)

The recipe for these pretty stuffed chicken slices was given to me by a Japanese diplomat's wife who was an authority on entertaining bentō-style. They are the perfect party fare. Serve them with other picnic foods, tucked into regional American baskets, on pottery or in *washi*-covered boxes.

4 chicken breast halves, skinned, boned and slightly flattened
1 tablespoon saké
1 tablespoon mirin
2 tablespoons light soy sauce (*usukuchi shoyu*)
1 tablespoon ginger juice (see *Graters,* page 257)

4 small green onions
1 large carrot, cut into 4 strips and blanched 1 minute
1/2 red bell pepper, cut into 1/2-inch-wide strips
1 celery stalk, cut into 4 strips
Salt and black pepper to taste

◉ Score chicken breast halves slightly on both sides; place in a large glass baking dish. Sprinkle with saké, mirin, soy sauce and ginger juice. Cover tightly and let stand 1 hour, or cover and refrigerate several hours.

◉ Preheat oven to 350F (175C). Drain chicken. Trim vegetables to width of chicken breasts. Place 1 green onion and 1 strip each of carrot, bell pepper and celery in middle of each chicken breast. Sprinkle with salt and pepper. Roll up chicken, enclosing vegetables. Secure openings with small bamboo skewers. Arrange chicken in a baking pan.

◉ Bake 22 to 25 minutes or until chicken is cooked through. Cool, then cut into 1/2-inch-thick slices, or cover uncut rolls and refrigerate up to 8 hours.

◉ *Makes 10 to 12 servings.*

PICKLES &
CONDIMENTS

(Tsukémono & Yakumi)

Under cherry trees
Soup, the salad, fish and all
Seasoned with petals

—BASHO

◙

The art of *tsukémono,* or pickling, began as a vital method of food preservation. For centuries, pickling was a seasonal household activity; ingredients and methods varied from region to region. *Ko-no-mono,* "fragrant things," is the old Japanese name for pickles. The name for miso was *ko;* vegetables pickled in miso were one of the early types.

Pickles are often served as accompaniment to saké and tea. In northern Japan, there are "tea parties" in which guests come proudly bearing a colorful assortment of their finest homemade pickles. Besides the pickles, Japanese tea cakes and green tea are served to complete the meal.

A bowl of rice, a cup of green tea and a side dish of pickles often constitute the last course of a Japanese meal. If you add a cup of miso soup, many Japanese consider this a satisfying, complete meal. It may be difficult to convince you of the deliciousness of such a simple meal, unless you are already familiar with the incredible range and depth of flavors of Japanese pickles. Just try the Glazed Vegetable Pickles and see what I mean. A small portion of the crunchy teriyaki-flavored vegetables makes a companionable topping for a bowl of cooked rice.

Pickles are appreciated in remote mountain villages where much of the arable land is terraced and suitable only for growing rice. In the cold winter months when the country folk are knee-deep in snow, pickled autumn vegetables are a means of extending the season and adding rich variety to the diet. Pickled vegetables often serve as a much-needed source of vitamins and minerals.

Throughout Japan, the preference has been for quick pickling so the fresh taste of each seasonal vegetable can be enjoyed. It is said in Japan that "to eat *tsukémono* is to fully enjoy the changing seasons." The salty taste, the crisp natural textures and the characteristic flavor and aroma of fermentation are the qualities of pickles the Japanese most enjoy.

Several important pickling methods are *shio-zuké,* or salt pickling; *miso-zuké,* or miso pickling; *nuka-zuké* or rice bran pickling, and *kasu- zuké,* or fermented-rice pickling. Fermented rice, or saké lees, is a by-product of saké production. *Su-zuké* is pickling with vinegar, and *karashi-zuké* involves preserving vegetables with soy sauce, mustard, sugar and vinegar.

The simplest form of pickling (*shio-zuké*) occurs when salted vegetables, fruits or flowers are put under pressure until their liquids are extracted. The resulting briny solution preserves the vegetables. The Japanese have invented the *shokutaku tsukémono ki,* a special crock with a built-in press especially for salt pickling. It is available in some Asian markets, but this equipment can easily be duplicated in your own kitchen.

Sun-dried vegetables are layered in a pickling bed to ferment and ripen. Rice bran mash, miso paste, saké lees and steamed rice inoculated with *koji* mold are the major types of pickling beds. An enzymatic reaction causes lactic acid fermentation, which gives this type of pickle its special taste and crunchiness. Salt prevents the growth of harmful toxin-producing bacteria. *Nuka-zuké* is a quick form of pickling in dry rice bran and salt. Commercially pickled daikon radish, or *takuan,* is an example of *nuka-zuké.*

Sample the many varieties of Japanese pickles from your local Asian market. Japanese department stores and supermarkets are famous for their attractive displays of open barrels, crocks and tubs filled with colorful, unusual pickles. Regional specialties are given as housewarming gifts and purchased as souvenirs. Japanese pickles can be served as a condiment or appetizer. Rinse off excess salt and add to soups and simmered dishes.

Condiments

Compared to other herb- and spice-infused cuisines, Japanese dishes are seasoned with a gentle hand. Condiments and seasonings, or *yakumi,* are added sparingly to enhance the natural flavors of foods, never to disguise or diminish them. Unlike pickles, they are not eaten for their individual taste alone. The most important seasoning is soy sauce, which has the ability to blend with and accent the flavors it is added to. Fresh ginger and *wasabi* complement the flavors of Japanese foods and cut through oiliness and the strong tastes and odors of fish or meats. Seven-Spice Powder adds zest to noodle dishes, yakitori and *nabé-ryōri*. The pretty green herb shiso adds a clean, fresh taste to any dish to which it is added. Shiso's unique flavor hints of the springtime and fresh mint.

I have been using all of these seasonings and herbs in my Western recipes with wonderful success. They have transcended the cultural barrier and secured a permanent place on my pantry shelf.

A few drops of shoyu, a tiny mound of ginger, a sprinkle of spice—seasonings so distinctive, yet they blend harmoniously with the taste of foods to create a whole. Japanese condiments and seasonings provide a magical dusting of flavor, as subtle as cherry blossoms falling on the tongue. This is the art of Japanese cooking.

SPICY MUSTARD

(Karashi)

Traditionally, mustard is ripened to full flavor in the bottom of an upside-down bowl.

2 tablespoons Japanese mustard
    powder (*karashi*)
1 tablespoon saké

1 teaspoon mirin
1/2 teaspoon soy sauce

◉ In a small bowl, combine mustard powder and saké. Cover and turn bowl upside down. Leave for 10 minutes. Turn bowl upright and stir in remaining ingredients. Serve immediately. Use in small amounts.

◉ *Makes about 1/8 cup.*

SEVEN-SPICE POWDER
(Shichimi Tōgarashi)

There is a paved stone road in Kyoto that leads to the entrance of a magnificent eighth-century temple, Kiyomizudera. On this road lies Shichimiya Honpo, a famous shop selling *shichimi tōgarashi*. Here is a recipe for the seasoned chili powder blend that is popular in Kyoto cuisine. Keep it on hand to add a touch of spice to grilled meats, noodle dishes and one-pot cookery.

1 1/2 tablespoons grated clementine tangerine peel or navel orange peel

1/2 teaspoon dried *sansho* pepper pods

1 oz. (1/2 cup) dried, whole red chiles, about 1 1/2 inches long

1 teaspoon toasted sesame seeds

1 teaspoon toasted flax seeds

1 teaspoon toasted poppy seeds

1/4 teaspoon powdered green seaweed (*ao-noriko*)

◉ Preheat oven to 200F (95C). Spread grated tangerine peel over the bottom of a pie plate. Dry in oven 30 minutes. Place *sansho* pepper in a grinding bowl, mortar or small electric coffee mill; grind to a powder. Remove to a small bowl.

◉ Break open chiles; remove and discard most of seeds. Grind chiles to a powder. Add to *sansho* along with tangerine peel and sesame seeds. Place mixture in a grinding bowl, mortar or another sturdy bowl. Pound 4 or 5 times to bruise seeds and blend mixture. Add flax seeds, poppy seeds and powdered seaweed. Blend well; do not continue crushing seeds. Spoon spice mixture into a small jar. With a paper towel, loosen any remaining mixture left in the ridges of the grinding bowl; add to jar. Cover tightly; store in a cool place 4 to 6 weeks.

◉ *Makes 1/4 cup.*

PICKLED GINGER SLICES

(Amazu Shōga)

This is the tangy pink pickle that always accompanies sushi. The pink color comes from a food coloring additive. The natural color is a golden blush. Purchase a package of pickled red shiso leaves and shred 1 or 2 for your next batch of *amazu shōga*. You will love the wonderful flavor and appreciate the natural pink color.

1/3 pound large gingerroot knobs, preferably with thin skin, scraped	1/3 cup rice vinegar
	1/4 cup sugar
	1/4 teaspoon salt

◉ Using a sharp knife or a Benriner cutter, shave gingerroot into paper-thin slices. In a small airtight container, combine vinegar, sugar and salt. Blanch gingerroot slices 30 seconds in boiling water. Drain gingerroot; cool. If desired, reserve ginger blanching liquid for soups or other cooking uses.

◉ Add ginger to vinegar mixture; mix well. Refrigerate in the marinade. Pickled ginger can be eaten after 24 hours. It will keep several weeks. Serve with sushi and rice or noodle dishes. Save the flavorful marinade for salad dressings, pickles and sauces.

◉ *Makes 1/2 cup.*

VARIATION

◉ One or 2 fresh shiso leaves, whole or in thin strips, can be added to pickled ginger to add pink color.

SALT-PICKLED VEGETABLES WITH RAISINS
(Yasai No Ama-zuke)

Currants add a natural sweetness to these crunchy pickled vegetables.

1 small Japanese cucumber or
   1/2 European cucumber
1/2 medium-size carrot, cut into
   thin strips
1/2 lb. napa cabbage, cut
   lengthwise into strips
1/2 red or green bell pepper, cut
   into 3 strips
1 medium-size Japanese eggplant,
   halved lengthwise to within
   1 inch of stem

2 tablespoons sea salt
3 tablespoons currants or 1/4 cup
   golden or dark raisins
1 (1/4-inch-thick) slice peeled
   gingerroot, crushed
Peel of 1/2 lemon, cut into thin
   strips
1 small dried, whole hot chile
   (optional)
Soy sauce (optional)

◉ Discard ends from cucumber. Cut in half lengthwise. If using European cucumber, scrape out seeds with a small spoon. Peel off narrow strips of cucumber skin lengthwise. Rinse cucumber, carrot, cabbage, bell pepper and eggplant; shake dry. Sprinkle with salt; rub into cut surfaces. In a Japanese screw-top pickling jar, layer salted vegetables, currants, gingerroot and lemon peel; tighten lid. Press mixture 24 to 48 hours; do not refrigerate. Tighten lid once or twice as vegetables soften, releasing liquid. After pressing, remove vegetables from jar; reserve liquid. Pack vegetables into a sterilized 1-quart jar. Add pressing liquid. Add chile. Tightly cover jar; refrigerate up to 2 weeks. To serve, remove as much as needed. Rinse; cut into thin slices or strips. Arrange a few pieces of each vegetable on small serving dishes. Add a few drops of soy sauce.

◉ *Makes 6 to 8 servings.*

VARIATION

◉ If a Japanese screw-top pickling jar is not available, layer vegetables in a crock or glass bowl. Place an appropriate-size plate on top of vegetables. Place a 3-pound weight on top; gradually increase weight to 5 pounds. Press vegetables 24 to 48 hours. Continue as directed above.

CABBAGE & SHISO PICKLE WITH LEMON

(Kyabetsu No Shiso-zuké)

Minty shiso leaves are easy to grow and make an excellent fragrant addition to your herb garden.

1 medium-size head green
    cabbage, core end trimmed off
2 pkgs. fresh shiso leaves (about
    18 leaves), rinsed and dried
1 teaspoon salt

1/2 teaspoon freshly grated
    lemon peel
About 1 tablespoon toasted
    sesame seeds

◉ Separate cabbage leaves. Select 6 to 8 attractive green leaves. Refrigerate remaining cabbage for another use. Cook cabbage leaves, 3 at a time, 1 minute in boiling salted water. In a medium-size bowl, rinse leaves in cool water. Drain well; pat dry. Trim off any tough parts. Trim stems from shiso leaves. In a 9 x 5-inch glass loaf pan, layer 2 or 3 cabbage leaves. Sprinkle with 1/4 teaspoon salt. Cover with a layer of shiso leaves. Add another layer of cabbage leaves; sprinkle with 1/4 teaspoon salt. Add a final layer of shiso leaves. Place remaining cabbage leaves on top. Sprinkle with 1/2 teaspoon salt.

◉ Place a piece of plastic wrap on top; press layers firmly together. Place 2 to 3 pounds of weight on top. Two 1-pound salt boxes make excellent weights. Press at room temperature 1 hour or up to 4 hours. Remove wilted cabbage and shiso, still layered, to a cutting board; pat dry. With a large sharp knife, cut in half lengthwise. Cut crosswise into matchstick shreds. In a medium-size bowl, toss shreds with lemon peel. Place a small mound of pickles on each serving dish. Sprinkle each with 1/4 teaspoon sesame seeds. Refrigerate leftovers in an airtight container.

◉ *Makes 6 to 8 servings.*

LEMON-FLAVORED MISO PICKLES
(Lemon Miso-Zuké)

Many vegetables can be pickled in this fragrant pickling bed. Try scraped burdock, strips of small Western eggplant, sliced lotus root, bell pepper strips, sliced daikon radish or tender cabbage leaves. I like to choose from the colorful bounty of organic vegetables from a local natural-food store. These quick, easy pickles add a harvest of flavor to every meal.

Lemon Miso Pickling Bed
  (see below)
2 Japanese cucumbers or 1
  European cucumber, ends
  trimmed
2 medium-size Japanese
  eggplants, halved lengthwise
  to within 1 inch of stem
1 carrot, scraped and thinly
  sliced diagonally
1 tablespoon sea salt
Soy sauce (optional)

LEMON MISO PICKLING BED
  1 cup white miso or red miso
    or a blend
  1/4 cup sugar, or to taste
  2 tablespoons saké
  2 tablespoons sea salt
  Peel of 1 small lemon, cut into
    thin strips
  2 dried, whole hot chiles
  3 (1/8-inch-thick) slices peeled
    gingerroot, crushed

◉ Cut cucumbers in half lengthwise. Scrape out any seeds. Cut crosswise into 4 pieces. Peel off narrow strips of cucumber skin lengthwise. Rinse vegetables; rub with salt. In a Japanese screw-top pickling jar, layer vegetables; tighten lid. Press overnight in a cool place. Tighten lid once or twice as vegetables soften, releasing liquid. Pour off liquid when pressing is complete. Remove vegetables from jar; pat dry with a clean kitchen towel.

◉ Bury vegetables in pickling bed. Cover tightly and refrigerate. Pickles can be eaten the next day, but are better after 48 hours or longer. Scrape pickles from miso mixture, rinse and pat dry. Cut into thin slices. Serve in small dishes with soy sauce. If miso bed becomes low or watery, add more miso. Continue adding vegetables as pickles are removed. Flavors improve as bed matures.

◉ *Makes 8 to 10 servings.*

LEMON MISO PICKLING BED

◉ In a medium-size bowl, stir together all ingredients. Scrape mixture into a medium-size crock, glass jar or plastic container with a tight-fitting lid. Cover and store in a cool place until needed.

RED MAPLE RADISH

(Momiji Oroshi)

This spicy hot condiment adds pizzazz to noodle dipping sauces, tempura broth and *nabémono* dishes.

1 (3- to 4-inch) piece daikon radish, peeled	1/2 teaspoon grated gingerroot (optional)
3 to 4 small dried, whole hot chiles	

◉ Using a chopstick, push 3 or 4 holes through piece of daikon. Push a chile into each hole. If not used at once, wrap whole daikon tightly in plastic wrap; refrigerate up to 2 days. At serving time, grate daikon on a fine grater using a circular motion. Daikon will be speckled with red chile flakes. Serve in individual condiment dishes, or serve in a single dish with a mound of grated gingerroot on top.

◉ *Makes 8 to 10 servings.*

KOREAN WINTER KIM CHEE

(Hakasui No Kim Chee)

Like the Japanese, the Koreans value a nutritious supply of pickled vegetables. Preservation of winter vegetables begins after the autumn harvest. In the old days, the preparation of *kim chee* was a social event which lasted for days. Today, great quantities of *kim chee* are still buried in huge earthen jars beneath the cold ground to ferment through the winter. I am often asked how long the *kim chee* will keep. My answer is, "How ripe do you like it?" Some connoisseurs enjoy the strong, sour flavor of aged *kim chee*. Personally, I prefer a crunchy fresh taste, so I discard the old stuff after 10 to 12 days. If you live near a Korean market, look for an airtight metal *kim chee* pot to keep renegade odors under control. Here is an excellent version shared by a well-known cooking professional I once visited in Seoul.

1/4 cup salt
1 large head napa cabbage,
   halved lengthwise
Seasoning Mixture (see below)
6 green onions, shredded
1 lb. daikon radish, cut into
   matchstick strips
1 large carrot, cut into
   matchstick strips
1 Asian pear (*nashi*) (optional),
   shredded

SEASONING MIXTURE
3 garlic cloves, minced
1 tablespoon minced gingerroot

1 tablespoon dried Korean hot
   red chile threads (*shile kochu*)
3 to 5 tablespoons ground
   Korean hot chiles (*kochu*)
1 small onion, halved and cut
   into strips
2 tablespoons sugar
2 tablespoons toasted sesame
   seeds
1 tablespoon salted shrimp
   paste (optional)

◉ With your hands rub salt in between and over cabbage leaves, especially near core. Place in a large bowl; add water to cover. Soak several hours or overnight. When cabbage wilts, it is ready to be pickled. Rinse under cool water; drain well.

◉ Prepare Seasoning Mixture. In a large bowl, place cabbage, onions, daikon, carrot and pear. With your hands, rub seasoning over cabbage and between the layers. Fold cabbage halves into 2 neat bundles. Place into a stainless *kim chee* pot or jar with a tight-fitting lid. Pour in any liquid from bowl.

◉ Cover tightly; refrigerate several hours or overnight before serving. Flavor matures daily. To serve, slice bundles and arrange on a serving platter in their original shape, or coarsely chop. Especially good with Korean or Western beef barbecue and Asian rice dishes.

◉ *Makes 10 to 12 Western servings.*

SEASONING MIXTURE

◉ In a small bowl, combine all ingredients.

QUICK DAIKON PICKLES
(Daikon-zuke)

Begin with this easy recipe if you have not made Japanese pickles before. Daikon is one of Japan's most popular vegetables for pickling. Well-scrubbed, slivered radish peelings are delicious stir-fried alone or with other vegetables and seasoned with soy sauce, mirin and Seven-Spice Powder (page 228).

1 1/2 to 1 3/4 lbs. daikon radish,
    peeled and halved lengthwise
Generous 1/4 cup sea salt
Pickling Syrup (see below)
1 (4-inch) square good-quality
    dried kelp (*dashi konbu*), wiped
1 to 2 small dried, whole hot chiles

PICKLING SYRUP
    1 cup water
    1/2 cup rice vinegar
    1 1/4 cups sugar
    1 teaspoon salt

◉ Cut daikon into thin slices. Place in a large bowl; mix in salt. To press daikon, place an appropriate-size plate on top. Top with a 3-pound weight; gradually increase weight to 5 pounds as vegetable softens, releasing liquid. Press overnight.

◉ Pour off liquid. If desired, rinse daikon to remove excess salt. Squeeze out as much liquid as possible. Place in a 1-quart sterilized jar. Prepare Pickling Syrup. Pour hot syrup over daikon. Cool; add kelp and chiles. Cover jar with a tight-fitting lid; refrigerate up to 3 months. Pickles can be eaten within 3 or 4 days; flavor improves daily.

◉ *Makes about 1 pint.*

PICKLING SYRUP

◉ In a medium-size saucepan, combine all ingredients over medium-high heat. Boil 1 to 2 minutes or until sugar is dissolved, stirring constantly.

◉ *Makes about 2 cups.*

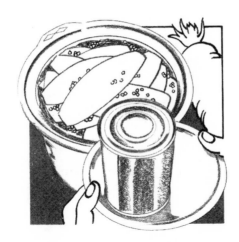

WASABI

Wasabi is the fiery condiment that is a traditional accompaniment to sushi and Sashimi (page 63).

1 tablespoon *wasabi* powder
3 teaspoons water or saké

1/2 teaspoon rice vinegar

◉ Place *wasabi* powder in a small dish. Add remaining ingredients; blend until a thick paste forms. Cover and turn bowl upside down. Leave for 10 minutes for flavors to develop. *Wasabi* should be thick enough to be molded in a small cone shape. Use sparingly.

◉ *Makes 1 tablespoon.*

VARIATION

WASABI LEAVES

◉ Prepare Wasabi. Press into a sheet, about 1/4 inch thick. Using a tiny leaf-shaped cutter, cut out leaf shapes. Lift onto serving plates with a small narrow spatula. Or cut and score with a small knife.

GLAZED VEGETABLE PICKLES

(Sanbai-zuke)

Flavorful shreds of dried kelp, eggplant and daikon are simmered in a vinegar-soy mixture. This recipe is similar to a method for preparing *tsukudani,* a Tokyo Bay condiment made by simmering small fish in a soy sauce mixture. Richly glazed, sweet, spicy and crunchy describe these unusual pickles. They are a favorite with Japanese students who always seem to turn up at my door.

1 (2-oz.) pkg. shredded dried
    konbu (kizami konbu)
1 (3-oz.) pkg. dried daikon
    radish *(kiriboshi daikon)*
1 (2-oz.) pkg. dried eggplant
    strips
1 1/2 cups soy sauce
2 cups rice vinegar

2 cups sugar
2 tablespoons mirin
3 (1/8-inch-thick) slices peeled
    gingerroot, crushed
1 tablespoon toasted sesame
    seeds
1 or 2 small dried hot chiles,
    seeded

◉ Place *konbu,* daikon and eggplant in 3 separate large bowls; add enough water to cover. Swish *konbu* around in the water several times. Rinse *konbu* quickly in cool water; drain and squeeze dry. With a large knife, cut 2 or 3 times into shorter lengths. Set aside. Soak daikon and eggplant 20 minutes. Rinse each vegetable separately in several changes of water. Squeeze dry. Cut daikon 2 or 3 times into shorter lengths. Chop eggplant into small pieces.

◉ In a large saucepan, combine soy sauce, vinegar, sugar, mirin and gingerroot. Boil 5 minutes over medium-high heat, stirring often. Add vegetables. Boil 5 minutes. Pour vegetables and liquid into a colander set inside a large bowl. Press vegetables to remove liquid. Pour liquid back into saucepan. Boil 5 minutes to reduce. Add vegetables back plus any liquid that has dripped into the large bowl. Cook 2 minutes. Drain again into the colander set in large bowl. Press out liquid. Boil liquid 5 minutes more. Add vegetables to hot mixture a final time. Bring vegetables and syrupy mixture to a boil. Strain vegetables; cool.

◉ Stir in sesame seeds. Pour liquid into a smaller saucepan. Add chiles. Boil over medium-high heat until reduced to about 1/2 cup. Discard chiles. Cool to room temperature. Pack cooled vegetables into a 1 1/2-quart sterilized jar. Pour in syrup. Cover and refrigerate. Pickles are good several months. Recipe can be cut in half.

◉ *Makes 1 1/2 quarts.*

SESAME SALT
(Goma Shio)

Goma shio is a nutty-tasting blend of toasted ground sesame seeds and sea salt. Sprinkle this condiment on noodles, vegetables, rice or rice balls. It tastes especially good on brown rice. Sesame seeds are high in calcium, iron, protein and vitamins. Fresh *goma shio* tastes best, so don't double the recipe unless you are feeding a crowd. If you don't have a Japanese grinding bowl, crush the mixture between sheets of parchment paper with a rolling pin.

1/2 cup unhulled white sesame seeds	2 to 3 teaspoons sea salt

◉ Place sesame seeds in a dry skillet over medium-high heat. Toast seeds about 1 minute or until they become aromatic and start popping in the pan. Shake pan to keep the seeds in constant motion. Pour into a Japanese grinding bowl. Toast salt in same skillet about 30 seconds. Add to sesame seeds. With a grinding stick, lightly crush seeds and salt by rotating it in a circular motion. When mixture is about 75 percent crushed, remove to a storage jar. Store in a cool place.

◉ *Makes about 1/2 cup.*

Desserts &
Confectionery

(Okashi)

In Japan, all types of sweets and cakes fall under the collective name *okashi*. Confectionery began sometime after sugar was introduced from China, around the eighth century. Before that, fresh fruits, dried fruits, honey, vegetables, nuts and other naturally sweet foods had to satisfy the sweet tooth. Historians believe confectionery developed extensively around the Kyoto area and was primarily enjoyed by the upper class.

As they are today, traditional sweets were made with rice, rice flour, sweet bean paste and seaweed gelatin. Tokyo became famous for its tasty, substantial type of sweets. A more refined confectionery had developed around the Imperial Court of Kyoto.

When the tea ceremony became popular, traditional sweets called *wagashi* were created to balance and enhance the astringent taste of the green tea. Chinese characters for *wa* indicate *yamato,* or "ancient Japan"; *gashi* is a variation of *kashi,* or "confection."

Many types of *wagashi* based on *an* or sweet red bean paste have survived through the centuries. Red Bean & Macadamia Jelly is a modern version of yokan, a type of firm jelly-like confection made from *an* and agar-agar. *Mizuyokan* is a softer version, often eaten chilled. *Manju,* a poorman's wheat bun, is filled with *an,* then steamed. Okinawan Sweet Fritters are spice-scented fried dough balls which stay moist from the addition of *tsubushi-an,* or chunky bean paste.

Japanese Cakes— a Different Tradition

The most beautiful sweets of the *wagashi* family are *namagashi,* or "fresh confections." Highly perishable, they are made daily. The famous tea cakes of Kyoto (*Kyogashi*) are miniature works of art, often with cultural significance. *Wagashi* are inspired by art and literature. They are an expression of the Japanese sensitivity toward seasonal change, shaped to evoke sentiments of flowers, birds, leaves and other objects of nature.

Imagine a goldfish-sweet swimming in a block of transparent jelly or an egg-shaped rice cake "blooming" with a hand-painted miniature garden. "Spring Shoots under Snow" and "Studious Blossom" are lyrical names of *namagashi* at the famous Toraya Confectioner in Tokyo. Shaped like a plum blossom, the latter refers to a fourteenth-century scholar who began and ended daily studies by opening and closing plum blossom petals. Japanese confectioners say *wagashi* should appeal to the five senses: taste, appearance, texture, scent and sound—the at-traction of the last coming from the melodious sound of their poetic names as they are spoken aloud.

Dry sweets, or *higashi,* include rice crackers and colorful molded hard candies. The latter are served with thin green tea during the tea ceremony. Many are tinted sugar cakes molded into seasonal shapes such as maple leaves, butterflies, dragonflies, gingko leaves and snowflakes.

The Portuguese and Dutch introduced the *kasutera,* a golden sponge cake from Castile, a region in Spain. The original version was modified to suit the flavors and cooking methods of Japan. Honey Ginger Sponge Cake is a special version shared by a housewife from Yokohama.

The Japanese have satisfied a growing passion for Western-style sweets with European-style pastry shops throughout Japan. (Home ovens are rare.) Pastries are less sweet and lighter than their European counterparts. Bread has become an important part of the Japanese diet, and a favorite breakfast food of the younger generation. Bread slices are larger and often richer-tasting than the Western equivalent, requiring larger toasters to accommodate them. The ends of bread loaves are considered undesirable by the Japanese and packaged in bags for feeding birds.

Partly in response to increasing health awareness by young Japanese women, there has been a resurgence of interest in *wagashi.* The high-fiber, low-calorie, often fat-free confections have great aesthetic appeal. They are beginning to attract exclusive new markets in Paris and New York. Japanese confectioners are modifying *wagashi,* adding Western spices, flavoring essences, nuts and liqueurs.

In Japan, sweets are served as a snack with tea or coffee rather than as a dessert. Fresh seasonal fruit might be served as a dessert. Ice cream or sherbet is the perfect light ending, especially if it tastes as good as the Strawberry Tofu Sherbet or Banana-Orange Tofu Sherbet.

Sweet Rice Saké is a traditional beverage which I first tasted at a 300-year-old Kyoto teahouse. It is low in alcoholic content, and its rich creamy taste is a favorite with both children and adults. Young girls delight in drinking it with colorful puffed-rice crackers during the Doll Festival. It can be chilled in the summertime for a refreshing drink.

STRAWBERRIES IN SNOW
(Awayukikan)

"Snow jelly" is a spectacular molded gelatin dessert which brings back wintertime memories of very large strawberries, simply bursting with flavor. Each strawberry is often hand-wrapped, then boxed in a single layer. The dish is traditionally made with firm *kanten;* this recipe uses gelatin to create a texture as delicate as newly fallen snow.

2 (1/4-oz.) envelopes unflavored
    gelatin
1/2 cup cool water
2 cups water
1 1/4 cups sugar
1/4 cup fresh lemon juice
Pinch salt
3 large egg whites, at room
    temperature
1 tablespoon sugar
2 1/2 cups fresh strawberries

CUSTARD SAUCE
3 egg yolks
1 1/2 cups milk
3 tablespoons sugar
Pinch salt
3/4 teaspoon potato starch or
    1 teaspoon cornstarch
1/2 teaspoon vanilla extract

⦿ Lightly oil a 5- to 6-cup ring mold. In a small cup, soften gelatin in 1/2 cup water. In a medium saucepan, heat 2 cups water and 1 1/4 cups sugar over medium heat. Stir in gelatin. When sugar and gelatin are dissolved, remove pan from heat. Stir in lemon juice and salt. Pour mixture into a medium bowl; set into a larger bowl of water and ice cubes. Refrigerate until slightly thickened; stir occasionally. When gelatin begins to thicken, remove bowl from iced water.

⦿ In a medium bowl, beat egg whites until foamy. Sprinkle in 1 tablespoon sugar; beat until egg whites are stiff but not dry. Slowly pour gelatin mixture into egg whites, beating constantly on low speed. Beat a few seconds until mixtures are completely combined. Decorate bottom of pan with 8 to 10 strawberries if desired. Pour mixture into mold; refrigerate until set. Prepare Custard Sauce. To unmold dessert, dip bottom of pan quickly in and out of warm water once or twice. Place serving dish upside down on top of mold. Invert dish and mold; gelatin should slip out. Fill center with strawberries. Serve with sauce.

⦿ *Makes 6 to 8 servings.*

CUSTARD SAUCE

⦿ Place egg yolks in top of a double boiler. Whisk in milk, sugar, salt and potato starch. Place over simmering water. Cook, stirring constantly, until mixture thickens slightly and coats a spoon. Stir in vanilla. Cool to room temperature. Cover and chill until serving time.

⦿ *Makes about 1 3/4 cups.*

STRAWBERRY TOFU SHERBET
(Ichigo Dofu Sha-be-to)

Visiting Japanese students just love the idea of tofu sherbet or ice cream. One young guest even photographed his portion, then sent the photo back home to share with Mom! His pronouncement: Fabulous, but next time add chocolate chips, please!

2 cups fresh strawberries, hulled
1 (14- to 16-oz.) pkg. silken
    tofu, rinsed and patted dry
1 cup corn syrup
1/2 cup fresh orange juice

2 tablespoons fresh lemon juice
1/8 teaspoon salt
1 teaspoon pure vanilla extract
1 teaspoon freshly grated
    orange peel

◉ Puree strawberries and tofu in a blender or food processor fitted with a steel blade. Add remaining ingredients; process until blended. Depending on size of blender, mixture may have to be processed in 2 batches. Refrigerate mixture until chilled. Freeze in an ice cream machine according to manufacturer's directions or follow directions on page 247. When frozen, serve immediately or store in the freezer. To store, remove dasher from canister. Cover lid with foil. If necessary, scoop sherbet from canister and pack into airtight containers for freezing.

◉ *Makes about 1 1/2 quarts.*

RED BEAN & MACADAMIA JELLY
(Macadamia Yokan)

Lily Hataye's modern version of this traditional Japanese *wagashi* includes macadamia nuts and amaretto. The Toraya Tea Room in New York City offers a special tea sandwich of soft fresh bread, cream cheese and a thin slice of red bean jelly. Lily's nutty bean jelly would be lovely served this way. Don't forget to toast the nuts lightly to bring out their best flavor.

2 (0.25-oz.) sticks red agar-agar (*kanten*)	1 cup chopped macadamia nuts, walnuts, almonds or peanuts
1 1/2 cups water	1/4 teaspoon salt
1 cup sugar	1 tablespoon amaretto liqueur or 1/2 teaspoon almond extract
2 cups smooth Japanese bean paste (*koshi-an*)	

◉ Tear each agar-agar stick into 4 pieces; place with water in a medium saucepan. Press agar-agar into water several seconds to soften. Shred pieces with your fingers. Soak 30 minutes. Simmer agar-agar and water over very low heat until dissolved, about 10 minutes. Stir once or twice while simmering. Stir in sugar. Cook until mixture comes to a boil. Add bean paste. Stir mixture until blended. Cook over very low heat 30 minutes or until mixture is thick and fudgy, stirring frequently to prevent burning. A metal heat diffuser may help prevent burning.

◉ When thick, remove mixture from heat. Stir in nuts, salt and amaretto. Rinse a 6 1/2 x 4 1/2-inch *nagashi-bako,* 8-inch-square pan or round pan with cold water. Tap out excess liquid. Quickly pour mixture into prepared pan; jelly sets at room temperature almost instantly. Or refrigerate until serving time. To serve, cut into thin bars or other shapes.

◉ *Makes 12 servings.*

SWEET RICE SAKÉ

(Amazaké)

This teahouse specialty is delicious at teatime or as a sweet course, after a meal. Long slow cooking of the raw rice is essential to break down the grains in preparation for fermentation. The base can also be used as a sweetener, much like honey. For a smooth texture, puree the base in a blender. Chopped fresh strawberries, tangerines, toasted almonds or pine nuts can be mixed into the *amazaké*.

1/2 cup short- or medium-grain
    rice, well rinsed
1 1/2 cups water
1 cup granular rice *koji* starter
1 cup water

1/8 teaspoon salt
1 teaspoon grated gingerroot
1/4 cup saké, brandy, almond
    liqueur or orange liqueur
    (optional)

◉ Place rice and 1 1/2 cups water in a small saucepan over low heat. When water boils, cover pan; reduce heat to low. Cook 1 hour, stirring often. A metal heat diffuser may be helpful to prevent burning. When soft, cool the rice to 140F (60C). Sterilize a 1-quart wide-mouth jar or heatproof glass bowl in boiling water. Add rice; stir in *koji*. Cover tightly with a lid or plastic wrap. Place in a 140 (60C) oven. Do not allow temperature to rise above 150F (65C). It may help to turn the oven on and off occasionally to maintain the temperature. If you have one, use a warming drawer. Incubate mixture 10 to 12 hours; do not disturb. The mixture will develop a rich sweet flavor. Consistency will be like rice porridge. In a saucepan, boil mixture 1 minute; cool. Refrigerate in an airtight container several days. To make *amazaké*, pour 2 cups of base mixture into a saucepan with 1 cup water, salt and gingerroot. Water amount can be adjusted to taste. Stir in saké. Serve hot in Japanese teacups.

◉ *Makes 8 to 10 servings.*

BANANA-ORANGE TOFU SHERBET

(Banana Orenji-dofu Shabeto)

I created this fantastic dessert for an Oriental appetizer party I created for *Cooking Light Magazine*. The sherbet has no cholesterol, is low in fat and high in calcium. Best of all, it tastes delicious!

2 large bananas
1/2 pound silken tofu, rinsed
   and patted dry
1/4 cup fresh lime juice
1 cup fresh orange juice
3/4 cup light corn syrup or
   rice syrup

1 tablespoon grated fresh
   orange peel
1/8 teaspoon ground turmeric
1/8 teaspooon ground nutmeg
1 teaspoon almond extract
1 teaspoon vanilla extract

◉ In a food processor fitted with a steel blade, process bananas, tofu and lime juice until pureed. Add remaining ingredients. Process until smooth. Freeze mixture in an ice cream machine according to manufacturer's directions or follow directions below. When frozen, serve immediately or store in the freezer. To store, remove dasher from canister. Cover the lid with foil. If necessary, scoop sherbet from canister and pack into airtight containers for freezing.

◉ *Makes about 1 quart.*

Making Ice Cream in the Freezer

If you do not have an ice cream maker, ice cream and sherbet can be frozen successfully in metal pans or in empty ice cube trays in the freezer. Set the freezer setting to the lowest temperature. Freeze prepared mixture until slushy. Scrape it away from the sides of the pan. Stir well to break up ice crystals. Freeze again until firm. Turn into a large bowl. Beat with an electric mixer 1 minute to incorporate air to lighten the mixture, or beat in a food processor fitted with a steel blade. Refreeze until firm. Serve as soon as possible. Ice crystals continue to form rather quickly, causing the texture of the frozen dessert to deteriorate.

OKINAWAN SWEET FRITTERS
(Sato Dango)

When I lived in Okinawa, these wonderful fritters seemed to be the specialty of every *obasan,* those incorrigible little grandmothers who are the darlings of their families. The nutritious red bean paste keeps this sweet snack soft and moist.

1 large egg	1/4 teaspoon ground cinnamon
1/2 cup evaporated milk	1/3 cup chunky or smooth
1 cup all-purpose flour	Japanese bean paste
1 teaspooon baking powder	6 cups peanut oil or vegetable
1/8 teaspoon salt	oil
1/3 cup light brown sugar	1/4 cup sugar (optional)

◉ In a small bowl, combine egg and milk. In a medium bowl, sift together flour, baking powder, salt, brown sugar and cinnamon. Add the egg and milk to the flour mixture; stir until blended. Stir in bean paste. In a wok or shallow pan, heat oil to 350F (175C). Drop batter into the hot oil by the tablespoonful. Fry fritters 3 to 5 minutes, turning often to brown evenly. Cut open one fritter to be sure the batter is cooked inside. Roll hot fritters in sugar or serve plain.

◉ *Makes about 12 fritters.*

PLUM WINE JELLY
(Umé-shu Kanten)

Fresh poached plums and Japanese plum wine are combined in an elegant jelly for a refreshing summertime confection. Serve small portions on your prettiest china.

1 cup water
1 (0.25-oz.) stick white agar-agar
　(*kanten*)
1/2 cup water
1/2 cup sugar
1 lb. ripe red or purple plums,
　pitted and quartered

Pinch salt
2 or 3 dashes ground cinnamon
1/2 cup Japanese plum wine
1/4 cup sugar

◉ Pour 1 cup water into a small saucepan. Tear agar-agar into 4 pieces. Press into water several seconds to soften. Shred agar-agar with your fingers. Soak 30 minutes. In a medium saucepan, bring 1/2 cup water and 1/2 cup sugar to a boil over medium-high heat. Stir to dissolve sugar. Add plum pieces; reduce heat to low. Cover pan; simmer 10 to 12 minutes. Strain plum syrup into a medium bowl; reserve.

◉ Place pulp into a blender or food processor fitted with a steel blade; process until smooth. Add puree to bowl of syrup. Stir in salt, cinnamon and wine. Simmer agar-agar and water over very low heat until dissolved, about 10 minutes. Stir once or twice. Stir in 1/4 cup sugar; simmer 2 minutes. Remove from heat. Using a fine strainer, strain agar-agar into plum mixture. Scrape agar-agar mixture from bottom of strainer into bowl. Quickly stir mixture.

◉ Rinse an 8-inch-square or round pan with water; tap out excess liquid. Quickly pour plum mixture into prepared pan. Mixture will set almost instantly at room temperature or can be refrigerated until serving time. When set, cut into plum-blossom shapes using Japanese 1 1/2-inch, flower-shaped metal cutters. Or cut into 32 (2 x 1-inch) rectangular pieces. Allow 2 pieces per serving.

◉ *Makes 10 to 16 servings.*

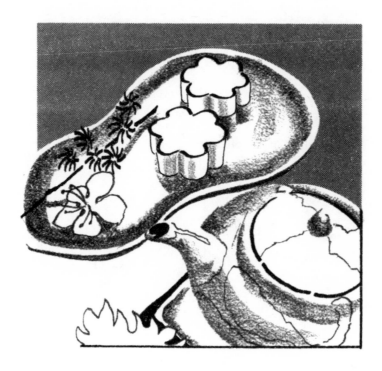

PLUM WINE SAUCE

(Umé-shu Sōsu)

This tangy dip complements any fresh fruit but especially fresh strawberries and
raspberries. Spoon it over cheesecake, molded custard or ice cream.

1/2 cup water	Dash salt
1/2 cup sugar	2 dashes ground cinnamon
1 lb. ripe plums, pitted and	1/4 cup Japanese plum wine
quartered	1/4 cup sugar

◉ In a medium saucepan, simmer water and sugar 1 minute. Add plums; reduce heat
to low. Cook 10 minutes. Pour cooked plums into a food processor fitted with a steel
blade. Puree until smooth. Combine with remaining ingredients in a large bowl. Refrigerate until chilled.

◉ *Makes about 2 cups.*

Agar-Agar (Kanten)

Brittle agar-agar sticks (*kanten*) are sold in pairs. The color may be white, red or green. Package weights can vary an ounce or two, depending on the manufacturer. Recipes in this book were tested with packages weighing 0.5 ounces (14 grams), each stick weighing 0.25 ounces (7 grams). If you are using packages of less weight (quite commonly 0.4 ounces, or 11 grams), adjust the amount of agar-agar in the recipe. For the 0.4-ounce package, you should use 1 stick and 2 1/4 inches of another, for each package called for.

Melted agar-agar must be blended into foods while still hot or warm. It gels at around 105–110F (40–45C), without refrigeration. Tiny bits of congealed agar-agar form quickly throughout the food being gelled. If the food is poured from pan to pan or stirred during this time, the gelling process will be interrupted. The consistency of the molded food will not be smooth and it will not set properly. Foods stiffened with agar-agar do not melt easily and are firmer than those made with regular gelatin.

One-half stick of agar-agar is equal to about 1 envelope regular gelatin. Substitutions are not recommended in certain recipes such as *yokan,* where the character of the dish depends a great deal on its firm texture.

GRILLED FRUIT KABOBS WITH PLUM WINE SAUCE

(Kushi yaki)

These refreshing fruit skewers go well with grilled meats or poultry. Plum wine, or *umé-shu*, is a summer drink, served over cracked ice. Purchase pale, clear Japanese plum wine, which is superior in taste to darker-hued plum wines.

Plum Wine Sauce (page 250)
Assorted Fresh Fruits (see below)
Plum Wine Marinade (see below)

1 large banana, cubed
1 cup fresh pineapple cubes
1 papaya, cubed

ASSORTED FRESH FRUITS

1 cup melon balls (watermelon, cantaloupe, honeydew)
1 (10-oz.) can lychee fruits, drained
1 cup fresh strawberries, hulled
1 or 2 peaches, peeled and cubed

PLUM WINE MARINADE

1/4 cup unsalted butter, melted
1/2 cup Japanese plum wine
1 teaspoon freshly grated orange peel
2 tablespoons tart, fresh orange juice

◉ Prepare Plum Wine Sauce; chill until needed. Soak 6- to 8-inch bamboo skewers in water 30 minutes. Select 3 or 4 types of fruit. Choose fruits that are ripe but not too soft. Lace fruit on skewers, 3 or 4 pieces per skewer. To prepare Plum Wine Marinade, combine marinade ingredients in a 13 x 9-inch baking pan. Add fruit skewers. Marinate 15 minutes, turning once or twice. Drain fruit. Preheat a hibachi or portable table-top grill. Place skewers over hot grill. Cook 3 to 4 minutes or until hot. Serve with sauce.

◉ *Makes 6 servings.*

HONEY GINGER SPONGE CAKE
(Kasutera)

This golden sponge cake was introduced by the Portuguese. It is sold in bakeries and department stores in a variety of tints and flavors. My favorite is a pale green cake flavored with the herb mugwort. In Okinawa, pineapple *kasutera* is a bestseller. The recipe here, from Meiko Yamazaki of Yokohama, is wonderfully moist and contains no fat. Bake the cake 2 or 3 days before you plan to serve it. It ages well. Serve small squares with hot green tea, or use it as a base for strawberry shortcake.

1 cup sugar
1/4 cup honey
3 tablespoons top-quality mirin
1 tablespoon fresh ginger juice
   (see *Graters*, page 257)
1 tablespoon fresh lemon juice

1/4 teaspoon salt
6 jumbo eggs or 7 large eggs,
   separated
1 cup sifted cake flour
1/8 teaspoon cream of tartar

◙ Preheat oven to 325F (165C). Use parchment to line a 10-inch-square pan with deep sides. Grease bottom, not sides. Reserve 1 tablespoon sugar. In a medium bowl, whisk remaining sugar, honey, mirin, ginger juice, lemon juice and salt into egg yolks. Place bowl in a large pan of hot water. Stir constantly 1 minute or until warm. With an electric mixer, beat 8 to 10 minutes on medium-high speed until tripled in size. Gently fold in sifted flour.

◙ Wash beaters. In a large bowl, beat egg whites in electric mixer on low speed 1 minute, increasing speed to medium-high. When foamy, sprinkle in reserved sugar and cream of tartar. Beat until stiff but not dry. With a spatula, fold 1/3 of egg whites into batter. Fold in 1/2 of the remaining egg whites. Fold in final amount of whites until just blended. Pour batter into pan; tap lightly on counter.

◙ Bake on middle rack of oven 25 minutes or until golden brown. When done, cake sides will pull away from pan slightly; top will be flat and feel spongy when pressed with finger. Cool 20 minutes. Run a small knife between edge of cake and pan. Invert on slightly damp kitchen towel and remove pan. Pull off parchment; cool. Serve or wrap airtight and refrigerate.

◙ *Makes 10 to 12 servings.*

GREEN-TEA CREPES

My sister, Dee Bradney, makes green tea-tofu crepes as a treat for her three sons. *Matcha*, the powdered green tea used for the tea ceremony, is made from the tender young leaves from the first tea picking. Dee often fills the pale green crepes with green-tea or ginger ice cream. They are especially delicious filled with fresh fruit macerated in orange or ginger liqueur topped with whipped cream. Or fill the centers with chunky bean paste, pull up the edges to form small pouches and fill with candy strings. Dee, a tea ceremony enthusiast, enjoys serving this East-West *wagashi* to her Japanese friends, also devotees of *cha-no-yu*.

2 large eggs
2/3 cup silken tofu, mashed
3 tablespoons melted butter
1 2/3 cups milk
1/2 teaspoon pure vanilla extract

1 cup all-purpose flour
1 teaspoon *matcha* green tea
  (optional)
About 1 quart of your favorite
  ice cream

◉ Place all ingredients except ice cream in an electric blender or food processor fitted with a steel blade; process until smooth. Pour batter into a bowl. Heat a crepe pan or an 8-inch nonstick skillet over medium-high heat. Wipe pan lightly with oil. Measure about 3 tablespoons batter; pour into pan. Roll pan to evenly coat the bottom. If pan is too hot, batter will not swirl to proper size. Cook 30 seconds or until set. Turn and cook the other side 30 seconds. Cook remaining batter. Cool crepes. In the center of each crepe, place about 1/3 cup ice cream; fold sides over.

◉ *Makes about 12 filled crepes.*

TRICOLORED AUTUMN RICE BALLS

(San-shoku Ohagi)

Ohagi is a simple tea sweet with homespun appeal. Soft rice balls are enclosed in red bean paste. *Ohagi* was once served during the autumn equinox celebration. The name comes from a type of bush clover that only blooms in the fall. Serve these rice balls with your finest cup of tea.

Steamed Sweet Rice, page 195
1/4 cup toasted black sesame
    seeds, lightly crushed
1 tablespoon sugar
1 cup smooth Japanese bean
    paste (*koshi-an*), chilled

1/2 cup roasted soybean powder
    (*kinako*) or toasted ground
    pecans

◙ Prepare rice. Mix sesame seeds and sugar in a small bowl. Moisten your hands with water. Divide warm rice into 12 equal portions. Shape 4 portions into balls. Moisten a clean dish towel; squeeze dry. Place 2 1/2 tablespoons bean paste on damp towel; pat into a 4-inch circle. Place 1 rice ball in center of bean-paste circle. Use towel to mold bean paste around the rice ball. When rice is covered, press mixture into an oval shape; set aside. Do 3 more times, using another 1/2 cup bean paste and the remaining 3 rice balls. Place on a lacquer serving tray. Flatten remaining 8 rice portions. Form remaining bean paste into 8 balls, using about 2 teaspoons per ball. Place a bean-paste ball in center of each piece of flattened rice. Shape rice around bean paste. Mold stuffed rice balls into oval shapes. Roll 4 ovals in sesame-sugar mixture. Roll remaining 4 balls in roasted soybean powder. Add balls to serving tray. Allow 2 balls per serving.

◙ *Makes 6 servings.*

GLOSSARY

Japanese Kitchen Equipment

Bamboo basket (zaru) Woven bamboo baskets are used in Japan for rinsing, cooking and serving food. Round baskets are used in place of a colander for rinsing foods, such as rice, shellfish and vegetables. Baskets are excellent for holding arranged foods for tabletop cooking; small baskets for serving individual portions of noodles. Cooking baskets (seiro) are used for dipping foods into boiling water, for soaking and for steaming doughs and grains.

Bamboo mat (sudaré) Mats of various sizes are used for rolling foods, such as sushi rolls, omelet rolls and spinach rolls. Slats are lashed together with string. Rinse mat well under cool water after each use; dry thoroughly. Many sushi chefs line their mats with plastic wrap before making sushi rolls, especially those where rice is rolled on the outside. If a bamboo mat is unavailable, substitute a piece of heavy foil, a folded kitchen towel or a bamboo place mat with tied wooden slats. Bamboo mats are called maki-su in sushi bars.

Benriner cutter Rectangular plastic box; the lid is fitted with several interchangeable blades for thin-slicing, shredding and grating. Substitute a mandoline or a large sharp knife. A food processor cannot duplicate the long thin vegetable shreds and slices, traditionally cut by hand. Finely shredded daikon radish and carrot are traditional garnishes for sashimi.

Domburi Large deep pottery or porcelain bowl with matching lid, used for rice-based one-bowl meals, which are also known as domburi. Soba and udon in soup can be served in domburi bowls. Use bowls for serving other foods including stews and even chili.

Donabé heatproof earthenware casserole Traditionally used for cooking one-pot dishes. Soak donabé in water 1 hour to prevent cracks during cooking. Raise the temperature of the cooking liquid in the pot slowly to prevent breakage. Hot cooking broth is poured into the donabé, then it is placed over a portable tabletop burner. Substitute an electric wok or electric skillet.

Drop lid (otoshi-buta) Cypress or cedar lid which can be dropped into a slightly larger straight-sided cooking pot to rest directly on simmering foods. Lid holds food in place in simmering sauce, keeping it moist. Lid also helps to prevent boiling, which in turn helps retain shape of vegetables. Excess moisture is allowed to escape between edge of lid and side of pot, preventing sauce from becoming diluted. Soak lid in water before use; pat dry. Do not put in the dishwasher. You can make a drop lid by cutting appropriate-size circles from thin sheets of cypress or cedar. Or use circles of waxed paper, slightly larger than diameter of pan, for cooking times up to 15 minutes; use parchment paper for times up to 30 minutes. Both waxed paper and parchment are likely to disintegrate during longer cooking. You can also use a flat lightweight cover, such as a metal lid or pie plate.

Fan (uchiwa) Paddle-shaped fan used frequently in Japanese cooking but most often for cooling sushi rice as it is tossed with vinegar dressing. Substitute a folded newspaper, cardboard or small electric fan.

Fine strainer (uragoshi) Traditional strainer made from a fine-mesh horsehair net stretched over a round wooden frame; fine metal strainers are also widely available. To puree foods, press food through strainer using a rice paddle or wooden spatula. After use, rinse strainer under hot water; if necessary, soak in hot soapy water to remove pieces of food.

Fish scaler (uroko-tori) Handy item to own if you clean your own catch. Grasp fish by the tail, using a kitchen towel to get a good hold, then run scaler down fish toward head. Continue scraping all around fish until scales are removed. Rinse fish and fish scaler. The back of a knife can also be used.

Graters (oroshi gané) Flat aluminum or stainless-steel graters vary in size and purpose. Graters with widely set ridges are used for grating daikon radish. Closely set ridges are for finely grating wasabi (Japanese horseradish) and gingerroot. For best results, grate in a circular motion. Well at bottom of each grater is designed to catch grated pulp with its juices. Tilt grater while holding grated gingerroot in place with your fingers. Pour off ginger juice for cooking purposes.

Grinding bowl and pestle (suribachi and surikogi) Earthenware bowl, usually coated on outside with a dark brown glaze. Unglazed interior is patterned with raised ridges to make an abrasive surface for grinding foods in the bowl. Pestle is made from unfinished cedarwood. Use bowl for grinding seeds and spices and for pounding and blending foods. Set bowl on a damp cloth to keep it from sliding around during use. Grinding bowls come in a variety of sizes ranging from a few inches wide up to 12 inches wide. They are excellent for grinding small amounts of spices which would be difficult to do in a blender or food processor.

Hand-pressed-sushi molds Use for quickly forming sushi rice into a variety of traditional shapes. Molds come in a variety of whimsical shapes, such as flowers and butterflies. They come in stainless steel, wood or plastic. Before use, soak wooden molds in vinegar water; quickly dip metal or plastic molds in vinegar water.

Hangiri Handsome shallow cypress-wood tub bound with copper hoops, used for mixing warm sushi rice with vinegar dressing. Wood does not react with vinegar and affect taste of rice. It also helps rice to cool evenly and absorbs excess moisture, adding to luster of rice. Some tubs come with lids and make excellent serving containers for rice dishes. Do not store onions, garlic or other aromatic vegetables in your sushi tub or your rice will have an unintended flavor! Before use, wet inside of tub with vinegar water. Substitute an unseasoned wooden salad bowl or a glass or plastic bowl.

Kim chee pot Stainless-steel pot, sold in a variety of sizes. Clamps on the side hold lid tightly shut. Usually available in Korean markets.

Nagashi-bako Stainless-steel metal mold with removable inner-lining tray for easy removal of foods. Used for steaming egg dishes and custards and molding jellied desserts. To remove food, simply lift out inner tray and if necessary, loosen edges with a small knife.

Oshiwaku Three-piece cypress pressing box for making pressed sushi. Soak frame in vinegar water before use, then pat dry. Fit wooden frame over bottom section of mold. Pack rice and other ingredients inside lined mold; put pressing lid into place. Press rice firmly. Remove lid and frame, leaving molded rice resting on bottom of mold. Turn molded rice off frame. Substitute a loaf pan, cake pan or small springform pan.

Pickling jar (tsukémono-ki) Plastic container for pickling vegetables. Lid contains a built-in screw top for pressing salted vegetables. As vegetables exude their liquid, lid is tightened several times. Substitute a bowl, crock or plastic tub and use a plate or flat pan of the appropriate size to fit into container on top of vegetables. Set a heavy object on top for pressing.

Wooden rice paddle (shamoji) Flat round paddle. Dampen and use to scoop cooked rice from cooking pot, to toss sushi rice with vinegar dressing and to press ingredients through a fine strainer. Substitute a wide wooden spatula.

Japanese Knives

The skill of the professional Japanese chef or *itamae*, which means in front of the cooking board, is judged by his ability to cut and arrange food artistically. This is especially important in Japan, where cooking is often a secondary consideration, the primary concern being the preservation of natural tastes and textures. The Japanese feel that the understanding and mastery of cooking cannot come about without first understanding the tools. To achieve success in the kitchen, the proper use of top-quality knives is the first step.

The Japanese chef is the samurai warrior of the kitchen, and treasures his kitchen knife (*hocho*) as much as the ancient samurai once treasured his sword. A kitchen knife is a treasured personal possession, almost an extension of the chef's arm. Special prayers of thanks are offered to the spirit of the knives each year on January 28 during the Hocho-Shiki festival. At this time, the most skillful chefs are allowed to display their carving talents at a special performance at the Imperial Palace.

Top-quality knives (*hon-yaki*) are forged from hard steel using methods perfected by the Japanese for producing some of the world's finest swords. *Hon-yaki* blades are hand-fashioned for professional chefs and can cost hundreds of dollars each. Ordinary good-quality kitchen knives (*hon-gasumi*) are made from layered iron and steel. They are forged with a single cutting edge, usually located on the right side of the blade. This type of knife, used in Japan for over a thousand years, cuts quickly and cleanly. Double-edged Western blades are not as popular in Japan. High-carbon steel knives are preferred because it is not difficult to maintain their cutting edge and they are stain-resistant. Recently ceramic knives have come into favor.

Japanese knives are designed for specific purposes. Although a variety of types and shapes exist, most fall into the following basic catagories:

Vegetable knives (nakiri-bocho, usuba-bocho) The nakiri-bocho has a thin blade with a dark-colored, straight, double cutting edge. It resembles a small lightweight cleaver. It is used for paring, chopping, slicing and mincing. It is an indispensable knife for the Japanese home kitchen. The usuba-bocho is a professional-quality vegetable knife with a single cutting edge. It is excellent for paring vegetables and for cutting paper-thin slices and shreds. To slice raw vegetables properly, use a forward thrusting cut (tsuki-giri). The bent fingers of the opposite hand should guide the knife and hold the food securely in place. When cutting, you should establish a smooth, rhythmic, continuous cutting motion. You can substitute a lightweight Chinese cleaver, although cutting will be harder work.

Fish-cutting knife (deba-bocho) A versatile, thick, heavy, triangular-blade knife used for gutting and filleting fish and for cutting some meats and chicken. Cutting and slicing are done with the front portion of this knife; chopping requires the use of the thick base. A top-quality Western boning knife and a chef's knife are good substitutes.

Fish-slicing knife (sashimi-bocho) This long narrow thin knife is used for slicing fresh fish for sashimi and for cutting some cooked foods. The willow-leaf-blade knife (yanagiba sashimi bocho) has a pointed end and is favored in the Osaka/Kyoto area. The octopus knife (tako-biki bocho) has a blunt end and is popular in the Tokyo area. Sashimi knives are used with a long drawing cut called hiki-giri. Place the knife blade on the fillet of fish and draw it the full length of the blade toward you as the food is cut. A vertical cut, called oshi-giri, is used for making swift clean cuts. The center of the blade is pushed straight down into the food. This cut is perfect for slicing rolled sushi. Wipe the blade with a damp cloth between cuts. It is important that the knife be well rinsed after sharpening to avoid a metallic taste on the fish. A top-quality Western slicing knife is a good substitute.

Soba knife (soba-bocho) This knife is designed solely to efficiently cut sheets of dough into thin noodles.

Caring for Knives

If you keep your knives sharp, they will serve you well and reduce much of the effort usually associated with cutting chores. Ideally, good knives should be honed on a whetstone before each use. To sharpen a knife, wet the knife and the whetstone with water. Place the stone vertically on a damp kitchen towel to hold it in place. Hold the knife in your right hand and place the cutting edge of the blade facing left on the stone. With your fingertips on the blade, push the entire length of the blade-edge up into a curved motion over the stone. Bring the knife back to the starting point and repeat the sharpening process several more times. Turn the knife over and run it over the stone a few times. Rinse the knife well before use.

Carbon-steel knives have a tendency to rust and discolor. Carefully dry the blades after washing and wipe them with a lightly oiled paper towel. If knives do rust, scour the blades lightly with a mild abrasive cleanser. A damp cork will help "erase" any rust spots from the blade. Never put your knives in the dishwasher. For storing, place in a knife rack or wrap each blade in a soft kitchen towel.

Japanese Knife Cuts

A large number of knife cuts are used in Japanese cooking; here are some of the most frequently used:

Sen-giri (matchstick strips) Cut desired food into 1 1/2- to 2-inch lengths. Make thin slices along the grain using a straight vertical cut. Stack several slices, then cut into matchstick strips. Fineness of strips can be varied according to personal preference.

Katsura-muki (wide strips and shreds) With a gentle sawing motion, cut carrot, daikon radish and cucumber into a paper-thin continuous sheet. This cut requires skill and is easier if the vegetable is soaked in a strong saltwater solution several hours before cutting. For easier handling, cut vegetable pieces into 2- to 3-inch lengths. Stack sheets and cut into fine shreds. Soak shreds in iced water. Use as a garnish for sashimi and other dishes. Sheets can be rolled and cut into curly thin shreds called kaminari.

Hangetsu-giri (half-moon cut) Cut cylindrical vegetables in half lengthwise, then crosswise into half-moon shapes. A popular cut for takuan (pickled daikon radish).

Namami-giri (diagonal cut) Cut vegetables diagonally. Vegetables cut on the diagonal are more attractive, absorb more flavors in cooking and cook more evenly because more surface is exposed.

Tazuna (braids) Cut food into thin rectangular pieces. Make a slit in the middle of each piece. Stick 1 end through slit, pulling it gently through to form a braided shape. This attractive cut can be used for devil's-tongue-jelly noodles (konnyaku) or steamed fish loaf (kamaboko). Braids make an excellent addition to braised and one-pot dishes.

Kika-kabu (chrysanthemum cut) See Marinated Radish Mums, page 37.

Sasagaki (shavings) In one hand, hold vegetable and cut at it with a knife as if you were sharpening a pencil. A common cut used for carrots, gobo (burdock) and similar-shaped root vegetables.

Mijin-giri (mincing) Pieces of fish, meat and vegetables are chopped to the finest consistency. They lose their individuality and blend into a single mass. When mincing garlic, gingerroot and green onions, smash them first with the side of the knife to break down fibers and release flavor oils. Garlic skins can be easily lifted off and discarded after smashing.

Hana-gata (flower shapes) Cut vegetables into attractive flower shapes with flower-shaped metal cutters (yasaino nuki-gata).

Sué-hiro (fan shape) Vegetables are cut into fan shapes.

The Traditional Flavors of Japan

Since ancient times, natural fermentation has played an important role in the development of Japanese cuisine. Originally promoted as a vital means of food preservation, fermented foods came to be appreciated for their own delicious taste and high digestibility. During the fermentation process, bacteria, yeast and molds work like busy little chemists, breaking down the original components of foods, altering their tastes and textures.

Fermented foods are more nutritious than when in their original form. They aid in the digestion of other foods and help keep our body's natural supply of antibodies and bacterial flora healthy.

Fermented rice wine, sweet rice wine, rice vinegar, miso paste and soy sauce are used as seasonings or condiments in almost every Japanese meal. They are produced in state-of-the-art factories using sophisticated, modern technology. But throughout Japan, a small number of skilled craftsmen still produce these foods using organic ingredients, traditional techniques and without preservatives. Referred to as "natural foods," Westerners are beginning to regard these handmade products as the culinary treasures of Japan. They are to be valued as much as the national treasures important to Japan's cultural heritage.

These fermented products can be purchased in Asian food stores and in most supermarkets across the country. To purchase traditional, handmade products, you may need to visit a natural food store in your area. Or check the mail-order section of this book for resources (page 269). These natural products meet the rigid standards set by the international macrobiotic community. Although the Japanese enjoy eating a variety of other fermented foods, I have listed a few of the most important ones used daily.

Mirin Slightly syrupy, this fine rice wine is made from sweet glutinous rice (mochi gomé), a mold (koji) and fiery distilled 90-proof liquor (shochu). Mirin is the traditional sweetener of Japanese cuisine. Highly valued in cha-kaiseki, or tea ceremony cuisine, mirin gives foods an attractive glaze and adds a delicate sweetness. It balances and adds depth to salty seasonings like shoyu and miso. It contributes luster to sushi rice and adds depth of flavor to noodle broths, teriyaki sauce, seafood and vegetables. For the finest mirin, look for hon-mirin or naturally brewed "true mirin." Good enough to drink, it is brewed with medicinal herbs to make otoso, a symbolic beverage drunk at New Year's celebrations. Do not expose mirin to direct sunlight or it will darken. Good-quality mirin can be purchased in natural-food stores.

Miso Paste Miso, fermented soybean paste, is one of Japan's most important foods. It is rich in amino acids, vitamins and minerals. After years of research, Japanese scientists have concluded that miso may reduce smoking's effects on the body, help decrease serum cholesterol and fight against heart disease and certain cancers. Like fine wine, miso can vary in color, flavor and aroma from region to region. Textures range from smooth to chunky and whole-bean. All contain salt, necessary to inhibit growth of undesirable bacteria. Each type has its own use and can successfully be incorporated into Western recipes.

Miso came to Japan in the thirteenth century with Buddhist monks returning from China. For centuries, balls of mashed cooked soybeans hung under the eaves of Japanese farmhouses, developing a natural mold covering. Upon completion of the process, the Japanese would say, "The flower has opened." Today, miso is made by inoculating cooked soybeans with a starter (koji) of cultured soybeans, rice or barley. The variance in miso types depends on the blend of soybeans, type of koji starter and salt.

Generally, miso can be classified as light or dark, with a few in-between shades. Light miso is high in koji, lower in soybeans and salt. Carbohydrate-rich light miso comes in white, yellow or tan shades. Sweet, white, rice-based miso is most popular in the Kyoto and southern areas. Look for the flavorful saikyo-miso ("western Kyoto miso"). Perishable; keep refrigerated and use quickly. Good for pickling vegetables, soups, salads or making Japanese sweets. A less-sweet, mellow, white miso variation comes from Hawaii. It is generally available throughout the country. Yellow Shinshu miso (chūmiso) is a popular mellow, high-salt blend. It is a good all-purpose miso, great for dressings, sauces, dips and marinades.

Red miso, or *aka-miso*, is also called barley or brown miso. It contains less *koji*, more salt and has more flavor depth. It may be fermented up to three years. Red miso is a farmhouse favorite. Because of high salt content, refrigerate indefinitely. Look for the popular reddish-brown Sendai miso, favored in northern Japan. *Mamé-miso* is made with beans, no grain. Rich, fudgy *hatcho-miso*, from Aichi Prefecture, might be aged up to five years. Popular in northern and central Japan, soybean *hatcho* was a favorite of the late Emperor Hirohito. Add this protein-rich miso to gravies, soups, stews, bean dishes, casseroles, meat marinades and stir-fry dishes. *Moromi-miso* is whole-bean miso used as a condiment. It is often served as an appetizer with cucumber. It may contain chopped, pickled vegetables.

Miso is eaten daily in some form. A traditional Japanese breakfast includes miso soup. Blend light and dark miso to develop complex flavors. Consider the salt content when adding miso to your favorite recipes; reduce suggested salt amounts. Low-salt miso is available for those with dietary concerns. Refrigerate miso in an airtight container, especially low-salt light miso and organic, unpasturized "natural" miso without preservatives.

Many fine miso companies exist in America, using organic ingredients and following traditional Japanese methods.

Saké Japanese wine (nihon shu) is brewed from steamed rice, a special mold (koji) and spring water. The alcoholic content ranges from 12 to 15 percent. Available dry (karakuchi) or sweet (amakuchi). Any saké can be used for cooking except I do not recommend that which is labeled cooking wine. Amino acids in saké act as a tenderizer on meats. Saké dispels fishy odors and acts as a balancing agent for other salty seasonings, such as soy sauce. Store in a cool dark place. Opened saké should be recapped tightly and refrigerated after each use. It will keep several weeks and can be used in cooking.

Soy sauce Soy sauce, or shoyu, is produced through fermentation from water, soybeans, wheat and salt. This distinctive seasoning brings out the natural sweetness in foods and enhances their flavors. Do not limit its use to Asian dishes; it adds real flavor to Western foods as well. To bring out the best qualities of soy sauce, add sparingly to foods. Brief cooking preserves its delicate flavor.

Both dark and light soy sauce are used in Japanese cooking. Dark soy sauce is favored in central Japan; light is favored in the Kyoto area. Kikkoman International produces quality dark soy sauce in Wisconsin; their excellent light soy sauce comes from Japan. Dark soy sauce, or *kokuchi shoyu*, is excellent for most cooking needs. Light soy sauce, or *usukuchi shoyu*, is salty and thinner. Use as a dipping sauce or on foods where flavor is desired but not a dark color. Use dark soy sauce for recipes in this book unless otherwise noted.

Low-sodium soy sauce is available for those who must reduce salt in their diet. Taste various brands to determine which taste best to you. An alternative way of limiting salt is to reduce the soy sauce amounts in recipes. Fill a spray bottle with soy sauce, then mist foods lightly to add a hint of delicate soy sauce flavor.

In the thirteenth century, Japanese priest Kakushin discovered that the rich dark liquid accumulating in miso kegs was a delicious seasoning. Mineral-rich tamari is more concentrated than other types of soy sauce. The name comes from the verb *tamaru*, "to accumulate." It is brewed from pure soybeans without wheat, unlike other types of soy sauce. In cooking, use about a quarter less than regular soy sauce. Tamari's distinctive flavor holds up well during lengthy simmering. Tamari is not used regularly in Japan except in commercial food preparation and around the Kyoto area in a dipping sauce for sashimi.

Around 1960, the Western macrobiotic community erroneously applied the name "tamari" to "natural" soy sauce produced through traditional manufacturing techniques. When authentic tamari was introduced to the West, the "natural" soy sauce was renamed "shoyu" (tamari shoyu). The addition of wheat is the main difference between "natural" soy sauce and wheat-free tamari. Somewhat expensive, both shoyu and pure tamari are available in natural-food stores. They may also be available in supermarkets along with regular soy sauce. Whichever you use, avoid synthetic nonbrewed Asian types produced by quick chemical means. Their flavors are not appropriate for Japanese or Chinese cooking. Do not use Chinese soy sauce for Japanese cooking. However, I find that Kikkoman is excellent for both. Read labels to find naturally brewed, aged soy sauce, made with soybeans, wheat, sea salt and water. Purchase small amounts of soy sauce; store in a cool place. Refrigerate shoyu and tamari after opening.

Rice vinegar (su) Rice is the staple food of Japan, so naturally the Japanese produce vinegar from rice. Rice vinegars come in a variety of strengths, most milder and sweeter than American vinegar. Rice vinegar neutralizes fatty flavors and fishy odors. It removes the slimy quality from vegetables such as taro potatoes (*sato imo*) and helps prevent enzymatic browning. Japanese research indicates that vinegar has the power to destroy bacteria. It is added to sushi rice as an antibacterial agent.

Rice vinegar from the first pressing is the most desirable. Natural brown rice vinegar (*genmai su*) is more costly but worth every drop. Delicate, fruity *umé su* (plum vinegar) is the brine from the pickling process of making *uméboshi*. Read labels to find pure rice vinegar. Some bottles of vinegar are preseasoned for making sushi. They are convenient to use and require no refrigeration after being opened. Sushi powder is a fairly new product for making a quick batch of sushi rice. It is a blend of powdered vinegar, sugar and salt.

Japanese Ingredients .

This is not a complete listing of Japanese food products but those used in this book. They are available throughout the United States in Oriental markets, supermarkets and health-food stores. Check the mail-order section (page 269) for items hard to find in your area.

Abura-agé (inari-agé) Golden brown puffs of deep-fried tofu. Available in square or rectangular shapes. Use for making inari-zushi. Check refrigerator or freezer section of Asian markets. Best texture is unfrozen. Stuff whole, cut in strips or open, fill and roll up like sushi. Tie with edible gourd strips called kampyo.

Asian pear (nashi) Same size as a pear but usually rounder. Juicy like a jicama and crisp like an apple. Ripe fruit can be refrigerated several months.

Azuki (adzuki beans) Small dried red beans, high in protein and B vitamins. Ranks second only to the soybean in nutritive value. Use to make sweet bean paste for Japanese sweets. Azuki beans are added to rice and vegetable dishes.

Agar-agar (kanten) Freeze-dried gelatin made from a blend of several red sea algae. Comes in stick form and in flakes. See page 251 for more information.

Amazu shōga Thin-sliced or shredded, young, pickled gingerroot. Usually tinted a pastel pink. After opening, refrigerate shōga in its vinegar marinade airtight; keeps several weeks. Traditionally eaten at the sushi bar as a palate cleanser between bites. Called gari by sushi chefs.

An or anko Sweet, pureed azuki bean paste used in traditional Japanese confectionery. It is sometimes the surprise ingredient in Western-style buns—even marshmallows! Koshi-an is the pureed form; tsubushi-an is the chunky whole-bean form. Excellent quality canned paste is available from Asian markets.

Ao-noriko Dried, powdery green seaweed flakes used as a seasoning for rice, noodles, salads, crackers, potato chips and other foods. Store at room temperature away from heat and moisture.

Ao-togarashi Small, sweet green peppers resembling hot green chiles in appearance. Bell pepper strips can be substituted. Togarashi are small, dried, hot red peppers; use whole or grind for seasoning.

Aramé Calcium-rich sea grass which resembles hijiki but has a milder ocean flavor. Rinse well, soak 30 minutes, press out water. Aramé triples in size when soaked.

Beni shōga Red-tinted pickled gingerroot; available sliced or shredded. Refrigerate airtight in its vinegar marinade. A delicious, colorful condiment.

Bifun Wheat-free Japanese rice noodles bound with potato starch. Use in salads, soups, stir-fries and spring rolls or eat plain with soy sauce, vinegar and grated ginger.

Burdock root (gobo) A wild root, now commercially harvested. A hallmark of the Japanese produce department, gobo has a unique, earthy flavor and crunchy texture. The dried leaves are added to soba noodles to lend a viscous quality. Rich in minerals and B vitamins, gobo can be eaten as a vegetable or pickled. I love the subtle flavor in tofu dishes and fried fish cakes. Simmer gobo before sautéeing to tenderize. The roots can be tenderized through energetic pounding. To store, refrigerate roots in damp newspapers or paper towels and plastic wrap. Rinse and scrape away the brown earthy covering just before use, or lightly peel with a vegetable peeler. Immerse in vinegar water to lessen discoloration.

Chikuwa Mild white-fish paste bound by a starch, shaped on metal rods, then steamed and grilled. The hollow rolls can be stuffed with a number of ingredients. Add to salads, soups and noodle dishes or serve plain with soy sauce and wasabi.

Cucumber, European Ten- to 12-inch-long cucumber. Fewer seeds than regular cucumber; better taste.

Cucumber, Japanese Short, thin seedless cucumber. Excellent flavor; buy when available.

Daikon radish This giant white radish is so beloved in Japan, it is wrapped and presented as a gift. I have purchased giant, round daikon in Japan weighing from 1 to 60 pounds. Daikon is an important aid in the digestion of fatty foods. The stems and leaves are rich in vitamin C. Daikon can be braised, steamed, pickled or grated in small portions for use as a condiment. It is fermented to make the pickle takuan and used in Korean kim chee. Shredded, dried kiriboshi daikon is sweet and rich in flavor. Kaiwari daikon are the crisp flavorful sprouts. Firm, unwrinkled, crisp daikon are best for grating as a condiment. For the zestiest flavor, grate from the tapering end. Older, slightly softened daikon are fine for cooking or pickling. Refrigerate after purchase.

Dashi Japan's basic soup stock and seasoning ingredient is made from dried bonito (katsuobushi) and good-quality dried kelp (dashi konbu).

Dashi-no-moto Instant dashi comes in granular form, premeasured powdered, liquid concentrate (memmi) or tea bags. Dilute concentrate to taste; use a few drops in cooking for additional flavor. If you don't have dashi on hand and need 1/2 cup or less for cooking, you can use instant dashi for convenience.

Denbu or soboro Pink or green sweetened, dried-fish flakes. Pretty for garnish.

Dried foods (kambutsu) For centuries foods have had moisture removed to prevent decay. The added bonus is a highly concentrated sweet flavor and in some cases, increased nutrition. Can be used as a seasoning in small amounts. In Japan, dried bonito, sardines and kelp are used for stock; the high amino acid content enhances flavors. The dried fungi, cloud ears and shiitake mushrooms are appreciated for flavor and texture. Other important dried foods include gourd strips (kampyō), wheat gluten (fu) and freeze-dried tofu (kōyadōfu).

Eggplant, Japanese Small elongated eggplant, starting at finger size.

Enokidaké (enoki or snow puff mushrooms) Clusters of long thin white stems and tiny round caps characterize these delicate crunchy mushrooms. Grown in California, they are shipped in tightly sealed plastic bags. Avoid darkened mushrooms, which are slimy. Keep refrigerated; use quickly. Rinse and trim off stem base before use. Add to soups, simmered dishes and salads.

Ginger (shōga) Pungent-tasting fresh gingerroot is a rhizome, or underground stem; indispensable to Japanese cuisine. Look for firm, heavy knobs of ginger with unwrinkled tan skin. Store on the counter in a cool, dry place. For long storage, refrigerate in a paper bag wrapped in plastic. Frozen ginger is too fibrous and tough for most uses. Thaw and squeeze spongy root to obtain the juice. Fresh young ginger can be potted in sandy soil and grown in a sunny spot. Uncover roots where new shoots appear; break off a tender piece for use. Smash gingerroot slices before use to release maximum flavors. Powdered ginger is not a substitute for fresh.

Gingko nuts (ginnan) Mild-flavored white nuts. To shell, crack hard white shells with a nutcracker.

Soak in hot water to help loosen inner skins. Nuts turn light green when cooked. Use fresh nuts if possible; available canned.

Harusamé Called "spring rain" or bean threads, these noodle-like, dried vegetable strands are made from mung bean starch. Snip the wiry noodles into shorter lengths with scissors. Soften in warm water 20 minutes; simmer 10 minutes. If noodles are to be cooked again, reduce simmering time to 5 minutes. Noodles plump, turn translucent and resemble gelatin strings. They absorb flavors of foods they are cooked with. Unsoaked noodles puff up and expand dramatically when deep-fried. Store in an airtight container in a cool place.

Hijiki A brown sea grass, parboiled and wind-dried after harvesting. Hijiki rivals milk in calcium content and is mineral-rich. Its sweet flavor is enhanced by sautéing. Store airtight in a dry place. After soaking, hijiki expands three to four times its original size. Aramé is similar with a milder flavor. The two are interchangeable.

Hiyamugi Thin, white, dried wheat noodles slightly larger than somen. Noodles are usually eaten cold with a dipping sauce and condiments. Sometimes characterized by several pink and green noodles tucked into each package.

Kamaboko Fish paste, or surimi, formed into loaves on boards, steamed; sometimes grilled. Sizes vary from 6 to 8 ounces. Some tops are tinted pink, green or blue. Itatsuki ("board mounted") kamaboko was first made in old Edo. Sasa-kamaboko comes in an oval leaf shape. Kobu-maki kamaboko is rolled and steamed in a sheet of seaweed. Plain kamaboko is available in almost any Asian market. Slice loaves and serve with soy sauce and wasabi. Texture softens when added to noodle dishes, stews, soups or fritters. Do not overcook or product may toughen. See Naruto-maki, page 266; Surimi, page 268.

Kampyo White sun-dried strips of calabash or bottle gourd. Soften fibers in salted water 15 minutes, rinse and simmer in a seasoned liquid. A delicious edible string for tying foods.

Katsuobushi From the mackerel family, boiled, smoked, sun-dried bonito fillets are a primary ingredient for making dashi, Japan's soup stock. Many households have a special cutting box for shaving the petrified fillets. Fresh bonito shavings make an exceptional stock. Convenient preshaved bonito (hana-katsuo or kezuribushi) is available in Asian markets. Buy small amounts and refrigerate; use within three weeks. Ito-kezuri-katsuo, or thread shavings, are used as a garnish. Té-maki-katsuo are dried pink sheets used like nori for sushi. Also available in plum flavor.

Kelp (konbu) Kelp blades are harvested, sun-dried and folded into smooth sheets. Kelp is a primary ingredient for making dashi, Japan's basic stock. The best fronds are 4 inches or wider and come from cool Hokkaido waters. Ask for dashi-konbu. Do not wash away the powdery white coating; the soup flavor will be diminished. Kelp is high in potassium, vitamin A and iodine, which helps prevent goiter. Kelp contains the amino acid glutamic acid, a natural flavoring compound isolated from other sources for the production of monosodium glutamate. Kelp is a natural flavor enhancer; add to simmering foods. It enhances the flavor of dried beans, makes them easier to digest and speeds the cooking time. Shredded kelp can be pickled, braised, sautéed and deep-fried for snacks. Pale green, delicate tororo-konbu is shaved from dried kelp. Oboro shavings are wider. Both are good seasonings. Mild oboro can be used for maki-zushi or wrapping rice balls. Store all forms of konbu in a dry airtight container.

Kinako Roasted soybean powder has a nutty taste and is used for making traditional Japanese sweets. Powder is perishable; refrigerate several weeks or freeze several months.

Kinomé Delicate leaves from the prickly ash tree. Mint-like peppery taste complements sushi and sashimi. No taste substitute is available, but parsley, watercress or fresh mint leaves will suffice.

Kishimen Wheat noodles, a Nagoya specialty, similar to udon but flatter and wider. It is often added to one-pot dishes as the final course. Purchase dried; prepare like udon.

Koji Short-grain steamed rice inoculated with the mold Aspergillus oryzae. Used as a starter for making rice wines, rice vinegar, sweet rice saké (amazaké), miso and koji pickles.

Konnyaku or konjac Jellied vegetable paste made from a tuber called devil's tongue. Available in a pure white form or in a dark unrefined form, konnyaku is available in bars, slices and noodle-like strands (shirataki). Konnyaku is high in water, low in calories and contains calcium. It has no taste of its own but readily absorbs flavors of other foods. Before use, blanch in boiling water to firm the texture and remove the odor of milk of lime, used in processing.

Kuzu The fast-growing kuzu (kudzu) plant was imported from Japan as a source of fodder in the American South. In Japan, kuzu starch is processed from the roots. It produces clear, translucent sauces and gives fried foods a crispy, delicate coating. Produces silken-textured puddings. Small chunks must be crushed before use. Use kuzu like cornstarch. Available in natural-food stores.

Lotus root (renkon or hasu) The root of a perennial aquatic plant which grows in water ponds. Beautiful water lilies are pink and white. When peeled and sliced, hollow canals running the length of the sausage-shaped roots form an attractive pattern. Soak cut pieces in water with lemon juice or vinegar to prevent discoloration. Lotus root can be pickled, stir-fried, braised and candied.

Matsutaké Highly prized expensive large autumn mushrooms. Wipe clean and sauté quickly for maximum enjoyment.

Mirin Sweet rice wine mainly used for cooking. For detailed information, see page 260.

Miso Fermented soybean paste. For detailed information, see page 260.

Mitsuba Trefoil, or wild parsley, is an important native vegetable and garnish used in many dishes. Flavor resembles a blend of parsley and celery. A single stem with a leaf is often knotted and added to a bowl of soup. Leaves and stems are cooked as a vegetable. Add to soups and other hot foods during the final minutes of cooking to avoid any bitter taste. Cook only 1 or 2 minutes or the delicate flavor will be lost. To store fresh leaves, rinse and shake dry. Refrigerate in an airtight plastic bag. Substitute flat-leaf parsley or watercress.

Mochi gomé Short-grain sweet glutinous rice. It has the highest starch content of any rice, causing grains to lose shape and become very sticky when cooked. Used for rice cakes, confections, and bean and rice dishes.

Mochiko Rice flour made from finely ground, cooked, sweet glutinous rice. Used for making instant rice cakes and traditional confections.

Monosodium glutamate (MSG) MSG is a monosodium salt of glutamic acid, one of the most common amino acids found in nature. Natural sources of glutamate (dried mushrooms, shrimp and seaweed) have enhanced food flavors for thousands of years. Glutamate is the basis for the "fifth taste," known in Japan as umami, or savory. In 1908, Japanese scientist Kikunae Ikeda extracted the amino acid from kelp. Today it is produced by a fermentation process using corn sugar or sugar beet molasses. In Japan, MSG is added to table salt to enhance flowing capabilities. Also found in seasonings, soup mixes, pickles and packaged snacks such as rice crackers. Hydrolyzed vegetable protein, used in the manufacture of chemically fermented soy sauce, is closely related. (Many people have reported suffering from "Chinese restaurant syndrome" after ingesting large doses of manufactured MSG in Chinese restaurants. For more information about research done by Ajinomoto USA on the safety of MSG, see mail-order sources.)

Mountain yam (yama imo) One variety of this long tuber slightly resembles an animal paw. Interior white flesh becomes gummy and adhesive when grated. Often eaten with soy sauce as a delicacy or used as a binding agent for buckwheat noodles and other foods. Wear rubber gloves if mountain yam irritates your skin.

Mustard cabbage From 12 to 18 inches in length, this tonic-tasting cabbage resembles bok choy. Available salted and pickled. Good in soups and stir-fried dishes. Substitute spinach, kale or Swiss chard. Purchase in sealed packages in the refrigerator section or in cans at Asian markets.

Nananegi Mild-flavored large green onions. Substitute green onions.

Napa or Chinese cabbage (hakusai) This popular, elongated, crinkly-leaf cabbage has a mild but distinctive taste. Leaves require little cooking and are good eaten raw or pickled. Refrigerate in an airtight plastic bag.

Naruto-maki is a decorative version of kamaboko with a pretty pink spiral design when sliced. Naruto means "whirlpool." Layers of colored fish paste are rolled up and steamed. Another pretty fish paste is daté-maki, with an egg-yellow swirl. See Kamaboko, page 264; Surimi, page 268.

Natto Steamed fermented soybeans with an impossibly sticky texture and flavor similar to over-ripe cheese. A popular breakfast food over rice. Try mixed with mustard, green onions and soy sauce. Some forms are dried and highly salted. For some, an acquired taste.

Nira Flat green chives with a pleasant garlic-onion taste.

Nori (laver) This prized alga is rich in protein, calcium, iron, minerals and vitamins, with almost no calories. Fronds are washed, chopped and sun-dried on screens. Quality is rated by the number of tiny pieces per square inch. The best nori is shiny black with a faint green and purple iridescence. Some sheets or strips come seasoned with soy sauce or pretoasted. Toast nori for better aroma and flavor. To store, refrigerate or freeze in airtight container. Price indicates quality; purchase the best you can afford. Nori is used as a wrapper for sushi rice or rice balls.

Panko Pressed coarse dry bread crumbs used for coating foods for deep-frying. Foods coated in panko have a wonderful crispy texture which holds up well after frying.

Potato starch (katakuriko) A popular inexpensive starch made from white or sweet potato. Similar to cornstarch; use slightly less potato starch than cornstarch. Potato starch thickens at a lower temperature; do not cook beyond thickening or it will break down. Excellent for extra-crisp coatings on foods and in smooth sauces.

Ramen Ramen, a type of modified wheat noodle, was introduced from China and popularized during the Meiji era (1868–1912). Primarily a soup noodle, ramen has a richer flavor than traditional Japanese noodles; often contains lard. Alkalized water kneaded into the flour makes the color yellow. Three-minute instant ramen is available in all markets. Steamed, oven-dried, fat-free ramen is available in supermarkets and natural-food stores. Available in whole wheat or regular.

Rice The Japanese prefer Japonica-type medium-grain and short-grain rice. In 1994, California grew 71 percent of the U.S. medium-grain rice crop and 95 percent of the short-grain crop. California rice is available in supermarkets, natural-food stores and ethnic markets throughout the country. Look for medium-grain rice under names such as: Hinode Calrose, Nishiki, New Rose, Kiki and Miyako Calrose. Less short-grain rice is sold because of the popularity of medium-grain rice. One California short-grain rice is Silver Pearl. Another, introduced in October 1994, is Tamanishiki, an outstanding premium short-grain rice, which I find similar to rice grown in Japan. For sweet glutinous rice, see Mochi gomé, page 265. Store rice in a cool, dry place in an airtight container. Properly stored, it keeps one year. Water amounts for cooking rice can vary slightly, depending on the moisture content of each bag. The time of harvest, storage, age and even the cooking method are all determining factors. See Cooking Rice (page 193).

Rice vinegar (su) Mild rice vinegar distilled from white rice. For detailed information, see page 262.

Saké (nihon shu) Japanese rice wine. For detailed information, see pages 10–11 and 261.

Salt Perhaps the most valued and frequently used mineral in the world. The Japanese do not view salt as sodium chloride but as "dehydrated ocean." Additives to table salt can cloud pickling brines. Use sea salt, unrefined, if available, and finely ground pickling salts.

Sato imo (country potatoes) In Asia, several varieties of taro are grown in wet and dry paddy fields. Tubers have hairy dark exteriors and grayish mealy interiors. Sizes range from tiny to large Okinawan tubers ranging from 1 to 2 pounds. Small potatoes in American markets are called *koimo*. Peel and soak in lightly salted water 15 minutes. Cut up and simmer in rice soaking water or water with a little vinegar until tender. They can be steamed, boiled, deep-fried and candied like sweet potatoes. Used for making poi in Hawaii. Mild delicious flavor.

Sansho Greenish aromatic pods of the prickly ash tree. Ground sansho gives foods a peppery spicy taste. Especially popular on grilled foods, it also adds zest to noodle dishes, soups and one-pot dishes. Related to Szechwan peppercorns.

Seasoning powders Dried herb and vegetable powders are available in several forms in Japanese cooking. Make shiitake mushroom powder by grinding high-quality dried mushrooms in a small electric coffee or spice grinder. Stir into sauces, soups or gravies to enhance flavors. Instant kelp and bonito soup base, dashi-no-moto, is used as a seasoning in the Ryūkyū Islands. Kinako is roasted soybean powder; use to coat mochi. Sun-dried, ground konbu (konbu tea), available in clear bags, is sprinkled on rice or other foods.

Sesame oil (goma abura) Aromatic pressed oil of toasted sesame seeds. Adds a nutty taste and fragrance to foods. Rarely used alone as cooking oil but sometimes added to other vegetable oils for frying tempura. Add sparingly to marinades, salad dressings, sauces, cooked vegetables, noodles and meats.

Sesame seeds (goma) Sesame seeds are abundant in protein, vitamins, calcium and phosphorus. High amounts of vitamin E stabilize the oil and help prevent oxidation. White and black seeds are available; white seeds are hulled (pure white) or unhulled (mottled color). Seeds are used as a delicious garnish or ground into a paste for salad dressing. Toast (or dry-roast) seeds as needed, just before use. Place in a small heavy skillet over medium-high heat. Stir seeds until they turn golden and become fragrant. Do not allow to burn. Crush lightly to release flavor oils. Use at once. Watch black seeds very carefully as they toast.

Shiitake Black, forest mushrooms prefer to grow on dead hardwood trees. Available fresh or dried, shiitake are rich in amino acids and lysine, often lacking in grains. Scientific studies indicate shiitake may lower blood cholesterol and help the body's immune system fight cancer. Dried shiitake have an intense, earthy flavor. The best quality have thick caps with cracks. Rehydrate in hot water at least 30 minutes or as long as overnight. Trim off tough stems; add to the stockpot. Strain and use the flavorful liquid in broths, soups, sauces and glazes.

Shirataki Jelly-like noodles made by an extrusion method from konnyaku, or devil's tongue jelly. Use in sukiyaki.

Shiso The flavorful leaf of the beefsteak plant (perilla) comes in two varieties: green and red. Green leaves are delicious added to soups, noodles, tempura and sushi. The Japanese believe shiso counteracts parasitic illness from raw fish. Red leaves stain foods pink and add delicious flavor. Pickled in brine and sold as a condiment, red shiso is used for making uméboshi (pickled plums) and pickled gingerroot. Shiso has a faint minty taste and is an excellent addition to the summer herb garden. Refrigerate in a plastic bag 5 or 6 days. Use leaves before they darken.

Soba Buckwheat, a cold-weather crop; yields a flour that is an excellent source of essential vitamins and minerals. It is used to make soba noodles, a favorite in Tokyo and northern Japan. Té-uchi, professionally made fresh organic noodles, are incomparable. Enjoy with dipping sauce, in hot broth, in salads or in rolled vegetarian sushi.

Somen Delicate, vermicelli-like wheat noodles made from a sesame oil–scented dough. It is the favored noodle in shojin-ryōri, an elegant vegetarian cuisine. Hiyashi-somen is a summer favorite served in iced water with cucumber, tomato and a cherry, with dipping sauce and condiments on the side. A creative Kyoto restaurant sends somen down a bamboo shoot into a miniature stream; guests "fish" out their portions. Chefs like to boil a bundle of somen tied at one end. The cooked noodles are arranged as if they were flowing in one direction. Only available dried, somen also comes in pink plum, golden egg or green tea flavor. Okinawans stir-fry somen Chinese-style with fish and vegetables.

Soy sauce (shoyu) Salty brown soybean-based liquid. For detailed information, see page 261.

Surimi ("minced meat") A refined form of fish paste, often made with pollock in the United States. An intermediate raw material from which the Japanese have made kamaboko and chikuwa for over 1,000 years. You are probably familiar with a similar product, surimi seafood analogue, or "imitation seafood." I never use surimi foods as a substitute for fresh seafood, but consider them a versatile, low-cost food that can stand on their own in the Asian or Western kitchen. To taste homemade surimi fish cake, try Fish Cake Tempura (page 158).

Takuan Distinctive-tasting pickled daikon radish is rich in vitamins and minerals, and believed to be an excellent aid to digestion. Fresh whole daikon are sun-dried, then packed into crocks of salt and rice bran for pickling. It is one of the most popular pickles in Japan.

Tempurako Low-gluten wheat flour primarily used for making tempura batter. Cake flour can be substituted.

Tofu Tofu is a white custard-like food substance made from soy milk that has been expressed from soybeans, then coagulated. See page 136 for more information.

Tosaka nori An attractive, dried, red, curly sea alga sold in its natural red color, bleached white, or treated with lime ash to turn it bright green. Rehydrate in warm water.

Tree oyster mushroom (shimejitaké) Beige mushroom with a cap vaguely resembling an oyster. Mushrooms grow in clumps and have a deep, rich oyster flavor. Shimeji have small brownish-gray caps. Use the freshest available for the best flavor. Rinse mushrooms quickly just before use. Pat dry; cut into smaller pieces for cooking.

Trefoil See Mitsuba, page 265.

Tuna (maguro) A member of the mackerel family, sliced raw tuna is one of the most popular toppings for hand-pressed sushi. Fat-bellied yellowfin tuna (hon maguro) is considered the finest. Yellowtail (kiwada) and pale albacore

tuna (binnaga) are also popular. Albacore is the top grade of canned tuna. Young people in Japan enjoy canned tuna in various types of rolled sushi. Buy only the freshest, top-quality seasonal fish for serving raw. Tuna is one of the few fish that retain their quality when frozen, thawed and served raw.

Udon A cream-colored, chewy noodle made from wheat flour, water and salt. A favored noodle in the ancient Imperial Court of Kyoto, udon is still a southern wintertime favorite. Udon noodles are square, flat or round like linguini. Available fresh or dried. Serve in hot broth, stews, one-pot dishes, salads and stir-fries. Seven-Spice Powder (page 228) is a favorite udon seasoning.

Uméboshi (pickled plums) One of the most popular condiments in Japan. Green plums are pickled in brine with red shiso leaves. Available in paste form. The salty, sour flavor is a breakfast favorite with plenty of rice. Expensive, top-quality uméboshi are tinted with red shiso leaves, not food dye. Uméboshi is very salty; limit your intake. The pickling liquid is processed into a flavorful vinegar.

Wasabi This perennial plant grows wild in Japan around streams in mountainous areas. The pungent flavor of fresh wasabi is incomparable. Hard to find in America, but sometimes available frozen in markets that cater to large Japanese populations. Available in tins in dry powdered form; usually blended with horseradish and cayenne. Reconstitute the powder with water or saké. Paste form is also available. Pickled wasabi, or wasabi-zuké, is made with saké lees, a saké-making by-product. Serve wasabi as a spicy accompaniment to sushi. Known as sabi or namida ("tears") in sushi bars.

Wheat gluten (fu) Fu is a chewy, low-starch substance made from gluten flour. The high-protein food is a welcome addition to vegetarian cookery. Sweet, doughy, fresh wheat gluten (namafu) is hard to obtain. Crisp, dried wheat gluten (yakifu) is readily available and comes shaped like coins, flowers, wheels and croutons. Soak dried wheat gluten in water a few minutes until spongy; squeeze out excess water. Add to soups or use as directed in recipes.

MAIL-ORDER SOURCES

To locate Japanese ingredients or utensils in your area, check the yellow pages of your telephone directory for Oriental markets, specialty cookware stores and natural-food stores. Visit your library and local bookstores for Japanese cookbooks. Check with local Japanese restaurants or contact the food department of your local newspaper for additional shopping information.

Eden Foods, Inc.
701 Tecumseh Rd.
Clinton, MI 49236
Importers of high-quality Japanese natural foods and seasonings, found in natural-food stores and supermarkets. If you can't locate a source near you, write for assistance.

Rafu Bussan, Inc.
326 E. 2nd St.
Los Angeles, CA 90012
Japanese foods, cookware, lacquerware, dishes.

Premier Japan Trading Company
P.O. Box 3150
Union, NJ 17083
Traditional Japanese food products.

Joyce Chen Products
411 Waverly Oaks Rd.
Waltham, MA 02154
Sushi tool kit, sushi food kit, vegetable knives, cleavers, cutting boards, woks, steamers.

Katagiri Company
224 E. 59th St.
New York, NY 10022
Japanese foods, cooking equipment.

Apcon International, Inc.
420 Boyd St. Suite 502
Los Angeles, CA 90013
(213) 680-9101

Palate Pleasers Magazine
Magazine of Japanese cuisine and culture.

Japan Yellow Pages

Mangajin
(800) 552-3206
200 N. Cobb Pky, Suite 421
Marietta, GA 30062
Magazine on Japanese pop culture and language learning.

Maid of Scandinavia
3244 Raleigh Ave.
Minneapolis, MN 55416
Kitchen supplies, cake decorating, vegetable cutters. Write for catalog.

Anzen Hardware & Supply
220 E. 1st St.
Los Angeles, CA 90012
Cooking equipment.

Japan Food Corp.
445 Kaufman Ct.
San Francisco, CA 94080
Write to the Consumer Service Supervisor for a list of supermarkets that carry Japanese foods.

Mountain Ark Trading Co.
120 South East St.
Fayetteville, AK 72701
(800) 643-8909
Japanese foods and cooking equipment. Call for catalog.

Erewhon
236 Washington St.
Brookline, MA 02146
Japanese natural foods, cooking equipment, *koji* rice starter.

The Wok Shop
c/o Tane Chan
804 Grant St.
San Francisco, CA 94108
(415) 989-3797
Chinese, Japanese, international cooking equipment, sushi-making equipment, plastic and stainless rice molds.

Macrobiotic Company of America
799 Old Leicester Hwy
Ashville, NC 28806
(800) 438-4730
Macro-Direct natural-food co-op. Foods, kitchenware, knives, books.

Iwatani & Co. (USA), Inc.
60 E. 42nd St. Suite 1740
New York, NY 10165
Casset Feu grill, burner unit and gas canisters.

Uwajimaya
P.O. Box 3003
Seattle, WA 98114
(206) 624-6248
Large supermarket. Japanese foods, cooking equipment, books, housewares.

Kitazawa Seed Company
356 W. Taylor St.
San Jose, CA 95110

Le Marché Seeds
Box 190
Dixon, CA 95820

Shepard's Garden Seeds
6116 Hwy 9
Felton, CA 95018

Mikado Seed Growers
1203 Hoshikuki
Shiba City 280 Japan

Zojirushi America Corp.
5628 Bandini Blvd.
Bell, CA 90201
(213) 264-6270
Rice cookers and other specialty cookware. Catalog available.

Sakura Horikiri
15480 S. Western Ave.
Gardenia, CA 90249
Japanese paper craft shop. Handcrafted papers and kits for making and covering boxes with *washi* paper.

Ajinomoto USA, Inc.
Glenpointe Center West
500 Frank W. Burr Blvd.
Teaneck, NJ 07666-6894
(201) 488-1212
Research studies on MSG.

American Allergy Association
P.O. Box 640
Menlo Park, CA 94026

The Food Allergy Network
4744 Holly Avenue
Fairfax, VA 22030
(703) 691-3179
Newsletter and food allergy publications.

G.E.M. Cultures
30301 Sherwood Rd.
Fort Bragg, CA 95437
(707) 964-2922
Tofu-making equipment and coagulents, terra alba (white earth—natural calcium sulfate), nagiri (magnesium chloride), amazaké, pickle, miso and saké koji starters. Catalog available.

Metric Conversion Charts

When You Know	Comparison to Metric Measure		To Find	Symbol
	Symbol	Multiply By		
teaspoons	tsp	5.0	milliliters	ml
tablespoons	tbsp	15.0	milliliters	ml
fluid ounces	fl. oz.	30.0	milliliters	ml
cups	c	0.24	liters	l
pints	pt.	0.47	liters	l
quarts	qt.	0.95	liters	l
ounces	oz.	28.0	grams	g
pounds	lb.	0.45	kilograms	kg
Fahrenheit	F	5/9 (after subtracting 32)	Celsius	C

Fahrenheit to Celsius

F	C
200–205	95
220–225	105
245–250	120
275	135
300–305	150
325–330	165
345–350	175
370–375	190
400–405	205
425–430	220
445–450	230
470–475	245
500	260

Liquid Measure to Liters

1/4 cup	=	0.06 liters
1/2 cup	=	0.12 liters
3/4 cup	=	0.18 liters
1 cup	=	0.24 liters
1-1/4 cups	=	0.3 liters
1-1/2 cups	=	0.36 liters
2 cups	=	0.48 liters
2-1/2 cups	=	0.6 liters
3 cups	=	0.72 liters
3-1/2 cups	=	0.84 liters
4 cups	=	0.96 liters
4-1/2 cups	=	1.08 liters
5 cups	=	1.2 liters
5-1/2 cups	=	1.32 liters

Liquid Measure to Milliliters

1/4 teaspoon	=	1.25 milliliters
1/2 teaspoon	=	2.5 milliliters
3/4 teaspoon	=	3.75 milliliters
1 teaspoon	=	5.0 milliliters
1-1/4 teaspoons	=	6.25 milliliters
1-1/2 teaspoons	=	7.5 milliliters
1-3/4 teaspoons	=	8.75 milliliters
2 teaspoons	=	10.0 milliliters
1 tablespoon	=	15.0 milliliters
2 tablespoons	=	30.0 milliliters

INDEX

JAPANESE RECIPE INDEX

About the Author

Susan Fuller Slack lives in Columbia, South Carolina, where she is a food consultant, food stylist and food writer. She teaches cooking to adults and children on a local television station. Susan has written eight cookbooks. An authority on Japanese cuisine, Susan is a Certified Culinary Professional with the International Association of Culinary Professionals.

Susan's interest in Japanese cuisine began 20 years ago when she moved to Japan with her son and her husband, a Marine Corps pilot. It was a world apart from her childhood home in the Smoky Mountains of Tennessee, yet Susan felt she had "come home." The people of both regions share strong agricultural traditions, a deep love of nature and prepare delicious foods utilizing available resources.

Susan explores the unique facets of Japanese cuisine and offers insight into Japanese tastes, cooking techniques and the deep cultural significance that food plays in daily life.